The Utah Entrepreneur's Guide

How to Start and Manage a Business in Utah

Dr. Paul Larson, University of Montana
Dr. Roger H. Nelson, University of Utah

University Press
1719 Dearborn
Missoula, MT 59801
(800) 243-6840

The Utah Entrepreneur's Guide
How to Start and Manage a Business in Utah

Printed in the United States of America

ISBN 0 9624819 3 9

Published by:

University Press
1719 Dearborn
Missoula, MT 59801
(800) 243-6840

Contents

Introduction

There is a difference between a small business and a small entrepreneurial company that is growing. The difference lies in the dreams of the owner. Small business owners are seeking independence and a decent-paying job. Entrepreneurs are seeking more. They want growth. They want to be challenged.

Running a small entrepreneurial firm is different than running a large business. The following encounter illustrates the difference in managers' motivation in running each:

*Two men sat next to each other at a truck stop counter. Both were proud of the fast automobiles they owned. The one who owned a Mercedes bragged that his car could go 150 miles per hour. The other man, who owned a Toyota Celica Supra, was unimpressed. He said "Its not the speed that counts, its the **acceleration**."*

Small companies may not have huge sales, but they can accelerate quickly. You have to change gears rapidly. This is what excites more entrepreneurs, but this is also what imperils them.

This book is for entrepreneurs. It describes ways to get your company to grow. It also describes the stages through which growing companies move and what you must do to manage the firm in those stages.

This book is written specifically for the Utah business community. Most of the examples describe Utah companies. Resources cited are those available to business owners in the state. Utah has a unique business environment and the suggestions in the book are in essence inspired by this environment.

Acknowledgements

We are greatly indebted to the many people who assisted in the writing of this book. To each of them, we offer our deepest appreciation. We thank:

Steven P. Grizzell, Utah Technology Finance Corporation
Rebecca R. Porter, Secretary, Programs in Emerging Business, David Eccles School of Business
Jurij Prizemin, Research Assistant, Programs in Emerging Business, David Eccles School of Business
R. Kent Moon, Sr. V.P., Zions First National Bank
Josie Valdez, Assistant Business Director of Business Development, Small Business Institute
Bruce A. Wambheim, Small Business Department, Zions First National Bank
Larry Gianchetta, Dean, University of Montana School of Business Administration
Sanjib Chowdhury, Research Assistant, University of North Texas
Kirsten Thompson, Research Assistant, University of Montana

Dedicated to our families

1

The Stages of Business Growth

Entrepreneurs thrive on growth. Growth brings challenges, variety, a sense of moving forward, and usually increased net worth. In fact, if your company is not growing it may be at risk. You may not be able to attract or retain quality managers and employees. The innovation of your company may stagnate. Competitors may move right past you. Your company may *have* to grow to be able to survive.

Growth may destroy your company

Although growth is wonderful, it brings with it problems. Cash flow is usually troublesome. Jobs don't get done because people are spread thin. Quality control can lapse because of the emphasis on getting more products out. People burn out because of the increased workload. If you grow too fast, the strain may destroy your company.

The purpose of this chapter is to help you manage the growth of your company. Most growing firms pass through identifiable stages with predictable characteristics. This chapter describes the stages and the common pitfalls, so that you can anticipate problems and hopefully be able to avoid them. You want to enjoy the growth of your company, not be overwhelmed by it.

The Stages of Growth

Existence

The first stage of a small company is Existence. The basic questions at this stage are, "Do you have a viable product?" and "Will enough people buy your products to keep the new venture alive?" The organization is made of yourself and any other partners and a few, if any, employees. You are involved in all aspects of the business, including product design, marketing, raising capital, etc. *You* are the business at this stage and it depends almost entirely on your energy and dedication. If you have a patentable product, this is the stage where you should work on obtaining a patent. You also need to research the market to gauge what potential customers are looking for and to determine if enough people will buy from you so you can stay in existence.

At startup, *you* are the business

Money is difficult to raise at this stage. Banks and venture capitalists are very leery of startup companies. The Small Business Administration (SBA) guarantees some loans to startup firms, but considerable equity and collateral are required. In many cases, the only sources of startup capital are your own resources and those of other individuals who are willing to back you.

Survival

Your business is able to survive if people start buying your products and you generate enough cash to continue paying the bills. At this stage you may hire a few people because you want to stop working sixteen hours a day. Although they may have some special skills for which you hired them, almost everyone in the company needs to be a "jack of all trades" at this point. You delegate some responsibility, but basically you make almost all decisions and you are still involved in all areas of the business. At this stage the company may be only marginally profitable, and you probably aren't able to pay yourself a decent manager's salary or a dividend check as an investor. Nonetheless, your business is generating enough cash to stay alive.

When you have a startup company, capital is hard to find

Capital is still difficult to raise at this stage. You at least have generated some sales, which bankers and venture capitalists appreciate. If you have a business plan that looks promising, you may be able to get a loan or equity financing at this stage from these sources.

The organizational structure is loose. You generally won't have set job descriptions, and people "chip in" on almost any job that has to be done. Planning emphasizes the short-term, usually pointed at staying in business another month. However, this is when you need to rise above the day-to-day pressures and write a longer-term business plan.

Early Success

You have reached the Early Success stage when your business consistently generates enough profits to pay you as a manager and investor. Usually the company has grown to the point that you can no longer make all of the decisions. Other people need to be recruited or promoted to management positions.

Now that you are in less need of capital, banks are happy to loan you money. If your company has the chance of significant growth, venture capitalists may be interested in investing. Cash flow may be an occasional problem, but it is not a constant worry.

Many businesses reach this stage and remain here for long periods of time. If you can find good managers, you may be able to spend much less time with the business. You may choose to disengage yourself from the business and pursue a more comfortable lifestyle, or you may decide to pursue other business ventures. You may decide to sell at this point and pursue something completely different. Or, if the opportunity is there, you may decide to forge ahead and really push the company to grow.

The success stage may be a real plateau and you will need to consciously commit to going beyond that point. For a retail store, it may mean opening several other outlets. For a manufacturer, it may mean design and production of new products after success with an initial product. For some ventures, the success stage may come very quickly and there is almost no time to think about ensuing growth—it just happens. Although the growth may come in different forms and at different rates, it poses similar problems to just about any firm experiencing it.

Once you have achieved some success, you can choose to stay there or forge ahead

High Growth

In this stage, companies experience real growing pains. If you aren't aware of potential problems in advance and don't prepare for them, they can make your life miserable. The first realization you must make is that you have to delegate more responsibilities. You can't have your hand in every decision. You need to give subordinates authority and be able to trust their decisions. You must consciously take the role of a leader and manager and be less involved in the details of the company. If you haven't taken any management courses, you definitely should at this point. You need to be able to set goals, give feedback, and monitor performance. The need for *people* skills is critical. You may be the most technically knowledgeable person in your firm at this point, but if you can't relate well to people and manage them they will be frustrated and your firm will lose productivity. You now need to learn "how to manage managers".

The organizational structure of your company needs to change as the enterprise grows. During the infancy of the firm, the few people involved worked on just about any job that needed to be done. Job responsibilities need to be better defined at this later stage. Job descriptions should be written so that employees have a clear idea of what is expected of them. Employees will become more specialized in their tasks. You may have to hire someone fulltime just to manage accounts receivable, for example. With this increased specialization, you need to promote communication between the different positions and departments so that people do not develop "tunnel vision." Many a company has been plagued by employees who believe that the company exists for the sake of the accounting department, or the sales department. You need to force the different specialists to communicate with each other and you also need to be a cheerleader to remind everyone of where the whole ship is headed. Overall, you are trying to bring structure to a growing organization whose natural tendency is to greater disorder. In the process, however, you are trying not to squelch the entrepreneurial spirit which brought about the growth.

The organizational structure of your company needs to change as the enterprise grows

Growth brings the need to hire or train a few specialists. With few exceptions, you need a skilled marketing person and a skilled finance person. If you are a manufacturer, you also need an experienced production manager. At the early stages one or two people may fill these roles. As growth occurs, each of these positions is so important that one person should be responsible for each area.

In the frenzied atmosphere of a growing firm, you as a manager can be so consumed with the demands of everyday life that you don't allow time for long-range planning. A strategic plan, including a finance and a marketing plan, is extremely important during a period of growth. They serve as road maps for where you are trying to go and keep your energies focused on high priorities. Regardless how busy you are, you must find time to formulate and update strategic plans.

A growing company usually has cash flow problems, even if it is profitable. Growing inventories, accounts receivable, and equipment expenditures cause cash flow problems. You need to set up a cash management system to avoid it. You also should have a financial management system. With the growing number of expenses of the business, you will be hard pressed to keep track of the financial condition of the company "in your head." A financial management system should include budgets, ratio analysis, and financial statement analysis. The purpose of these financial controls

You need to set up a cash management system

is to prohibit your accelerating train from running off of the track— a common occurrence for growing businesses.

Maturity

The Maturity stage is a second version of the Early Success stage. After dramatic growth, sales are leveling off. The company is on firm financial ground and cash flow is not usually a problem. The owner(s) has built considerable wealth and the company can usually run pretty well without the lead entrepreneur being there. Many entrepreneurs lose interest at this stage and seek to sell the business or get cash out of it. A common problem here is the direct opposite of that facing the high growth firm— how to get the large train accelerating again. The size of the organization inhibits its ability to innovate and move quickly.

A problem you face at maturity is how to get the train accelerating again

Conclusion

Most growing companies pass through recognizable stages. You, as the lead entrepreneur of your organization, need to be aware of them. Although the stages may be of different duration for different firms, the problems at each stage are fairly predictable. In this book, the chapters are presented in the order in which those issues normally surface in a growing enterprise. That order is:

Existence

1.	Developing Business Ideas	Chap. 2
2.	Patents, Trademarks, and Copyrights	Chap. 3
3.	Marketing Research	Chap. 4

Survival

1.	Regulations on Doing Business	Chap. 5
2.	Choosing a Form of Business	Chap. 6

Early Success

1.	Raising Capital	Chap. 7
2.	Gathering Your Forces	Chap. 8

High Growth

1.	Strategic Planning	Chap. 9
2.	The Marketing Plan	Chap. 10
3.	Cash Management	Chap. 11
4.	Financial Management	Chap. 12
5.	The Business Plan	Chap. 13

Maturity

1.	Harvesting a Business	Chap. 14

Don't be afraid to "jump ahead" of where your company is currently and read ensuing chapters. Some topics, such as Marketing Research and Cash Management, are always relevant, regardless of the stage of company development. These topics are merely presented at the earliest stages where the need for them is critical.

References

1. Baird, Bruce F. *The Technical Manager.* Belmont, California: Lifetime Learning Publications, 1983.

2. Churchill, Neil C. and Lewis, Virginia L., "The Five Stages of Small Business Growth," *Harvard Business Review*, May-June 1983, pp. 30-38.

3. Timmons, Jeffry A. *New Venture Creation*, 3rd Edition. Homewood, Illinois: Irwin, 1990.

4. Vesper, Karl H. *New Venture Strategies,* Englewood Cliffs, Prentice-Hall, 1990.

5. Vesper, Karl H. *New Venture Mechanics,* Englewood Cliffs, Prentice-Hall, 1993.

2

Developing Business Ideas

To create a successful business, *you must provide something that is unique*. You will not succeed by being average. There are unlimited ways to differentiate your business. It can be the product itself, how it is marketed, the services provided, or the price you charge, to name a few. As an entrepreneur, your head is full of creative business ideas already. It doesn't hurt, however, to look at how other companies have succeeded in differentiating themselves. This chapter presents a variety of approaches that firms have undertaken to make themselves unique.

Ways to Make Your Company Unique

Quality

Quality is the obvious place to start. For any product or service, can you make it more functional? Brakes that stop a car more quickly. A computer monitor that is easier to read. A golf ball that flies further. An accountant who gives you more timely information. A teacher who is better able to communicate. Each of these illustrates an improvement in quality.

You must provide something that is unique

Quicker Response to Customers

Your boat breaks down and you call around to local marinas to get it fixed. If you are lucky, you can get it done before summer is over. Sorry, no loaner boats are available. Some industries have traditionally had very slow response times. A new competitor with a "quick turnaround" strategy would do very well.

Although there are many employment services, Karen E. Chellis believed she could build a differentiated employment agency by giving better attention to quality, service and quick response. In 1989 she started Excel Personnel. It had $5.5 million in revenues in 1994—with the company experiencing a sales increase of 59 per cent in the last two years. The company has assisted more than six thousand people in getting employment over the past five years.

Less Maintenance to Customers

The Maytag repairman epitomizes this form of differentiation. Sell a product which requires less maintenance. If you are an oil driller and are working far from civilization (and from oil rig service businesses), more dependable drilling hardware is worth a lot.

Better Warranty

The car industry has experienced "warranty wars." They are trying to gain your business by assuring you that you will not have to pay for repairs for a longer period of time. Forget the fact that they warrant only about 2 percent of the parts on the car. Customers pay attention to warranties in many industries. Make sure the quality of your product is high enough that warranty expenses will not break you.

Better Service

Listen to customers and dedicate yourself to meeting their needs

Tom Peters, author of *A Passion for Excellence*, says in his presentations, "It has gotten to the point that if you expect good service, people think you are some kind of weirdo!" Nonetheless, some companies excel in service. Nordstroms built its reputation around customer service. The basics of this approach are a willingness to listen to customers' concerns and a dedication to meeting their needs.

Better Trade-in Policy

Some car dealerships give better trade-in values to customers who have bought cars from them. If you are in a business in which customers are constantly changing products or "trading up," this strategy may differentiate you.

Better Compatibility With Other Products

Some products need to work with other components. Computer hardware has to work with software. Automobile parts need to work on automobiles. If your product is more compatible with other units, you have a competitive advantage.

More Flexible Usage

Arm & Hammer is the world champion in this category with its baking soda. It is used to bake, deoderize, disinfect, put out fires, clean, de-acidify, and for untold other applications. Mazda's new mini-van is a passenger, off-road, and towing vehicle all in one unit. With this approach, you design your product to have more applications than your competitors'.

Safer

Safety is a big issue these days, especially as government becomes more involved in legislating it. Volvos are safer for car passengers in collisions. Reinell boats are heavier and thus safer in high waves. Michelin tires protect precious babies. Many products are sold on the basis of higher safety.

Healthier and More Environmentally Conscious

Today there are many customers who respond positively to companies marketing healthy and environmentally friendly products. If in your marketing you stress your environmental consciousness, these people may buy from you, even at higher prices. Can you make products that are healthier, or at least less health-threatening, and more environmentally friendly than your competitors? Salt Lake City's Fountain Fresh dispenses soft drinks from hi-tech, computer-controlled machines into refillable bottles right in groceries and convenience stores. The company encourages customers to save money and do their part in reducing the waste from throw-away containers.

If in your marketing you stress your environmental consciousness, people may buy from you, even at higher prices

More Compact and More Portable

The battleground in electronics industries is over who can make products smaller and lighter. Notebook computers now have more power than desktop models three years ago had. Sony created a new industry when it developed the Walkman portable cassette stereo. Portability is important in non-electronic industries also. Bikes that can be folded up and carried around easily are now being sold. Baby strollers can be broken down into small portable units.

More Attractive

Even if you don't change the functionality of a product, you can change its appearance. The trends in fashion colors change nearly every year, and if you keep producing with the same old colors you may be in trouble. Do you remember the old Opel GT's? The cars were pretty much gutless wonders but they looked like mini-Corvettes, and hence they sold. With many generic products, packaging is what convinces a customer to purchase a particular brand.

More Status Appeal

Let's face it, some people buy certain products because of the status associated with them. Calvin Klein jeans weren't popular because of their rugged durability, rather because of the Calvin Klein name, their high cost, and because Brooke Shields wore them. People travel to Sun Valley and pay "big bucks" for everything because of the reputation the area has gained. Oil of Olay probably may not lubricate your skin any better than does Vaseline Intensive Care, but people buy it because of the mystique the company has built around the product.

Better Service to Dealers

You need to service dealers as well as customers

Sometimes differentiation is pointed not at the end user, rather at the intermediate resellers. Frito-Lay's chips may not be any better than anyone else's, yet the timeliness and reliability of their delivery trucks prompts retailers to buy from them. Some companies offer better credit terms to dealers, and thus influence them to carry their products. Perhaps you can provide better display racks than your competitors and thus get resellers to carry your products.

More Convenient Hours

We occasionally see businesses such as grocery stores and banks announcing new evening hours to provide more convenient access. They must balance the extra cost of operating such hours against the new business they get from additional customers. Convenience stores charge substantially higher prices to operate 24 hours a day profitably. Granted, if you change your hours and are successful, other stores will probably copy your idea. Nonetheless, you probably brought more people into the market.

More Fun for the Customer

People love to have fun

Bennihana's Restaurants have been successful around the world. Probably the most distinctive part of their meals is the fact that they are cooked right in front of you. The cooks dazzle customers by juggling knives, cutting vegetables, and tossing food onto plates. McDonald's attracts so many customers because kids love to go there— it's fun!

Friendlier Environment

Do you ever patronize a certain business because the people are friendly and nice to deal with? Some business managers set goals for friendliness and courtesy and give rewards to employees based on their performance in these areas.

Getting the Wheels Turning

Sometimes all you need to create a unique product or service is a little inspiration and some innovative ideas. The following approaches to innovation might work in your business.

Adapt Features of Other Products

Do you know where the idea of roll-on deodorant came from? Of course, from the ballpoint pen. Diffusion of technology gives new opportunities for adaptations of products in other industries. Since the advent of computer aided technology, many industries have undergone revolutionary changes in how they design and manufacture new products. The graphic arts industry is jumping on the band wagon of revolutionary change and is embracing computer aided technology. Onyx Graphics of Salt Lake is a good example of a highly adaptive company. Onyx is the world leader in the development of large format (any printing larger than 18" x 22") digital color printing software. You've probably seen and been impressed with marketing displays created by this innovative company. This Company was founded in 1989 by Charles Edwards and Dean Wittman and now has revenues of several million dollars. Onyx markets its systems to reprographic bureaus, photographic labs, service bureaus, outdoor advertising, etc.

The company holds a proprietary color enhancement algorithm that accurately reproduces photographic images and graphics on a variety of color printers. The system automatically compensates for inefficiencies of the input and output devices like scanners and printers respectively. Onyx has developed a new patented printing algorithm that dramatically enhances resolution and color quality for use with conventional computer printers. The company has also developed high speed interfaces for high resolution scanners and a wide variety of color printers.

Modify the Product

Product modification may involve only a very minor change

Product modification may involve only a very minor change. Adding a new color to a tool-handle may give a product a "new" and attractive appeal. Alternatively, a change may be one that is technologically superior. The Utah CFA company produces and markets an advanced hybrid air bag system (stored argon gas). The result is a more environmentally safe system which is a low-cost alternative to the capital-intensive solid pyrotechnic systems (sodium azide) now generally used in air-bag production.

The typical floral shop has been around for years, but Lorraine A. Miller decided she could put a novel twist to that business and created Cactus and Tropicals in 1975. Specializing in the narrow niche of cacti and other exotic plants, it now has the largest variety of cacti of any other similar business. Starting with only $2,000, the business grew into a 29-employee company with annual revenues in excess of $1.1 million by 1994. Cactus and Tropicals now occupies over 10,000 square feet, including greenhouses, an office building and a retail gift shop. The founder, Lorraine A. Miller was awarded the distinction of The National Small Business Person of the year in 1994 by the Small Business Administration.

A variety of creative approaches can be used to develop new products

Product modifications are often necessary to achieve growth in a company. Too often new ventures start with a single product or service, and the entrepreneur becomes complacent and slow to react to the competition. Other firms copy the product and improve it, and the originator of the product is left behind. Teletrust of Utah demonstrates the opportunity in modifying products. The Company started in 1986 with about $5,000 and saw its future in the cellular phone market. Faltering in its original business concept, it diversified with 800-line telemarketing, debit calling cards and other services, making needed changes in management as it went along. The Company now has $1 million plus in earnings and employs hundreds.

Substitute Components

For those of you with children who have recently been in diapers, you probably noticed a change in diaper technology in the last several years. You can now buy "super absorbent" diapers which are wafer thin but absorb incredible amounts of moisture. If you forget to change diapers, your child won't get wet from leakage, she'll get bowlegged from walking around with so much weight between her legs. One of the major diaper producers developed this incredible diaper by putting a new substance in them— gelatin. It absorbs the water and turns into Jello!

Combine Features

Can you introduce a product which has features which appeal to different segments of the market? Miller Brewing Co. has used this approach with its Lite beer. "Less filling, tastes great" brings together what used to be incompatible features. Composite tennis rackets bring the "feel" of wood plus the strength of graphite to tennis players.

Revive What is Dead

Some products seem to be resurrected periodically. Hula Hoops are back in. So are skateboards, Black Jack gum, troll dolls, and short skirts. You don't have to invent something new, you just have to be there ready when it returns to popularity.

Copy the Trend Setters

You do not need to be creative to copy someone else. However, it does take ingenuity to shape the concept so that it will work in your city, state or region. Go to areas with reputations for setting the trends and keep your eyes open. Some of those ideas may work well locally, and you could be first in introducing them.

Conclusion

You cannot put a box around creativity. Therefore, you cannot derive a complete checklist of creative options. The ideas in this chapter will prompt you to think of ways of making your business unique.

Be aware that the world is full of copiers (you were encouraged to do it yourself.) Therefore, any uniqueness you gain will probably only be temporary. You must therefore *consistently* search for new ways of standing apart from the pack. This is the fun of entrepreneuring.

References

1. Baird, Bruce F. *The Technical Manager*. Belmont, California: Lifetime Learning Publications, 1983.

2. Peters, Thomas J. and Austin, Nancy K. *A Passion for Excellence*. New York: Warner Books, Inc., 1985.

3. Thompson, Arthur A. and Strickland, A. J. *Strategic Management*, Sixth Edition. Plano, Texas: Business Publications, Inc., 1992.

3

Patents, Trademarks, and Copyrights

Free competition is the backbone of America's capitalistic system. From your company's perspective, however, you are wise to deter competition by inhibiting other firms from copying you. There are various means of inhibiting others from copying you, and this chapter discusses three: patents, trademarks, and copyrights.

Patents

If your business will be based on a novel invention, you need to become familiar with at least the basics of patent law. Patents are a complex subject, and this chapter can only provide an overview. A patent is "a right guaranteed by the government to a person or corporation which gives its holder the right to exclude others from making, using, or selling the invention "claimed" in the patent deed."

There are three types of patents

There are three types of patents— utility, design, and plant. A utility patent can be granted for a "new, useful, and nonobvious process, machine, manufactured article, composition, or an improvement in any of these items." A design patent can be granted for a "new, original, and ornamental design for an article of manufacture. A design patent only protects the appearance of an article and not its structure or utilitarian features." Filing an application for a design patent is significantly easier than filing one for a utility patent. A plant patent can be granted to anyone who "has invented, or discovered and asexually reproduced any distinct and new variety of plant, including cultivated spores, mutants, hybrids, and newly found seedlings, other than a tuber-propagated plant or a plant found in an uncultivated state." Utility and plant patents are in effect for seventeen years from the date of issue, while design patents are in effect for only fourteen years.

The government does not seek out patent infringers

A patent may be compared to a hunting license. It enables you to legally "go after" a patent infringer through a suit filed in federal court. The government does not seek out patent infringers; rather, you must take action against them. In such a suit, you ask the judge to order that the infringer no longer make, use, or sell the invention claimed. You also typically ask for monetary damages to compensate for the loss of income sustained during the period when the patent was infringed.

Be aware the patent is merely a license to sue, not a guarantee that the suit will be successful. There are many reasons why the suit might not be successful, including the fact that the patent might be shown by the infringer to be invalid, despite having already been issued by the government! Even if your law suit is successful, the legal fees—$200,000 or more is typical—for pursuing infringement action could be greater than the infringer is ever able to pay. And this says nothing for the loss in your time and energy during what may be a very long, frustrating process, particularly if more than one infringement action needs to be filed at the same time. There is intellectual property insurance that is available to help defray the costs of enforcing intellectual property rights. Check with insurance agents to see if this option is worth exploring.

You have to spend a significant amount of money to obtain a patent, even if you do a large amount of the work yourself. You can perform a search yourself, otherwise you may pay someone else from $400 to $1000. Depending on the complexity of the patent application, you may pay an attorney from $2500 to $5000 to prepare the patent application. The cost can go considerably higher.

A patent is only a starting point in the entrepreneurial process

Fewer than one patent in ten pays for even its own filing cost, let alone a significant profit to its inventor. A patent is *no guarantee of commercial success*. Most people who file patent applications are not business people— they are inventors. A patent is only a starting point in the entrepreneurial process.

This introduction is not intended to dissuade you from pursuing a patent. It remains one of the best forms of insurance available to inventors and companies which generate proprietary products or processes. You need to be aware, however, that receiving a patent requires money and effort, and that you still have a long way to go in building a successful business.

The Patent Process

To be eligible to receive a United States patent, you must file a patent application *within one year* of the date on which you first publish, publicly use, sell, or offer your invention for sale. To be eligible for most foreign patents, you must file your application *before* you take any of the above steps. Patent materials are submitted to:

Patent and Trademark Office (PTO)
Washington, D.C. 20231

Once you file a patent application, you usually have to wait between one and three years for the Patent Office to review and decide whether or not to grant you a patent. By filing a patent you establish *potentially valuable* rights against any inventor who later conceives of the same invention and applies for a patent on it. However, during this waiting, or "pending" period, *you have no legal rights to file a suit against an infringer.* You may send the infringer a warning letter, but you only receive your right to sue when the patent is issued.

While in the "patent pending" stage, all documents relating to the invention are held "secret" by the Patent Office; however, if a patent is granted, the patent disclosure becomes public information.

If you plan to have your invention manufactured by another company or plan to sell your invention outright to them, filing for a patent may be a precondition for that company to look at your invention. They will usually insist that you sign a waiver agreement, which states that they will only respect the rights to your invention to the extent to which these rights are covered by the "claims" in your patent. Consequently, if your patent claims prove to be deficient, your protection may be limited or non-existent.

How Much Can You Do Yourself?

A good patent attorney can help you write an application that really protects you

You can do it all yourself, in spite of the fact that the legalities can be complex, but you need to be willing to invest a significant amount of time learning the process. You read about prison inmates who take law bar examinations without ever going to law school. They just read all the materials in the prison library. By the same token, you can teach yourself the field of patent law. However, most people turn the whole process over to an attorney and hope that the costs do not become exorbitant. They do not wish to become bogged down in all of the legalities of writing a good patent application.

It is generally not difficult to prepare a written description of an invention in a patent application, however, writing one that *really protects you* is a fine art. This is where the experience of a good patent attorney is invaluable. Appendix A contains a general description of the steps involved in patenting a product. If you are serious about doing it yourself, you should get the book *Patent It Yourself* (see citation at the end of the chapter.) It is a complete guide to the patenting process. Even if you hire an attorney to do your patent work, knowing this material can help you facilitate his work and can significantly reduce its cost.

Trademarks

You may spend a considerable amount of time and money developing a reputation for your company and products. You need to protect that investment from copiers. Trademarks provide such protection. Even if your name is John McDonald, you don't have the right to open a restaurant called McDonalds. You don't have the right to sell a "Big Mac," either. Both the company and the product name are trademarks. A trademark is "any symbol, sign, word, name, device, or combination of these that tells who makes a product or who sells it, distinguishing it from those made or sold by others." [2]

Registering a Trademark

You don't *have* to register a trademark, but it is a wise idea

You establish your trademark by being the first to use it for a certain category of goods. Some companies register their trademarks for an advertising message, as has Megahertz Corporation, a Salt Lake producer of data/fax modem cards for mobile computers. Their advertising trade mark message "Linking Your Worlds" and their logo "XJACK" are trademarks.

The official registration establishes rights throughout the United States, notifies others of your trademark and protects you from infringement of other parties. If, within five years of registration, old bills of sale or advertisements prove that someone else used your trademark previously, they still hold rights to it. Nonetheless, you should register your company name and major product names if you will be selling products outside of Utah. You register trademarks with the Patent and Trademark Office (PTO), whose address and trademark information hotline number are given below. The registration lasts twenty years, at which point you can renew it.

State Registration of a Trademark

Trademarks and service marks may be registered in Utah for a term of ten years. You have to be careful when choosing an attorney for filing for a trademark or patent. Fees may vary significantly and thorough research is therefore suggested.

Form:	Application for Registration of Trademark or Service Mark
Filling Fee:	Original Application - $20 Renewal Application - $20

Contact: Trademark Coordinator
Division of Corporations and Commercial Code
160 East 300 South
Salt Lake City, UT 84111
(801) 530-6026

Until just recently, you had to use a company or product name publicly and in more than one state before you could register them. The United States Department of Commerce now allows trademark registration applications based on "intent to use." If they approve this, you can apply for a trademark before the name is used and then later notify the PTO when the product is put into use. The filing fee for a trademark is $245. Application forms are available from the PTO.

Before applying for a trademark, you should make a *search* of registered names. There are several ways of doing it. A patent attorney will gladly have it done for you. She will hire a professional trademark search firm and then tack on her own fee. If you work directly with the search firm, you save the lawyer's add-on fee. Look in yellow pages under "Trademark Searchers" or "Patent Searchers." You may have to consult yellow pages in metropolitan areas to find some firms. If you look in the Washington, D.C. directory, you'll find plenty.

You can do a trademark search on your own without too much difficulty

Federal Registration of a Trademark and Patent

Contact: Trademark Information Hotline
(703) 557-3158
U.S. Commissioner of Patents and Trademarks
Washington, D.C. 20231
(703) 557-3158

Federal trademark information is also available at the Marriott Library at the University of Utah. *Caution: Federally registered trademarks may conflict with and supersede Utah registered business and product names* [8]. Businesses are encouraged to check for conflicts with federal trademarks." If you have questions about whether your trademark is infringing on others, an experienced patent and trademark attorney's opinion is important. The following issues are considered by courts in determining trademark infringement:

1. The distinctiveness of the complainant's mark.
2. The similarity of the marks.
3. The proximity of the parties' products.
4. The likelihood of the complainant bridging the gap between noncompeting products.
5. The similarity of the parties' trade channels and advertising methods.
6. The quality of the alleged infringer's products.
7. The sophistication of the particular customers.

Types of Trademarks

There are several types of trademarks

There are several types of trademarks. The first is for product names, such as "Cabbage Patch Dolls." A trademark for a company name is called a trade name, such as "Eastern Airlines." A service mark distinguishes a company's service, i.e. Hertz' "Drive Yourself Service." If a trademark contains some pictorial or design element, it is called a logotype, or logo. You can, and should, register your logo.

Using a Trademark

The successful trademark is one that complements, and distinguishes, your company and product images. It should be used in all advertising, packaging, and correspondence. Maintain the same logo over time, since recognition is crucial. Register trademarks, since the registration discourages copiers and gives you increased legal clout. Be aware that trademarks, like patents, do not provide ironclad protection. If you feel that someone has infringed on your trademark, *you* must initiate action, since the government won't do it on its own. The effort and expense in suing over trademark infringement can be considerable, $80,000 to $160,000 is not unusual.

Copyrights

Copyrights protect "original works of authorship" against copying and unauthorized public performance. They cover literary, dramatic, musical, artistic, and other intellectual works, including computer software. The protection is available to published and unpublished works. A copyright is in effect for the author's life plus fifty years.

How to Secure a Copyright

No registration is required with the Copyright Office to secure a copyright. Your work is "automatically" copyrighted when it is created. You would be wise, however, to file a formal copyright application with the Library of Congress. There are benefits to registration such as statutory damages and attorney fees for infringement lawsuits. This establishes a "public record" of your claim and it also helps you in any copyright law suit. The filing fee is only $20. For copyright forms and information, contact:

Your work is automatically copyrighted when you create it and provide notice of intent to copyright

Copyright Office
Library of Congress
Washington, D.C. 20559
(202) 287-8700

In anything that you copyright, you must give official notice of copyright, even if you do not officially file with the Copyright Office. The notice should contain three elements.

— The symbol ©, or the word "copyright", or the abbreviation "Copr."
— The year of first publication of your work
— The name of the owner of the copyright.

For example, © 1995 Microsoft Corporation

Conclusion

Patents, trademarks, and copyrights can protect valuable proprietary rights for your company. Take the necessary steps to register those elements of your business that can be protected under these programs. Realize, however, that in almost all cases *you* must initiate action when you feel there is an infringement. Legal action is slow and costly.

References

1. Jones, Stacy V. *The Inventor's Patent Handbook.* New York: The Dial Press, 1969.

2. Levy, Richard C. *Inventing and Patenting Sourcebook.* Detroit: Gale Research, 1990.

3. Pressman, David. *Patent It Yourself.* New York: McGraw-Hill Book Company, 1979.

4. Richardson, Robert O. *How to Get Your Own Patent.* New York: Sterling Publishing Co., 1981.

5. Russell, J. Thomas et. al. *Kleppner's Advertising Procedure*, 10th Ed. Englewood Cliffs, New Jersey: Prentice Hall, Inc., 1986.

6. Samuels, Jeffery M. *Patent, Trademark, and Copyright Laws.* Washington, D.C.: The Bureau of National Affairs, Inc., 1987.

7. *General Information Concerning Patents.* Washington, D.C.: U.S. Department of Commerce, Patent and Trademark Office, 1989.

8. USBDC Doing Business In Utah. *A Guide to Business Information.* Salt Lake City: SBA, 1993.

4

Marketing Research

"You don't become successful in business by trying to be successful, you become successful by meeting customers' needs."
Peter Drucker

One of the most common reasons businesses flounder or fail is that management is not in touch with what customers want. The company makes products that management wants, but not necessarily what people are willing to buy. The basic purpose of marketing research is *to give management a clear idea of who customers are and what they want.* Market research also provides information on the size of markets and whether or not they are growing.

Although market research should be an on-going project, it is especially critical in the following circumstances:

- As a business is being planned, before the doors open
- Before new products are introduced
- When sales are declining
- When new competitors enter the market

The market information you gather helps you formulate a marketing strategy, which includes how to design, price, promote, package, service, and distribute products.

Types of Marketing Research

The two major types of marketing research are *qualitative* and *quantitative* research. In general, qualitative research uses a small sample and does not employ statistical analysis to arrive at conclusions. It typically costs less, is more appropriate at early stages of the research process, and provides less precise conclusions than does quantitative research. Quantitative research is characterized by a large sample size, and results are considered representative of a larger population. The most frequently employed quantitative techniques include telephone interviewing, mall intercepts and mail questionnaires. Other distinctive features include controlled research data collection and the use of formal interviewing instruments (questionnaires). Quantitative research draws from a large enough sample so that researchers can analyze responses quantitively and employ statistical techniques. The primary types of qualitative research described in this chapter are:

- Expert interviews
- Case studies
- Focus groups

The main forms of quantitative research are:

- Secondary data studies
- Experiments
- Questionnaires

All of these research methods are described in this chapter.

The research method you choose should be based on the type of information you want to get

The research method you choose should be based on the type of information you want to get. Although the qualitative methods can generate in-depth information, it may be biased. In expert interviews, case studies, and focus groups you are hearing from only a few sources. If you feel confident of those sources, the research may be valid. In many cases, however, the opinion of a few is not representative of the way the entire market might respond, and therefore you have faulty information. Because quantitative techniques gather information from a greater number of sources, the data might be more reliable. In many cases, qualitative techniques initially generate ideas, and quantitative techniques are then used to substantiate initial qualitative findings.

The second issue in choosing a research method is how much money you are willing to spend. You can do any of the research methods yourself, or you can hire a marketing research consultant. A consultant typically charges $50/hour or more, so the research can easily cost $5000. Expert interviews, case studies, and secondary data are research methods you can do yourself— if you have the time. Focus groups, questionnaires, and experiments are more involved. You can do them yourself, but you must learn the techniques and invest quite a bit of time in the research process. The information in this book describes each of these research techniques, but you would be wise to read the books listed in the bibliography to gain more in-depth knowledge of them.

Qualitative Research

Expert Interviews

An *expert interview* is a discussion with someone who knows much about the industry you are researching, perhaps a person who has competed in the industry for some time. In some cases, that person may not be threatened by a newcomer to the industry and may freely offer information. You may have to talk to quite a few people before you find one willing to share her experiences, but your efforts will be rewarded if you perservere. Be honest when you approach such people and communicate your intentions of starting a business. They will quickly decide whether they want to talk to you. If you misrepresent the fact that you are a potential competitor, they will see right through you.

An expert may not be threatened by a newcomer

There are other places to search for experts. *Adjacent industries* are possibilities. Assume that you make furniture and want to find out more how to market it. If you call other manufacturers and ask them for help, they may not respond, especially if you have similar products. An industry adjacent to furniture building would be the lighting industry. Typically, lamps and furniture are sold in the same stores and through the same channels. If you spoke to a lighting manufacturer, they would not be afraid of giving you information that could be used competitively against them.

Retailers, sales reps, suppliers, and industry associations, as well as customers, can be experts on an industry. If you make furniture, speak to the most prominent furniture retailers about customers and their buying habits. Sales reps are independent business people who sell different manufacturers' products, usually to retail outlets (see Chapter 10). Since they are in contact with a large number of manufacturers and retailers, they often know the industry very well. If there are only a few suppliers to your industry, they often can tell you a lot about it. If you want to open a pizza restaurant, the few suppliers of food products to your area will be able to tell you quite a bit, including sales trends, which of your competitors does the most business with them, etc. Industry associations usually gather statistics on the industry and survey customers. The officers of an association, especially if they were involved with the research, are often experts on an industry. Experienced customers can tell you a lot about an industry. If you make boats, talk to some old-timer on the lake who has been buying boats for fifty years. He'll know a lot about the industry and customers. In an expert interview, you are seeking information from someone who knows your industry.

Focus Groups

Researchers use focus groups to generate ideas or gather information about customers. The advantage of a focus group over interviews with individuals is that the people can respond to each other. One of them may bring up a point that another had not thought about, and thus the group can provide depth of information that individual interviews cannot. A focus group is usually comprised 6 to 12 consumers and meets for up to two hours. In many cases a focus group is conducted as initial research. With the ideas generated from the group, a questionnaire is designed and customers are surveyed so that responses from a larger number of people are obtained.

Just about *any* business can get a group of its present or potential customers together and quiz them as to their product preferences, views about competitors, and buying habits. If you own a fitness center, call 12 members, offer them a free lunch, and tell them you want their honest opinions about your center and fitness in general. Many customers are anxious to express their opinions on any topic.

The advantage of a focus group over interviews with individuals is that the people can respond to each other

You need to plan a focus group. Invite 6 to 12 people. A group less than six tends not to have the interaction and idea generation that you would like. A group of more than 12 becomes hard to manage and some people do not get much chance to participate. In general, you try to have groups that are relatively homogeneous. For the health club, you might want to have separate groups for aerobics and weight lifters. If those two differing groups were together, they might be reticent to voice their true opinions (like weight lifters wanting to tear out the dance floor so that more weights could be added). You therefore first need to decide if you need several focus groups for the different types of customers that you serve. Strangers in focus groups tend to be less inhibited and express their opinions more freely. Try not to assemble a group of people who know each other well.

A focus group needs a *moderator*. She introduces the general topics for discussion and brings the discussion back on track if it wanders. The moderator should blend into the group and not appear different from the group. For example, male groups usually have male moderators and young groups usually have young moderators, etc. Although the moderator needs to have a well thought-out plan for the session, she tries to play a minor role and let the discussion sustain itself on the various topics introduced. She should attempt to tone down those who are outspoken and tend to dominate discussions. You should not have an employee of your company be the moderator. You want people to express honest opinions, including negative ones, and many are reticent to do so knowing a member of the organization is present.

Most focus groups are recorded on a tape recorder. This relieves the moderator or anyone else of having to take notes during the session. Some focus groups are video-taped, which helps you to review participants' reactions and gestures. Some professional marketing research firms have special rooms equipped with cameras and one-way mirrors, so that you see observe people's reactions "live." A problem with this is that some people become inhibited with a camera pointing at them or knowing that someone is watching them.

The primary drawback of a focus group is its sample size

Focus groups are excellent tools for gathering in-depth information on a variety of topics. You can usually obtain much richer data from these than from questionnaires. Their primary drawback is the sample size. You may get good information, but is it representative of all customers? To substantiate findings in focus groups, surveys are usually performed afterwards.

Case Studies

A *case study* is an in-depth research project of a particular person or situation. The advantage of this technique is the depth of information obtained. The disadvantage, similar to focus groups, is that you are studying only one or a few subjects and therefore the results may be biased. Assume that you manufacture fishing poles and you want to understand the mind set of potential customers. In a case study approach, you would pick one or only a few persons and seek to understand all of their considerations in purchasing a new fishing pole. Perhaps you would go fishing with them and quiz them about what features they like and dislike in poles. Perhaps you would talk to them about the poles they own and what their thought process was in deciding to buy them. Perhaps you would go with them to a local fishing shop and ask them about the products there and how they are merchandised. In a case study, you try to determine *all* of the relevant variables that affect your subject and the decisions that they make.

Assume that you own the same fishing pole company and are perplexed by the fact that some retailers to whom you sell are able to move many poles while others move almost none. A case study approach to this problem would be to go to both a retail store that has high sales and to one that has low sales and observe how the poles are sold. Do salespeople push them? Where are they displayed in the store? What competitive poles are stocked? These are only a few questions to be answered which could explain the different sales levels. The basic approach of a case study is to study only a few units but obtain in-depth information.

Quantitative Research

Secondary Data

Secondary data contain research information which is gathered by someone else but that you are able to use. The advantages of secondary data are that they are not expensive and in most cases are accurate (but check the sources). The disadvantage is that you rarely can find just the information you are looking for-- you have to settle for what you get.

Secondary data contain research information which is gathered by someone else but that you are able to use

Secondary data usually relate to industry structure. They include statistics on total industry sales, on number of businesses, on industry payroll, etc. These describe more the *suppliers* in the industry than the consumers. Some people believe that marketing research relates strictly to users of products and services, and therefore this type of information should be considered *industry structure*. Whether the information describes customers or the industry, it is still helpful to you in formulating a marketing strategy. Therefore, it is included in this chapter on marketing research. You will see reference to the same information in other sections that deal with industry structure.

The U.S. Government publishes incredible amounts of information, some of which is valuable to certain businesses. The Census Bureau publishes business industry statistics every five years in the *Census of Retail Trade, Census of Wholesale Trade, Census of Service Industries, Census of Manufactures, Census of Mineral Industries, Census of Construction Industries*, and *Census of Agriculture*. Each census provides data on the number of companies, sales, number of employees, total payroll, expenses, and other statistics. They are provided for the entire U.S., by state, and by county. State and county statistics are reported in large, general industries. Federal statistics are cited by specific, narrowly defined industries. Besides the business censuses, the U.S. Government also publishes the *Census of Population* and the *Census of Housing*. All U.S. Census documents are available at the Marriott Library at the University of Utah and at different libraries in Utah which are designated Official U.S. Publication

Depositories. The Internal Revenue Service publishes extensive financial information on industries in the *IRS Source Book of Statistics of Income*. Contact your local IRS office to obtain the book.

Industry Studies. There are two primary sources of industry studies. The first is exhaustive, book-length reports that are usually done by economists. You can look for such references in the card catalogs of major libraries. If you have access to a database system which provides references to other libraries, you can often get the study on "inter-library" loan from another library.

The second type of industry study is much shorter, typically done by consulting or investment companies. Examples of such companies are Wall Street research houses, Arthur D. Little, Stanford Research Institute, Business Trends Analysts, Business Communications Company, Martin & Martin, E.R.C. statistics, and others. Business Trend Analysts, Inc. in New York, prints a listing of over 150 industry studies that it will sell. The cost of such studies ranges from $800 to $1500. Business Trend Analysts, Inc.'s phone number is (516) 462-2410.

Company Directories. Several directories publish information on both public and private U.S. companies. The *Thomas Registry of American Manufacturers*, the *Dun & Bradstreet Million Dollar Directory* and *Middle Market Directory*, *Standard & Poor's Register of Corporations*, and the various Moody's publications list companies by industry. Some give limited financial information. Check your local libraries for these directories. Dun & Bradstreet compiles credit reports on all companies of significant size and charges a fee to member companies which want the information. You need to use this information with caution. It is not audited and some is self-reported, therefore there can be errors in the information.

Several directories publish information on both public and private U.S. companies

Company Documents. Some companies publish annual reports which contain company information. Write to the company and ask them to send one. If a firm has publicly traded stock, it must file Securities and Exchange Commission (SEC) quarterly report 10-Q and annual report 10-K. These are public information and can be obtained by contacting the SEC. The companies are required to provide complete financial data and also operating information.

Business Information Guides. Several guides to sources of business information are published. The following four are some of the more widely distributed ones.

Where to Find Business Information: A Worldwide Guide for Everyone Who Needs the Answers to Business Questions. This reference book lists over 5,000 publications of current interest.

An Annotated Guide for Harvard Business School Students. It is a superb guide to most of the business reference books found in libraries.

Encyclopedia of Business Information Sources. By industry, this book lists sources of information, trade associations, trade journals, and other pertinent industry information.

Check your local library to see if it has one of these information guides. If not, you should encourage them to purchase one of them. They are very helpful in finding industry information.

Financial Information Sources. Several companies publish industry financial data, which includes financial ratios and common-size financial statements. Most libraries will have one of the following sources of financial information.

Several companies publish industry financial data

- Robert Morris Associates
- Dun & Bradstreet
- Standard and Poor's

Chapter 12 discusses how this information can be used in financial analysis.

Databases. On-line computer databases are becoming increasingly popular. Some of them contain information on specific industries. The following resources provide information on databases.

Directory of Online Databases

Information Industry Market Place: An International Directory of Information Products and Services

Trade Associations. Just about every industry has one or more trade associations whose purpose is to promote the entire industry. They typically publish trade publications. The associations often conduct industry surveys and then print the results. Contact any associations in your industry and see what information they have available. If you are unsure what associations exist in your industry, consult the *Encyclopedia of Associations*, the *Directory of Directories*, or the

National Trade and Professional Associations of the United States and Canada and Labor Unions.

Experiments

An experiment is a situation where you manipulate a variable, hold others constant, and look at the effect on another variable. For example, assume you are trying to decide between two different types of packaging for a model boat kit you are manufacturing. You decide to try the first type of packaging at Douglas Models in Salt Lake City and the second type at the West Valley Hobbies in West Valley City. After three months, with permission of the stores, you reverse the arrangement to see whether one type of package tends to sell better in both stores. If so, and other factors seem to be equal, you adopt that package design for the ensuing production runs. Both stores have had similar sales of the product in the last year. After three months, the packaging that sells more will be the one you incorporate for ensuing production runs. The advantage of the experiment over other research techniques is that you can try different marketing approaches in a "live" situation. Asking people what they would do is one matter. Observing what they do is another. Like other research techniques, an experiment allows you to test different marketing approaches on a small scale before trying them on a broad scale.

The advantage of the experiment is that you can try different marketing approaches in a "live" situation

Experimental Variable. There are three general classes of experimental variables: independent, dependent, and control. In the boat example, the independent variable was the one you manipulated, which was the packaging of the doll. The dependent variable was the one which you observed to see the effects-- sales of the doll. Control variables are other factors which can affect the dependent variable, but you try to keep them constant.

The key to a successful experiment is to control other "confounding" factors to ensure that changes in the dependent variable (sales) are due only to changes in the independent variable (packaging). To control such factors as well as possible several steps might help. First, the stores should be comparable in sales, merchandise selection, type of customers and levels and types of advertising. Second, the experimenter in this case should make sure that the boat models were similarly priced and displayed in both stores. Third, the local economies of the stores should be assessed for similarity during the test period, including possible seasonality effects to assure that differences in sales were not the result of differences in those factors. Fourth, the experimenter should check to be sure that competing brands of boats were not introduced at just one of the stores and not at the other during the test. Fifth, the experimenter should also make sure that salespeople promoted the boats similarly at both stores. Failure to control for possible differences in such variables between stores can yield misleading results.

A variety of marketing questions might be answered through properly controlled experiments. Product features might be changed and customer reaction assessed. Prices can be changed. Different types of promotion might be used. In similar market areas, you might try newspaper advertising in one and television advertising in the other. If you are considering hiring inhouse salespeople, try one or two in a few areas to see how they do. Perhaps you are considering direct marketing your products and have obtained a large mailing list. Rather than mail to all of the people on the list, which is costly, mail to a small experimental group and gauge the response.

A multitude of experimental designs exists. Some have only two groups. One receives the experimental treatment (change in price, packaging, etc.) while a control group does not. Some designs can have as many as eight groups. To select a design, you must study a marketing research text which discusses in detail experimental design. Several books are listed in the bibliography at the end of this chapter. Marketing research consultants can assist you in design or they can perform the entire experiment for you, if you are willing to pay the fees. Experiments need to be carefully designed. You can do it yourself, but you need to be well versed in the different possible approaches.

Questionnaires

A questionnaire, or market survey, is a tool for gathering information about current or potential customers. It is one of the most widely used forms of marketing research. A questionnaire is usually considered quantitative research, which lends itself to statistical analysis, if a large enough sample size is used. A survey can range from an exhaustive phone survey of your current nationwide customers to a one-page questionnaire that customers fill out while in your store. Information gathered from a questionnaire is used to formulate the marketing strategy for the firm, which includes how products are designed, priced, promoted, packaged, serviced, and distributed.

Information gathered from a questionnaire is used to formulate the marketing strategy

Steps in Questionnaire Development. Listed below are the traditional steps in questionnaire development:

1. Decide on Purpose of Questionnaire
2. Select Sampling Method

3. Decide Number and Types of Questions on Each Topic
4. Design the Topic Sequence
5. Write Questions and Response Categories
6. Decide on Layout and Format
7. Pretest and Revise

The sequence may vary somewhat on different projects, and in many cases it is a cyclical process-- you proceed through several steps, then go back and revise what you did previously. For example, you may have decided that questions concerning customers' opinions of competitors should come near the end of the survey. However, after writing out the questionnaire you find that respondents cannot answer some other questions relating to the entire industry until they have thought about competitors. Therefore, you may need to back up and redesign the questionnaire so that competitor questions come earlier in the survey.

The process of designing a questionnaire is a cyclical one

There are many books and references on writing questionnaires. You can obtain a short handbook entitled, *How to Write a Questionnaire*, by contacting:

University Press
PO Box 4946
Missoula, MT 59806
(800)243-6840
Cost: $7.00

Before you begin a survey research project, you should read this or the many other references on questionnaire development.

If your plan to conduct business from your home, you can obtain additional information to help you frame appropriate marketing research by calling U.S. West's toll-free number: 1-800-898-WORK. Callers may request a *Home Office Resource Guide.*

Conclusion

Marketing research is important at all stages of company growth, but it is especially critical at early stages. As a young firm, you cannot afford to make marketing mistakes. Blunders can put you under. The purpose of marketing research is to understand your customers and what motivates them to buy. Since your customers' tastes and motivations change over time, the need for research is on-going.

References

1. Brownstone, David M. *Where to Find Business Information: A Worldwide Guide for Everyone Who Needs the Answers to Business Questions*. New York: Wiley, 1982.

2. Daniela, Lorna M. *An Annotated Guide for Harvard Business School Students*, revised edition. Boston: Baker Library, Graduate School of Business Administration, Harvard University, 1979.

3. Luck, Adele K., Wales, Mary F., and Rubin, Cynthia B. *Marketing Research*. Englewood Cliffs, New Jersey: Prentice Hall Inc., 1982.

4. Marlow, Cecilia A. *Directory of Directories*. Detroit, Gale Research Co., 1991.

5. Parasuraman, A. *Marketing Research*. Reading, Mass: Addison-Wesley Publishing Co, Inc., 1986.

6. Timmons, Jeffry A. *New Venture Creation*, 2nd Edition. Homewood, Illinois: Irwin, 1990.

7. *Annual Statement Studies*. Philadelphia: Robert Morris Associates, 1991.

8. *Encyclopedia of Associations*, 23rd Edition. Detroit: Gale Research Co., 1991.

9. *Encyclopedia of Business Information Sources*, Sixth Edition. Detroit: Gale Research Co., 1991.

10. *Encyclopedia of Information Systems and Services*. Detroit: Gale Research, 1989.

11. *Directory of Online Databases*. Santa Monica, California: Guadra Associates, 1989.

12. *Dun and Bradstreet Million Dollar Directory*, 1989 Edition. New York: Dun and Bradstreet, 1989.

13. *Industry Norms and Key Business Ratios*. New York: Dun & Bradstreet, 1989.

14. *Information Industry Market Place: An International Directory of Information Products and Services*. New York: R.R. Bowker, 1982.

15. *National Trade and Professional Associations of the United States and Canada and Labor Unions*. Columbia Books, 1979.

16. *Standard & Poor's Register of Corporations, Directors, and Executives*. New York, Standard & Poor's Corp., 1989.

17. *Thomas Register of American Manufacturers*, 76th Edition. Thomas Publishing Co., 1989.

5

Regulations on Doing Business

"It is better to beg forgiveness
than to ask permission in the first place."

Most entrepreneurs smile and nod when they read the quote above. There are times, however, when this philosophy will backfire on you. The Internal Revenue Service allows you to be ignorant of its rules, but it fines you heartily when they find you out. You can face severe consequences if you break certain laws regulating businesses. You don't need to be aware of a large number of business laws to start a business, but you do need to be aware of some of the basics. The first section of this chapter describes rules which apply to *all* businesses. The second section describes regulations which apply only to businesses which have employees.

You can face severe consequences if you break certain laws regulating business

Regulations For All Businesses

Most businesses need to be licensed with one or more institutions. You need to check with city, county, and state offices, each of which is described below. You are also responsible for paying income, Social Security, and property taxes, which are also described below.

City License

If your business is located within a legal "city limits," you need a city business license. This is the city's way of ensuring that zoning, fire, and building regulations are observed. Fees are usually assessed by the size of a company. If your business is located outside of a city limit you don't need the license. If it is inside, contact City Hall and ask to be connected with the licensing division.

Local City or County Business Licenses

All businesses must obtain a business license from the local city or county in which the business is being conducted. Contact your local city or county offices and ask about forms and fees. A directory of city and county license information is available at the Utah Department of Commerce, Division of Corporations and Commercial Code: (801) 530-4849.

State, Professional or Specialty Licenses

No single department has responsibility for all licensing, and licensing fees vary. Certain types of business activities require special permits (for example: transient vendors, food processors, franchise and distributorships, automated dialing companies, charities and professional fund raisers, credit services organizations, hotels and motels, health and fitness centers, nursing homes, warehousing operations, telephone solicitations and sales, and home based businesses). For a more comprehensive list of companies requiring special permits or licenses request, "A Basic Kit For Going into Business In Utah" from:

Division of Corporations and Commercial Code
Department of Commerce
160 East 300 South P.O. Box 45801
Salt Lake City, UT 84145-0801
(801)530-4849

If you want to protect your business name on a national basis, you have to register it as a trade name

Business Name Registration

All individuals and partnerships conducting business under an assumed name (DBA:"Doing Business As") must register within 30 days of starting business. This protects the owner against the use of the name by any other business, and provides consumers access to information about the owner or operator of the business. Renewal of the registration is required every three years.

Original application - $20
Renewal application - $20

Contact: Division of Corporations and Commercial Code
Department of Commerce
160 East 300 South P.O. Box 45801
Salt Lake City, UT 84145-0801
(801)530-4849

If your company is incorporated, you do not need to register the name as the incorporation protects it. If you would like to protect the name of your business on a national basis, you must register it as a trade name (see Chapter 3).

Income Taxes

All businesses must comply with federal income and Social Security taxes. You are required to pay estimated federal income taxes quarterly, based on projected profits. This is the IRS's way of getting periodic payments from you instead of waiting (and hoping) to receive one big check on April 15th of the following year. You must submit your estimated income taxes for each quarter on the following dates: April 15, June 15, September 15, and January 15. You are allowed some latitude if you underestimate taxes and pay the difference on April 15th, but you are fined if you underestimate by too large of an amount. While individual tax returns are due April 15, corporate federal returns must be filed on the 15th day of the third month after the end of the fiscal year. To receive IRS forms, visit your local IRS office or call (800) 829-3676. For assistance on tax questions, call (800) 829-4059 or (800) 829-1040.

All businesses must comply with federal income and Social Security taxes

State Tax Registration

When starting a business in Utah, an application must be filed with the Utah State Tax Commission if one of the following applies:

1. The business will be selling goods or services subject to a sales tax or will purchase goods subject to use tax.
2. In addition to the owner, there will be one or more employees.

This application will register the business for a sales and tax number and/or an employer's withholding identification number. When applicable, it will also register the business for transient room tax, resort community tax, tourism tax, or waste tire fee.

State tax forms may be ordered by contacting the State Tax Commission at the telephone number listed below. As a courtesy to the taxpayer, the State Tax Commission mails the necessary tax returns to all registered taxpayers. Returns must be filed by the due date even if no tax is due. Penalties and interest apply to late returns and underpayment of tax due.

Contact: Utah State Tax Commission
Heber M. Wells Building
160 East 300 South, First Floor
Salt Lake City, UT 84134
(801) 530-4848

	1-800-662-4335
Form:	TC-69 - Utah State Business Application Form
Filing Fee:	None

Social Security Taxes on Yourself

As a sole proprietor, you are to pay Social Security taxes on the net income of your business. Check with the IRS. You are required to remit Social Security taxes quarterly along with your quarterly estimated federal taxes.

Property Taxes

Taxes in Utah are levied on real and personal property. Real property includes land, buildings and other improvements. Personal property includes items which are generally moveable such as business assets, furniture, fixtures, machinery, equipment, supplies, etc. It does not include inventory held for resale.

Most business property is assessed by the county assessor. The necessary forms and filing instructions can be obtained by calling your county assessor. Additions and changes to your business equipment and other property must be reported annually.

Personal property taxes are due 30 days from the date the tax bill is mailed. Real property taxes are billed by November 1st and must be paid by November 30th. Contact your county assessor for further information.

Regulations For Businesses With Employees

All businesses must pay the taxes described above. If you have any employees, however, you are required to pay other taxes and comply with other government regulations. These regulations cover employee withholding amounts, employee social security payments, unemployment insurance, and workers' compensation insurance.

If you have any employees you are required to pay other taxes and comply with other government regulations

You should first obtain IRS Publication 15 *Employer's Tax Guide*. It describes in detail the generalities that you read here. You must first determine if you have employees. If you can pay people as "independent contractors," you need not be concerned with these other taxes and regulations. The IRS, however, is making it very difficult to classify someone as an independent contractor.

Anyone who performs services is an employee if you, as an employer, can control what will be done and how it will be done. This is so even when the employer gives the employee freedom of action. What matters is that you have the legal right to control the method and the result of the services. IRS Publication 539, *Employment Taxes*, gives examples of the employer-employee relationship. If you want a decision as to whether a worker is an employee, file the IRS Form SS-8, *Information for Use in Determining Whether a Worker is an Employee for Federal Employment Taxes and Income Tax Withholding*. Call (800) 829-3676 for any of these IRS forms.

If you have employees, you need to obtain an employer identification number. Go to your local IRS office or call the IRS forms number listed above. This ID number is used consistently in many government programs.

Employee Federal Income and Social Security Tax Withholding

You are required to withhold federal and state income taxes and also Social Security taxes from employees' paychecks. You withhold a certain percentage of employees' wages (7.65 percent in 1994 of first $60,600, and additional Medicare of 1.45 percent on all earnings) and are responsible for paying an equal amount in Social Security taxes. Certain restrictions apply, so be sure to review the IRS Social Security rules. You are required to complete W-4 forms which allow you to calculate how much federal income tax should be withheld from each employee's paycheck.

You may need to set up a federal deposit account for withholding

If the total amount you withhold in a year exceeds $500, you need to set up a federal deposit account with a local bank. Depending on the amount that you are depositing, federal guidelines determine how often you must make deposits. It ranges from monthly to every three days. The IRS gives you coupons that must be filled out when you make deposits. The bank sends the money directly to the IRS. At the end of each quarter, you file IRS Form 940 which summarizes the amounts that you withheld and submitted. You have one month to file the form at the end of the quarter.

If you have employees, you need to obtain an employer identification number

Unemployment Insurance

Unemployment insurance is administered at both the state (SUTA) and federal (FUTA) levels. The insurance provides payments to employees who have been terminated or in certain circumstances have quit a job. You pay FUTA and SUTA quarterly, and have one month to pay at the end of the quarter. If you have a Federal Deposit Account, you can deposit FUTA in the account along with the appropriate coupon.

The federal tax rate at the end of 1994 was .8 percent of wages. The (SUTA) tax rates are between .013 and 5.4 percent based on the average tax rates for businesses in your industry. New employers pay that established rate on the first $16,500 of each employee's annual wage to the maximum percentage (5.4). Information can be obtained from, and SUTA taxes remitted to:

Utah Department of Employment Security
140 East 300 South
Salt Lake City, UT 84111
(801) 536-7760

Workers' Compensation Insurance

You *must* provide workers' compensation insurance for all employees

Workers' Compensation Insurance is a state-mandated insurance program that provides compensation and medical benefits to employees injured on the job. By covering employees under the Workers' Compensation Act, the employer generally is ensured immunity from lawsuits due to any job-related injury or illness. The employee is paid a certain percentage of his/her wage while unable to work, subject to a maximum, and an additional benefit for any permanent partial impairment sustained due to the industrial injury. All medical bills are paid in full as long as they are related to the industrial accident. In addition, benefits are paid to the dependents of deceased workers, as well as some burial expenses.

The Industrial Accidents Division, a division of The Industrial Commission of Utah, will prosecute non-complying employers for violations of the mandatory insurance provisions of the Utah Code.
To receive information or to register with the state program, contact:

Workers' Compensation Fund of Utah (WCFU)
392 East 6400 South
P.O. Box 57929
Salt Lake City, UT 84157-0929
(801) 288-8020 or (800) 446-2667

You can also purchase coverage from any private insurance company authorized to write workers' compensation insurance in Utah. If you are a large employer with firm financial status and well-documented loss records, such as public utilities, government entities, and national corporations, you can apply to the Industrial Commission for permission to self-insure.

Conclusion

You have read about six areas of business regulations in this chapter: licensing, income taxes, Social Security taxes, property taxes, unemployment insurance, and workers' compensation insurance. Make sure that you abide by the regulations which apply to your company. You can write directly to these programs for information and forms. Otherwise, accountants usually stay current with these programs and can streamline the process for you.

There are many other legal matters that pertain to business. Bookstores usually carry several small business law books. You may have to call upon an attorney well versed in business law from time to time.

6

Choosing a Form of Business

One of the decisions you must make early in the life of your firm is the legal form of business. Sole proprietorships, partnerships, and corporations are the three primary forms of organization, and there are several types of partnerships and corporations. There is no *one best* form of organization; it depends on the company and its owners' situation. Nonetheless, one of the primary considerations in selecting a business organization is shielding the entrepreneur from liabilities incurred in running the venture. Other important considerations include (a) the ability to transfer ownership rights to the firm, (b) the continuation of the business in the event of death or withdrawal of one or more of the entrepreneurs, (c) the initial and later money or capital needs of the proposed business, and (d) tax implications—which are significant on-going concerns. A description of each of the legal forms is given below along with the considerations in making your final choice.

There is no *one best* form of business

A sole proprietorship consists of one person who owns and controls the business. That person alone receives the profit or loss from the company and is personally responsible for the debts. This can be risky for the entrepreneur if the business fails or incurs large debts. Profits are taxed at the individual's income tax rate. The owner may sell the business to someone else; however if only part of the business is sold to another party, that sale may create a new partnership. If the owner dies, the business is usually terminated unless willed to another person or persons, in which case a new sole proprietorship or partnership is created.

A *partnership* is owned by two or more persons. The most common form of partnership is a *general partnership*, in which all partners legally share equal right to manage the business. Each partner responsibility for *all* debts of the firm and liability may extend to other other personal debts of the partners. A partnership agreement dictates management responsibilities, how profits are to be distributed, and other issues important to the partners. The partnership itself is not taxed, rather profits are allocated to each of the owners and they are taxed at individual tax rates. Figure 6-1 at the end of this chapter lists common issues addressed in partnership agreements. One issue of critical importance is a provision for breaking up the partnership. If the business is doing well, most issues can be worked out between owners as they come up. However, if the business is doing poorly and somebody wants out, this is when things get difficult, and partners wish it had been clearly spelled out how to break up the partnership fairly.

A *limited partnership* has a general partner who is responsible for all debts of the partnership and who manages the company. There are one or more limited partners who are liable for no more than their investment and who do not participate in the day-to-day management of the firm. In the last decade limited partnerships have been used frequently as tax shelters, but current tax laws have restricted this usage. You should consult an attorney experienced in partnerships to set up a limited partnership.

A *Limited Liability Partnership* is a new form of business now available in Utah

A *Limited Liability Partnership* is a new form of business now available in Utah. The 1994 Legislature passed an amendment to the Utah Partnership Act (48, Utah Code Annotated), creating Limited Liability Partnerships. If you are establishing a service-type business—such as a consulting firm, or other professional services business, you may wish to consider this new business vehicle as opposed to the Limited Liability Company. This new business form does provide some liability shield for malpractice kinds of liabilities. While a Limited Liability Partnership is a "general partnership"; and, therefore, it as well as its partners are liable for business-type debts or liabilities, "a partner in a limited liability partnership is not liable, directly or indirectly, including by way of indemnification, contribution, or otherwise, for a debt, obligation, or liability chargeable to the partnership arising from negligence, wrongful acts, or misconduct committed while the partnership is registered as a limited liability partnership and in the course of the partnership business by another partner, or an employee, agent, or representative of the limited liability partnership." [1]

A *limited liability company* ("LLC") is a new form of business entity that combines the operational flexibility and tax status of a general partnership with the limited liability protection traditionally associated with limited partnerships and corporations. An LLC has far greater operational flexibility than either a subchapter C corporation, a subchapter S corporation or a limited partnership. The principal characteristics of limited liability companies are:

1. The LLC is not required to hold annual meetings or to comply with the many operational restrictions imposed upon corporations.

2. The restrictions on the number and types of shareholders applicable to a subchapter S corporation do not apply to the owners of an LLC (the "members"). The members of an LLC may also participate in management to a greater extent than limited partners.

An LLC has far greater operational flexibility than either a subchapter C corporation, a subchapter S corporation or a limited partnership

3. An LLC differs from a general partnership inasmuch as its members are not personally liable for the obligations of the LLC. It also differs from a limited partnership in that no member is jointly and severally liable for obligations of the LLC, unlike the general partner in a limited partnership. An LLC is subject, however, to disclosure, recordkeeping and reporting requirements that do not apply to a general partnership.

4. An LLC is a business entity consisting of two or more "persons" (meaning an individual, general partnership, limited partnership, association, trust, estate or corporation), conducting business for any lawful purpose. An LLC may be an incorporator, general partner, limited partner, applicant of a DBA, or a manager of any corporation, partnership, limited partnership or limited liability company.

5. LLC's consist of *members*, *managers*, and *employees*. Management of the company is reserved to the *members* or *managers* as specified in the Articles of Organization. Generally, neither members, managers nor employees are personally liable for any debt or obligation of the company.

6. LLC's are creatures of statute and become effective once having filed approved Articles with the Division. Like most business types filed with the Division, LLC's are formed by filing Articles (called Articles of Organization). Foreign LLC's may transact business in the state once having completed an Application for Registration. LLC's may amend their articles, file Articles of Dissolution, and must file an Annual Report. The floppy disc attached to the back cover of this book provides software to facilitate formation of a new limited liability company.

7. Utah LLC's will be treated as partnerships for tax purposes. Partnership tax treatment is advantageous because the earnings of a partnership are treated as the earnings of its partners. No separate tax is imposed on the partnership entity. In contrast, the earnings of a regular corporation are taxed at the entity level; and dividends which are distributed to the shareholders are also taxable to the shareholders. Thus, the distributed earnings of a corporation are taxed twice, the earnings of a partnership only once. Like a partnership, the earnings of the LLC are taxed only once.

The software supplied with this book includes Articles of Incorporation for the State of Utah

A *corporation* is a legal entity separate from its owners, who own shares of stock in the company. A company must comply with fairly stringent regulations in the state in which it is incorporated. Shareholders generally are not responsible for debts of the company beyond their investment in stock and are, therefore, insulated from claims against the company. Corporations are taxed on the income they make, plus dividends which are disbursed to shareholders are taxed, resulting in "double taxation." The "regular" type of corporation (as opposed to the special types described below) is called a "C" corporation. The software supplied with this book includes Articles of Incorporation for the State of Utah and can help you get a corporation legally organized.

An "S" corporation receives special tax treatment

An "S" corporation is a special type of corporation which receives special tax treatment. If a corporation qualifies for "S" status from the Internal Revenue Service, it is taxed like a partnership whereby corporate income "flows through" to shareholders and is taxed at individual rates. While you pay the normal payroll taxes (FICA, Social Security) on salaries to owners and others, profits over and above reasonable salaries to the entrepreneur(s) can be paid out as corporate dividends without payroll tax overhead. This is important if the corporation prospers and earns more net income than would normally be paid out in salaries. The corporation itself is not taxed, thus avoiding double taxation. To be considered an "S" corporation, a firm must:

- not have more than 35 shareholders;
- not have any non-individual shareholders (other than estates & trusts);
- not have a nonresident alien as a shareholder; and
- not have more than one class of stock.

To set up your new company as an "S" corporation, you need to incorporate as a regular corporation and abide by the guidelines indicated above. You then make an election for "S" Corporation status with the IRS. This is done on IRS Form 2553. A consent is required of each shareholder on this form, acknowledged with their signature(s).

A *closely held corporation* is a corporation with fewer than 35 employees that meets other requirements for being considered "closely held." The purpose of this designation is to allow smaller companies to incorporate more easily and have fewer reporting requirements. A closely held corporation could also have "S" tax status. The firm could therefore provide advantages of incorporation to owners, such as limited liability, while avoiding double taxation and burdensome reporting requirements. The "S" and "closely held" designations have made incorporation more attractive to smaller firms.

A *closely held corporation* is a corporation with fewer than 35 employees that meets other requirements for being considered "closely held."

Important and liberalizing changes are being proposed to Congress for "S" corporations. Therefore, you may want to check with your attorney or business advisor to update you on any changes that may have gone into effect between the time this book was published and the time you may incorporate.

The software included with this guide provides a sample Articles of Incorporation for a regular or an "S" corporation.

Choosing a Legal Form of Business

The choice of legal form of organization depends on a variety of factors, the most important typically being:

Laws affecting choice of legal form of business change often

- liability of the business owner(s);
- tax considerations, distribution of profits and losses;
- ability to raise capital;
- expense and complexity of organizing the business;
- amount of government regulation and reporting requirements;
- management control.

Each of these factors is discussed below. Be aware that the laws change frequently for some of these factors, and consultation with law, accounting, and/or tax professionals is a good idea.

Liability of the Business Owners

Most businesses with high-growth potential choose to incorporate for one overriding reason— limited liability. A shareholder in a corporation is not liable for more than his investment in the corporation. Creditors cannot seek individuals' assets for repayment of corporate liabilities. With proprietorships and partnerships, owners are personally liable, except in the circumstances described for limited liability partnerships and LLC's. In fact, general partnerships make each owner liable for debts for the entire company and may even extend to personal indebtedness beyond the business.

Lenders may require personal guarantees on loans when you are incorporated

Be aware that incorporation primarily protects you from liability suits. If your business is sued by customers, employees, or anyone else, your personal assets are protected (they can also sue you personally, however). Incorporation provides protection against creditors seeking to claim your personal assets because of your business' debts; however, many lenders require a *personal guarantee* to back up corporate loans. In that case, incorporation is not providing protection against those creditors. Therefore, even though incorporation legally protects owners from creditors and liability suits, outside parties may skirt around that protection through various means.

Tax Considerations and Distribution of Profits/Losses

Tax laws change frequently; therefore, you should consult an accountant or tax attorney about current tax considerations. One tax law has remained unchanged for a long period of time: owners of "C" corporations can be taxed twice, which is not the case for owners of proprietorships, partnerships, and LLC's. The corporation is taxed on net profits, and if dividends are declared to shareholders, each owner is taxed on his return. If a corporation has "S" status, however, this disadvantage disappears and it is taxed just like a general partnership. Since a corporation is a legal entity separate from its owners, profits of the company do not "flow through" directly to owners for taxation purposes. Owners are taxed only when dividends are declared, and owners cannot deduct company losses against their individual income. An "S" designation allows losses from a company to be applied towards owners' individual returns, reducing their tax liabilities. In summary, a "C" corporation is taxed differently than a proprietorship, partnership, an LLC, or an "S" corporation.

Amount of Government Regulation

Corporations are required to comply with a large number of laws, whereas partnerships and proprietorships are not as highly regulated. Furthermore, if a corporation issues publicly traded stock (see Chapter 7), the reporting requirements can be burdensome. If, however, a corporation is "closely held," the reporting requirements are reduced. Therefore, unless a corporation is "closely held," it has significantly more reporting requirements and is more closely regulated than proprietorships and partnerships.

Ability to Raise Capital

It is usually difficult for any business, regardless of the legal form of organization, to raise money at startup. In the long run, the corporation is best organized to raise capital, followed by a partnership, followed by a proprietorship. The corporation has the ability to sell stock to a relatively large number of investors (see Chapter 7 for a discussion of "going public"), and with a large equity base, corporations have less difficulty in obtaining loans. Partnerships allow a company to have more than one owner, allowing it to raise more money than a proprietorship (unless Bill Gates is the proprietor). Proprietorships can raise only what the owner has to invest or what the firm can borrow.

The corporation is best organized to raise capital

Management Control and Decision Making

A sole proprietor has complete authority to run the business as he sees fit, which many entrepreneurs appreciate. The drawback is that the entrepreneur is then responsible for doing just about everything in the company at startup, and that can be overwhelming. In a partnership, all owners have equal right to manage the company, regardless of what percentage of ownership they have. The decision-making process can become cumbersome. Unless specifically noted otherwise in the partnership agreement, each partner can act on behalf of the other partners, legally binding them without their knowledge. The advantage of the partnership is the pooling of skills and knowledge, which may be essential for the company to grow.

In a corporation, there is a distinction between management and shareholders, although in smaller corporations there is usually a significant overlap. The shareholders elect a board of directors who make general policy decisions and hire managers to conduct the business' affairs. The articles of incorporation usually include clauses on what types of decisions the board and managers can make. The advantage in this area of the corporation, like a partnership, is the involvement of different people in the decision-making process, although it can be cumbersome. In a corporation, an owner cannot legally bind another owner personally, as in a partnership.

Complexity and Expenses of Organizing the Business

A sole proprietorship can be started simply and cheaply. All that needs to be done is to get proper licenses (see Chapter 5) and a tax identification number (if employees will be hired). A general partnership agreement can be simple; in fact legally, it does not have to be written. An agreement should be written, however, for the partners' protection, but it does not have to be filed with any government agency. The last section of this chapter shows typical issues addressed in partnerships. You don't have to consult an attorney to draw up a partnership agreement, but you would be wise to do so after you have drafted an agreement. The corporation is the most expensive, time-consuming legal form to organize. A *for-profit corporation* is formed in Utah by filing Articles of Incorporation with the Utah Division of Corporations and Commercial Code. There is a $50 filing fee.

The sole proprietorship is the easiest legal structure to set up

To form a *Limited Liability Company*, you need to file the Articles of Organization with the Utah Division of Corporations and Commercial Code together with a filing fee of $50.

Other Considerations

There are other factors that may affect the choice of legal form of business, including provisions for retirement plans and fringe benefits. The regulations in both of these areas are quite complex and change frequently. Consult an attorney familiar with business law.

Summary

While the final choice of a legal form of business depends on a variety of factors, in general most entrepreneurs (with concepts having significant growth potential) would be well-advised to either (1) form a limited liability company or (2) incorporate, especially if they can receive "S" and "closely held" status. Both forms of business provide protection from business liabilities which is important both to the new-venture entrepreneur as well as any investor in that new enterprise. Neither form has any tax disadvantages.

More information about starting a limited liability company or a corporation can be obtained from:

> Division of Corporation and Commercial Code
> Department of Commerce
> 160 East 300 South, P.O. Box 45801
> Salt Lake City, UT 84145-0801
> (801) 530-4849

The Division of Corporation also has a number of free publications that are very useful in starting a new venture. Ask specifically for the booklet: "Doing Business in Utah." See also the computer files provided on the floppy disk in the back cover of this book.

References

1. Kamoroff, Bernard. *Small Time Operator*, 2nd Edition. Laytonville, Cal: Bell Springs Publishing Company, 1979.

2. *A Guide To Starting a Business in Minnesota.* St. Paul: Minnesota Department of Trade and Economic Development, 1988.

3. House Bill No. 5, *An Act Relating to Partnerships and Limited Liability Companies*, 1994, General Session.

Figure 6-1. Possible Issues in Partnership Agreements [2]

1. Name of the partnership.
2. Duration of the partnership.
3. Location of its place of business.
4. Capital contribution of each partner.
5. Whether partners may make additional contributions.
6. The level at which capital accounts of partners must be maintained.
7. Participation of each partner in profits and losses.
8. The amounts of any regular drawings against profits.
9. Duties, responsibilities, and sphere of activities of each partner.
10. Amount of time to be contributed by each partner.
11. Prohibition of partners' outside business activities which would compete with the partnership business.
12. Name of the managing partner and method for resolving management disputes.
13. Procedure for admitting new partners.
14. Method of determing the value of goodwill in the business, in case of death, incompetence, or withdrawal of a partner or dissolution of the partnership for any other reason.
15. Method of liquidating the interest of a deceased or retiring partner.
16. Age at which a partner must withdraw from active participation, and arrangements for adjusting his or her salary and equity.
17. Whether or not surviving partners have the right to continue using the name of a deceased partner in the partnership name.
18. Basis for expulsion of a partner, method of notification of expulsion, and the disposition of any losses that arise from the delinquency of such a partner.
19. Period of time in which retiring or withdrawing partners may not engage in a competing business.
20. Procedures for handling the protracted disability of a partner.
21. How partnership accounts are to be kept.
22. The fiscal year of the partnership.
23. Whether or not interest is to be paid on the debit and credit balances in the partners' accounts.
24. Where the partnership cash is to be deposited and who may sign checks.
25. Prohibition of partners' selling or pledging their interest in the partnership except to other partners.
26. Identification of material contracts or agreements affecting the liability or operation of the partnership.

7

Raising Capital

"A banker is a person who will loan you an umbrella on a sunny day and then demand it back if it starts to rain."
Mark Twain

Adequate financial resources are essential for a new venture's success, as are good people and products. Financing also encompasses more than merely obtaining money. It should involve realistic and strategic plans for the initial establishment of your business as well as cash-flow plans which coincide with a good business plan. Since your new firm may not spin off positive cash flows immediately, these shortfalls in cash should be carefully included in your up-front financing requirements. Unless you have a lot of money to put into the business yourself or have a wealthy family willing to assist in your venture, you will have to find sources for capital that are "affordable" as well as allowing you an acceptable level of ownership and control in your business. This chapter describes different sources of capital and how to approach them: banks and other lenders, governmental and quasi-governmental grant and lending programs, trade credit, finance companies, and different approaches to equity financing, including venture capital companies.

Don't try to raise money *just for the sake* of raising money

Don't try to raise money just for the sake of raising money. Some people feel like they don't have a bona fide business unless they borrow some money or get people to invest in their company. If you can avoid borrowing or bringing in investors, you are better off. Unfortunately, most businesses cannot avoid doing one or the other.

You have probably heard conflicting stories about raising new venture money. The newspapers run stories about entrepreneurs exasperated at how difficult it is to get bank loans. Some business people feel that Utah bankers are especially conservative. But on the other hand, you find small businessmen who say, "If you have a good plan and a sound business concept, there is money out there. You just need to know where to look and how to ask for it." In fact in a recent statewide survey of Utah small businessmen, the vast majority said their banks had supplied the necessary bank credit needed for their firms. So, while there is some truth to both arguments, with a good business plan and knowledge of where to look for money, your odds of being able to raise capital will be greatly improved.

Debt vs. Equity

Unless you can talk someone into *giving* you money, you need to decide whether you want debt or equity capital. When you borrow money, it is called *debt.* You are required to pay back the money by a certain date and under certain terms. The people who loan you the money do not own a part of your company, although they may have the right to take the business if you do not meet the terms of the loan.

***Equity* financing involves giving up part ownership of your company**

Equity financing involves giving up part ownership of your company. You do not make set payments to investors, rather they share in the profits of your company. The amount of money they invest and the percentage ownership of the company that you give to them is negotiable.

Debt financing has some advantages over equity financing. The most important is that you do not give up any ownership of the company. Many entrepreneurs give up significant portions of their company at startup for relatively small investments. These people later regret having given up equity which later is worth a lot of money, since the value of the company has increased substantially. Once you give up ownership, the only way to get it back is to buy it, which may become very costly. Second, if you borrow money, the origination fees are usually less than those associated with equity financing. Third, since you do not give up ownership in debt financing, you do not have to deal with other partners and their ideas on running the business.

Debt and equity financing each has its own advantages and disadvantages

Equity financing also has some advantages over debt financing. First, it is less risky to the business. Equity financing does not require set payments on certain dates. This takes the pressure off you to have enough cash to meet those payments. You also do not run the risk associated with variable interest rate loans. If the economy turns downward or your sales are lower than expected, a bank is not waiting to repossess the business. Second, equity investors are willing to give money to riskier business situations. Banks do not usually loan money to startups or to businesses which they consider to be risky. Therefore, equity financing may be the only alternative. Third, you can generally raise larger amounts of money through equity investments than through debt (but there are all sorts of exceptions).

Debt Financing

There are various types of debt financing. Loans through banks are most common, but leases, trade credit, loans from finance companies, and special loan programs are other possibilities. Each is described in this section.

Bank Loans. Bankers are infamous for being conservative. You need to understand why they are forced to be that way. They borrow money from depositors and loan it out to businesses. If they they borrow it at 7 percent and loan it out at 10 percent, their *spread* is three points. What happens if a business they loan money to does very well? They get their three points. What happens if the business goes bankrupt? They may lose their total investment. It only takes one bad loan to wipe out the proceeds of quite a few good ones; therefore, the bankers need to be very careful selecting their clients. Bankers are also under pressure from government loan evaluators. If the evaluators rate many of their loans as being quite risky, the bank is severely hampered in making loans. Yes, banks are conservative, and you cannot expect them to make a loan in a situation they consider to be quite risky.

You cannot expect banks to make loans to companies they consider quite risky

Types of Bank Loans. Banks make different types of loans and the terms of a loan are generally dictated by what the money is used for. *Short-term loans* are used to finance assets which are liquidated in the short term (one year maximum). For example, seasonal fluctuations in inventory are usually financed by short-term loans. You need money to buy inventory before the heavy selling season begins. Once you have sold the inventory and collected on them, you should be able to pay the bank back. Short-term loans are usually used to finance inventory, accounts receivable, and other situations where cash is needed for only a short period of time.

In the last year, there has been a noticeable trend for some banks to set up "factoring departments or units" which buy qualified businesses accounts receivables. There are also factor companies, niche lenders, which specialize in this type of lending. While historically, factors have operated mostly in the garment and apparel industries, they are now moving into electronics, toys, furniture, and medical businesses. This type of credit will be more costly from either a bank or a specialized factor company, but does give some extra flexibility to some small firms when special credit needs arise.

Factor companies are now loaning in new industries

Some people do not understand why a bank lends using a series of short-term notes instead of issuing longer-term debt. Consider the service station owner who borrows money to fill his underground tank with gasoline. The bank loans him the money for the gas, requires him to repay the loan when the tank is empty, and then will turn right around and re-loan the money to refill the tank. The bankers aren't stupid. If they gave a long-term loan for gasoline, chances are cash would eventually be used for a new pickup truck. Then there wouldn't be enough money to purchase gasoline when the tank is empty again. The bank would then be asked to make another loan. Short-term loans are used to finance assets that are liquidated in the short term.

Intermediate term loans are used to finance assets such as automobiles, furniture, and equipment. These are assets which are used for several years but wear out. You typically have one to five years to pay off this type of loan.

You don't see too many loans with terms longer than ten years these days

Long-term loans are usually paid off over long periods of time, anywhere from six to twenty-five years. Because of the risk to banks of interest rate fluctuations, they are offering fewer of these loans. They are also making payment schedules more compressed. You don't see too many loans with terms longer than ten years these days. Long-term loans are used to purchase real property— land and buildings. The banks are willing to loan over longer periods of time on these assets because they feel safe that the assets will retain their value if they need to be repossessed. In general, banks are willing to make long-term loans on long-term assets.

A line of credit is a long-term loan, because money can be borrowed, paid back, and then borrowed again, perhaps indefinitely. A bank typically allows a certain credit limit (with some restrictions) up to which you may borrow. When you have the cash, you pay the loan back down, but you still retain the right to borrow again if the need arises. This type of loan alleviates the pressure to go to the bank every time you need to borrow money— the credit is already established. Banks are very selective as to whom they will give a line of credit.

Choosing a Banker. You should spend some time choosing a banker. It is a shopping process, which you should do before you urgently need the money. Nothing will turn a banker off more quickly than a frantic applicant. Project your cash needs, and well in advance of when you need the money, talk to different banks.

Of course you want a loan with the best terms, but there are other factors to consider as you shop. Try to find a bank that can handle your needs as you grow. If you are right up against a bank's upper lending limit, you'll probably have to shop for another bank in the future. Also, try to find a bank that has lending experience in your industry and in working with young, growing companies. The bankers will understand the seasonal and cyclical variations that affect your need to borrow. Lastly, try to find bankers with which you have "good chemistry." You're dealing not with just a bank, but also with bankers. Their commitment to you may be invaluable.

Try to find a bank that can handle your needs as you grow

You can evaluate some of these issues simply by dealing with the bank. You may need to talk to outsiders to get accurate information on some issues. Fellow entrepreneurs, accountants, attorneys, and consultants can give you their assessments. Ask for small business references from the bank and talk to some of their current loan holders. Don't think that you should bank with the first institution that agrees to give you a loan. As with any product that you are selling, it doesn't hurt to let people know that others are interested in what you have to sell. Shop around. Have some alternatives.

Approaching a Bank. At the same time you are shopping for a bank, you are selling yourself. Yes, bankers do have common criteria they use in deciding whether to give a loan. However, their rules can bend if they "like what they see." The way you present yourself is as important as what you present.

Try to get an introduction to a banker as opposed to calling him "cold." If someone he knows introduces you and puts in a good word for you, the door is opened. Try to complete a business plan (see Chapter 13) even for a bank loan. Granted, many people receive loans without a full business plan. However, a loan officer will be greatly impressed if you do present one. If yours is a startup business, you *need* to present a complete plan.

If yours is a startup business, you *need* to present a complete plan.

The banker will be trying to assess your business acumen and ability to repay the loan. If you have a partner, accountant, or employee who can provide support and expertise, have them come to meetings with the banker. One of the concerns that bankers have is whether you, as an entrepreneur, can stay focused and pay attention to the financial end of the business. If you do not have strong financial skills, bring someone involved with your business who can emphasize the finances of the company. Avoid talking about the spectacular new plans for growth that you have and all of the new products or acquisitions that you are considering. The banker will fear that you will go off half-cocked and not keep track of finances. Emphasize the fact that there will be more than adequate cash flow to make loan payments. This is what they are concerned with.

What Bankers Need to Know to Give You a Loan. All bankers will want you to give them some basic information before they consider giving you a loan. Make sure you have answers to these basics:

- How much money do you need to borrow?
- When do you need the money?
- What will you use the money for?
- When can you repay the money?

Emphasize that there will be more than adequate cash flow to repay the loan

You need to generate a cash flow projection to be able to answer questions 1, 2, and 4. Review Chapter 11, Cash Management, and Appendix C, Computer Finance Templates, on how to formulate a cash projection. The banker will want to see a cash flow forecast, anyway.

The Bank's Decision. Each bank approaches lending decisions in its own somewhat subjective fashion. However, banks have traditionally evaluated the "5 C's of Credit" in determining whether to give a loan: Character, Capacity, Capital, Conditions, and Collateral. These criteria are standard enough in the banking world that each merits a description.

Character. The banker will try to determine if you are a trustworthy person. Have you paid back previous loans on time? Do you have the reputation of being an honest business person? Are you open and honest in your dealings with the loan officer? This criterion is the most subjective of the five, and yet one of the most important. Bankers know that when it is all said and done, your integrity will determine to a large degree whether or not the loan will be repaid.

Bankers intently evaluate if the business will have cash flow to repay the loan

Capacity. The banker evaluates whether the business has enough cash flow to repay the loan. You need to present a cash flow projection for him to make such a decision. In decades past, bankers were not as concerned with this aspect as they now are. Previously, if the loan was backed up by plenty of collateral, the decision to loan was easy. Recently, however, banks have become much more careful. In most cases, bankers don't want to have to sell your collateral if you can't make your payments. By their own admission, they are lousy salespeople and they would prefer you stay in business and make loan payments than for them to sell your collateral. They evaluate capacity through your projected cash flows.

Capital. The banker evaluates how much money you, or other investors, have in the business. The bank does not want to become an owner of the business; it wants to remain a lender. If it puts the majority of money into the business, it begins to feel more like an owner. Bankers want to ensure that the business owners put an adequate amount of capital into the firm for two reasons. First, if they do have to sell your collateral, they normally can't get a very good price for it. Therefore, they want a cushion. Your investment provides that. Second, an investment on your part tells them that you are committed personally to the venture. It is amazing how much more committed people become once their own money is tied up in a project. Different banks and loan programs require varying levels of owner investment. The range may be anywhere from 10 percent up to 50 owner investment. In *very few* situations can you expect to borrow all of the money you need. You need to put in a substantial amount yourself or get others to invest.

The bank does not want to become an owner of the business; it wants to remain a lender

Conditions. The banker evaluates the overall economy, your industry, and your competitive position before making a loan. If your business is highly dependent on the national economy and the forecast for it is down, you probably won't get the loan. Likewise, if companies are struggling in your industry and/or they usually react aggressively to a newcomer, the banker may be hesitant to make a loan. It is your job to point out the promise of the proposed business in the business plan.

Collateral. Bankers want to know what they will get from you if you are unable to repay the loan. If you have a startup business, they are very serious about collateral. If you borrow money for inventory, they usually want more than the inventory itself as collateral for the loan. They don't have much faith that they could sell it for enough to recapture the value of the loan. Therefore, they ask for secondary means of collateral, either other assets of the business or your personal assets. If you are at startup, you will almost always be required to pledge personal assets as collateral. Beyond that, you may be asked to give a personal guarantee, which allows the bank the right to seize assets not already pledged as collateral if you default on the loan. They can even garnish your future wages. It is not easy to risk losing your house, other personal assets, and even future wages, but you almost invariably will be required to make personal guarantees.

You may be asked to give a *personal guarantee* for a loan

Make sure you know what assets you are tying up in a loan agreement

Negotiating the Deal. A bank loan should be negotiated. The first time you deal with a bank, you may feel like you need to accept whatever they offer. Remember that they are a business and are trying to make the best deal for themselves. In most cases, they have some bend in them. Many an entrepreneur is ecstatic at receiving a loan, signs on the dotted line, and later regrets they didn't read the loan agreement more closely and negotiate it. First, banks will look to tie up as many of your assets as they can as collateral. If you allow them to do so, you may lock yourself out of any further loans down the road because no assets are free to be used as collateral. *Make sure you know what assets you are tying up in a loan agreement.*

Make sure you don't get boxed into a corner by a restriction of which you were unaware

Most loans are written with certain *restrictions*. After giving you a loan, bankers want you to operate in a fashion that preserves the safety of the loan. They may require that you not take on any further debt, make dividend payments, nor pledge your assets to anyone else without their prior consent. They may require you to maintain cash reserves or working capital at certain levels, submit periodic financial statements to them, maintain insurance on key people, or comply with other restrictions. *Make sure you know what the restrictions are.* They can be negotiated. You may not be able to change a lot of them, but you want to make sure you don't get boxed into a corner by a restriction of which you were unaware. By the same token, make sure that what the banker tells you is documented in the agreement. For example, if they tell you that you can have a line of credit up to a certain amount, make sure it is written in the loan agreement. Don't sign the loan form until you have had an accountant and/or an attorney review it.

Developing A Relationship With Your Banker. After receiving a loan, most entrepreneurs contact their bankers on only two occasions: when they need more money or when they are unable to make a payment. These are not bankers' favorite visits. *Do not surprise your banker!* Send him financial statements, new product releases, wedding announcements, etc. Invite him to your office or plant for a tour and discuss how the business is doing. Ask him for advice on running your business (you don't have to listen). After all, a banker spends most of his time in his office looking in on businesses from the outside. He gets excited when he feels like he is an insider. Make him feel like a part of your team, not an adversary. This will be important when you do go in to borrow more money or call to say that you will be late with a payment.

Although you want the banker to feel like an insider, you also should be careful to document your interactions with him. After any meeting in which you discuss terms of your loan, you should write a letter stating your understanding of the discussion and keep a copy in your file. It's a hassle, but in this day and age of law suits it can be important. Some business people have been shocked when their bank apparently changed the terms on loans, to the business people's disadvantage. If you have no record of dealings with your banker, you may not be able to justify your position.

Document your interactions with your banker

Governmental Programs

Small Business Administration (SBA) Loans

The vast majority of SBA's business loans are made by participating banks and other private lenders with the loans being guaranteed by the SBA. The SBA can guarantee up to 90 percent with a maximum guarantee amount currently of $500,000 (changes frequently). Loan maturities can range from 1 to 25 years, depending on the usage of funds. The SBA also offers a number of special loan programs (with limited funds) to eligible small business persons, including:

Small Loan Guarantees: To help businesses needing capital of $50,000 or less.

International Trade Loan Guarantees: To finance U.S. based facilities, equipment producing goods, or services for export.

Export Revolving Line of Credit Guarantees: For pre-export financing.

Seasonal Line of Credit Guarantees: For firms facing seasonal business increases.

Small General Contractor Loan Guarantees: For small construction businesses.

Energy Loan Guarantees: For firms that make, install, sell or service energy equipment and technology.

Physically Challenged Assistance Loans: For businesses owned by the disabled or private non-profit organizations that employ the disabled and operate in their interest.

Pollution Control Loan Guarantees: For firms involved with pollution control and reduction.

Disabled and Vietnam-era Veteran Loans: For veterans who are starting, operating, or expanding a small business.

Surety Bond Guarantee Program: Makes the bonding process accessible to small contractors who find bonding unavailable elsewhere. Contracts up to $1 million are eligible for an SBA bond guarantee.

For additional information about the above SBA loan or management assistance programs, call or write:

U.S. Small Business Administration
Room 2337 Federal Building
125 South State Street
Salt Lake City, UT 84138-1195
(801)524-3209

The following were SBA Participating Lenders as of July 1994. They may be contacted directly for information about SBA loans:

Bank of Utah	355-1701
First Western National Bank	259-5961
Barnes Banking Company	296-1010
Guardian State Bank	531-3400
Bonneville Bank	374-9500
Heritage Savings Bank	272-4438
Brighton Bank	943-6500
Key Bank of Utah	530-7050
Cache Valley Bank	753-3020
State Bank of Southern Utah	674-4164
Capital City Bank	486-4800
Sun Capital Bank	673-6177
Community First Bank	773-8600
United Savings Bank	530-1801
Dixie State Bank	673-4633
Utah Independent Bank	438-2433
Draper Bank and Trust	571-3141
Valley Bank and Trust	481-5000
Far West Bank	566-1275
Valley Central Bank	896-9285
First Commerce Bank	257-3613
Wasatch Bank	328-3081
First Interstate Bank	264-8020
West One Bank of Utah	534-6199
First Professional Bank	531-0400
Zions First National Bank	324-4870
First Security Bank	246-6449

SBA 504 Certified Development Companies

Two Utah development companies, located in Salt Lake City and Ogden, lend to small and medium-sized businesses at fixed rates for terms of 10 to 20 years. Companies must create one job for every $35,000 received in financing. A 504 loan is funded through the sale of a debenture that is guaranteed by the U.S. Small Business Administration for up to $750,000 or 40 percent of the total cost of land, buildings, and equipment.(7)

Contacts:

Deseret Certified Development Company
7050 Union Park Center, Suite 570
Midvale, UT 84047
(801) 566-1163
Fax: (801) 566-1632

Weber Capital Development Company**
2404 Washington Boulevard, Suite 1100
Ogden, UT 84401-2316
(801) 627-1333
Fax: (801) 392-7609

** The Weber Economic Development Corporation makes loans only in Weber County. The other Development Company handles all other areas in Utah.

The number of state programs that counsel and assist small businesses in every state is listed in the 1993 edition of *The States and Small Business: A Directory of Programs and Activities*. The programs described in this book provide a wide range of services; including business financing programs, procurement assistance programs, and business service centers that furnish information on licenses, fees, regulations, etc. The 1993 edition is available for purchase from the nearest U.S. Government Printing Office Bookstore. Written requests for the directory should be mailed to: Superintendent of Documents, P.O. Box 371954, Pittsburgh, PA 15250-7954, (202) 783-3238.

Utah Technology Finance Corporation

The purpose of the *Utah Technology Finance Corporation* is to encourage the growth of new and emerging high technology businesses throughout Utah and assist with product commercialization. UTFC is a state chartered, non-profit organization established by the legislature in 1983 to encourage high-growth, technology-based businesses in Utah. Although UTFC focuses on technology-based companies because of their propensity to create high quality jobs, UTFC's 100+ loan recipient firms represent a variety of industries located throughout Utah. One common characteristic that UTFC borrowers share is that, at the time the loan was approved, they were high risk companies with a lack of access to traditional financing.

Loan Programs. *Early Technology Business Capital* is an example of a loan program designed specifically for startup or growing high tech firms which are developing and marketing emerging technologies and new innovations. This three-phase program provides (1) up to $75,000 for research and development which leads to a working model or prototype; (2) up to $150,000 for commercialization and market entry; and (3) up to $175,000 for production guaranteed by purchase orders.

Matching Loans. Matching Loans combine local or federal funding and private investment to strengthen targeted regional economies. The purpose is not only to build the local tax bases but also to create new jobs for residents. Borrowers go to banks, family and friends, venture capital firms, the Small Business Administration, or private investors to obtain matching funds needed to obtain a loan. To facilitate further private investment, UTFC links borrowers to banks and other potential investors. The four matching loan programs UTFC offers are: Utah Revolving Loan Fund, Salt Lake County Revolving Loan Fund, Utah Rural Loan Program, and Defense Conversion Loan Program.

MicroLoans. UTFC is the administrator for the SBA's Microloan program, which provides funding from $5,000 to $25,000 for working capital, machinery, equipment, and inventory. The loans are not restricted to technology-based businesses but extend to a wide variety of operations, including home-based businesses.

Bridge Financing. While banks are invariably unable to offer loans on purchase orders, UTFC will sometimes provide interim financing to enable companies to fulfill valid purchase orders. For example, a company may need financial resourc4es to purchase component parts, raw materials, or even to purchase additional production equipment to enable the enterprise to fill a new large order. To qualify for such Bridge Financing, a company needs a proven track record in producing and filling orders and must bre able to demonstrate the feasibility of it meeting such an order in a timely fashion. The financial standing of the purchaser is also important to UTFC's decision. Bridge Financing is a short-term credit arrangement, and proceeds from the order are collateralized.

For further information or a UTFC loan application, contact:
Utah Technology Finance Corporation
185 South State Street, Suite 208
Salt Lake City, UT 84111
Tel:(801)364-4346
Fax:(801)364-4361

Revolving Loan Funds

In an effort to create jobs and improve the business climate of a community, some cities, counties, and Associations of Governments (geographical regions) will lend money to small businesses located in their areas. The amount available to a business ranges from a few thousand dollars to over $100,000. Typically, the money is used for plant and equipment, working capital, inventory or accounts receivable financing. Rates are usually less than or equal to conventional bank financing, and the term for repayment may be either short (6 months) or extended (many years). This type of financing is often used in conjunction with bank financing since most revolving loan programs will accept a second or third position on financed assets.

Contact: Your local county or Association of Governments Office.

Community Development Block Grants (CDBG)

CDBG loans are federal loans available to businesses that meet rather stringent criteria. The loans have very low interest rates and lenient payback schedules. Competition for limited funds in this program is intense. Payments on these loans go to the local community for its use in further economic development. The loans are therefore very attractive to both the business and the local community. Chapter 16 describes this program in detail.

Trade Credit

Trade credit can be used to finance inventory. It is a short-term loan from suppliers. Most suppliers will sell to you on credit. However, a new company has to work at getting it. Suppliers want to know the names of other companies with which you have accounts, so they can check with them to see if you have paid your bills. At startup, of course, you have no accounts. You need to get a few key accounts, and thereafter the others will fall into place. Offer to go on a COD basis with a major supplier. After several purchases, they will grant you credit. You then have them to list as a credit reference.

Trade credit is a short-term loan from suppliers

Listing yourself with Dun and Bradstreet often gives you credibility. They provide credit and financial information to member companies. Your suppliers could therefore check with D&B about your credit. To list your company, contact the D&B office at (215) 865-0204.

Be aware that trade credit is short term. Most companies give you thirty days to pay for purchases, but sometimes you get up to sixty or ninety days. You probably will not have liquidated your inventory that quickly. You therefore need to find another way to pay the bills. Line

Trade credit can be costly

up another source in advance. Don't get behind in your payments. Your inventory is the lifeblood of your business. If you get put on COD terms or suppliers refuse to ship to you because you are behind on your bills, your company is severely hampered. You may have great difficulty reestablishing trade credit once it is taken away.

Trade credit can also be costly. Most suppliers give you a discount if you pay early. A common credit term is 2/10 net 30. This means that you have thirty days to pay the bill, but if you pay within ten you get a 2 percent discount. If you don't pay early and take the discount, you are paying the equivalent of 36 percent interest on the borrowed amount. If you have the cash, you should pay early. It will improve your profits.

Finance Companies

Finance companies will sometimes give loans to businesses which banks consider too risky. They are not as concerned with your ability to repay as they are with their ability to liquidate your assets if they get them back. They are generally willing to loan on equipment, inventory, and accounts receivable. If you already have a bank loan, again, this is why you need to try to keep these assets unemcumbered. A finance company cannot loan against them if a bank already has claimed them as collateral. Finance companies will generally lend 70-80 percent on receivables, 40-50 percent of the liquidation value of inventory, and 60-70 percent of the liquidation value of assets. The equipment loans are usually for five years, while the receivables and inventory loans are for one year. Finance companies usually write stringent prepayment penalties into loan agreements. They don't want you to turn around and refinance the assets with a bank as soon as the opportunity arises.

Finance companies will sometimes give loans to businesses which banks consider too risky

Finance companies loan on a percentage basis of the liquidation value of assets. While finance companies don't like to get assets back any more than do banks, they are much better and experienced at getting rid of assets. They are willing, therefore, to make riskier loans if they feel that they can get their money out at auction. If you can't get banks to give you a loan, consider finance companies. Be ready to pay the price, however. Their interest rates are 2 to 6 percentage points higher than the banks'.

Equity investors consider growth potential and stage of development

Conclusion on Debt Financing

Debt financing enforces a set payment schedule upon your business. If you don't make payments according to the loan agreement, you risk losing the business and whatever else you pledge against the loan.

With a loan, however, no one else becomes an owner of the business. Shop around for a bank that can meet your long-term needs, and be prepared when you go in to ask for a loan. *Prepare your business plan.* The SBA may help the bank in making a loan to you. Ask your banker if they are certified with these programs. If banks are unwilling to give you a loan, consider finance companies. You'll have to pay higher interest rates, though. Lastly, trade credit can provide you with short-term credit, but don't depend on it for long-term financing of your business.

Equity Financing

An equity investor becomes part owner of your business. Such an investor doesn't require a set payback schedule, but rather shares in the business profits and growth in equity. There are different generic types of equity investors. The first and simplest type is a "friendly investor," such as a relative or friend who believes in you, gives you money, and takes a share of the business. Second, wealthy individual investors have provided the funding for many startup ventures. They are people with significant means and an interest in being a part of high opportunity ventures. Third, venture capitalists are professional fund managers who seek to invest in high-growth ventures. Fourth, stock offerings make stock available to a large number of investors. A public stock offering allows stock to be traded by investors in different markets. All of these forms of equity investment are discussed in this section.

An equity investor becomes part owner of your business

If you seek equity capital, you need to be aware of the criteria that investors use. Two critical elements that they consider are stage of development and growth potential. The stages of development are similar to the ones presented in Chapter 1, The Stages of Business Growth. Each is described below:

Seed Stage. This is the idea stage of the business. Work is done on completing product development. The stage ends when the business plan is written.

Startup Stage. The owner(s) actively pursues the business and seeks to make sales. The stage ends when commercial interest is shown in the product.

First Stage. The organization becomes established. Sales are made. The organization has sufficient cash flows to survive.

Rapid Growth. Sales of the company increase dramatically.

Investors also classify companies according to the potential that they demonstrate. These are:

Stable Small firms. These companies have sales less than $1 million. They have little potential for growth by choice, market size, or circumstance.

Foundation firms. These companies have sales potential of $1-20 million and have growth rates of ten to twenty percent per year.

High Growth firms. These companies have sales potential of over $20 million and grow in excess of thirty percent per year.

Figure 7-1 shows what type of equity investments are generally available to companies depending on their stage of development and growth potential of the firm.

Figure 7-1. Equity Capital Available for Different Ventures

Stage of Development	Stable Sm. Firms	Foundation Firms	High-Potential Firms
Seed	Pers svngs	Prs svngs, Frndly srces	Personal savings Wealthy people Venture capital
Startup	Pers svngs	Wlthy ppl	SBIC's Venture capital Wealthy people
First Stage	Pers svngs Frndly srces	SBIC's Wlthy ppl	Venture capital Wealthy people
Rapid Growth	Pers svngs Frndly srces	Vent cap Public stock	Venture capital Public stock

Most companies in Utah do not have a realistic chance of attracting money from wealthy investors, venture capitalists or a stock offering

The Reality for Most Utah Companies

Most companies in Utah or any other state are essentially small. Because of the nature of the business or, perhaps, by conscious entrepreneurial choice, they will probably not grow beyond $1 million in sales. According to the above chart, the only potential sources of equity investment are personal savings and friendly sources. Most companies do not have a realistic chance of attracting money from wealthy investors, venture capitalists or a stock offering.

Brad Bertoch, who heads the Wayne Brown Institute, made the following insightful comments regarding hi-tech companies and their need for capital and growth in a recent issue of *Connections*: "There are no small high-tech companies—only large companies in their early stages. This is due to the competitive environment, the constant need for innovation and the financial resources needed to capture significant market share quickly. A high tech community made out of small companies will not survive." Therefore, for high tech companies and others that do have the potential of significant growth, each of the following alternatives is a possibility.

Wealthy Individual Investors

Private investors known as wealthy individuals may range from family friends to extremely wealthy individuals who manage their money by themselves. Wealthy investors are usually found through a network of friends and acquaintances, or advisors like your personal accountant, lawyer, etc. A professionally prepared private offering document which includes a realistic business plan is a key for your legal protection as well as to making certain that you aren't misleading the prospective investor. Wealthy individuals commonly may not have time and expertise to get directly involved with business but legitimately may become very frustrated and impatient with their investment when things are not going according to your plan. It is always a good idea to let a competent securities attorney review your private offering circular to make certain you are adhering to State and Federal Security Laws.

Let a competent securities attorney review your private offering circular

Venture Capital

Venture capital is managed by professionals who are expecting high returns in exchange for equity, or any combination of debt, equity and equipment leasebacks. Typically, the venture capital firm stays very close to your business, may want one of its designated people on your board of directors, or in other ways gets involved in the management of your company. When approaching a venture capitalist, you need to have a short, concise, business plan which will capture their interest in the first few moments of their review. Moreover, a venture capital firm may have important contacts with other financial resources for later-stage financing as the business expands. It may likewise have critical linkages for marketing or technology development joint-venture which may greatly speed the growth of the company. These entities have an established capital base and good managerial and market savvy. Typically, these funds prefer to invest larger sums of money: the smaller venture entities look at deals between $500K to $1 million; most of the larger funds do not like to consider investments of less than $1 or $2 million—and may well want to see deals involving

$20 million or more. Many of the venture capital firms invest money for large pension funds, municipalities, or insurance companies—sometimes involving blocks of funds of $50 million or more. Since the venture capitalist will spend just as much time researching a $1 million deal as it will on a $20 million one, it obviously is more advantageous to serve the larger client.

Before closing any funding, the venture capital company will conduct an exhaustive review of the new venture

Often entrepreneurs are afraid of truly coming to grips with the large sums of money it will ultimately take to make their venture succeed nationally and globally. The venture capitalist will be impressed by realistic, long-term projections showing how the firm can grow—and when infusions of money will be needed to facilitate that growth. Even large funds may do a $1 million deal if they see that ultimately the business will need another $10-$20 million to make the venture a viable future company. If the venture capital company doesn't want to take all the risk of a deal, they may have other cooperating funds they can use to share the deal.

Before closing any funding, the venture capital company will conduct an exhaustive review of the new venture. Things the venture capitalist looks for are discussed later in this chapter.

The Mountain West Venture Group is a nonprofit organization which has been established to provide a public, nonaligned forum for business development. The group welcomes involvement of persons interested in the process of the establishment, funding, operations and success of business ventures. The Venture Group is comprised of entrepreneurs, investors, venture capital providers, attorneys, bankers, accountants, consultants, professors and others. Through the exchange of ideas and acquaintances, the group seeks to foster the investment of risk funds, the competence of venture management, the commercialization of technology and the rewards to those involved.

Contact: Mountain West Venture Group
P.O. Box 210
Salt Lake City, UT 84144

Utah Ventures is the only active venture group in Utah. It is a small venture fund which specializes in early stages financing of biomedical companies.

Contact: Utah Ventures
419 S Wakara Way
Salt Lake City, UT 84108
(801)583-5922

The Pro's and Con's of Getting Venture Capital. For a growing company, venture capital has its advantages. The primary one is that venture capital may be the only source of funds for the enterprise. Banks are usually hesitant to loan to young, growing companies. Venture capitalists understand that they are taking on high risk, but they are betting on a "big win." They may invest when no one else is willing to. Another advantage is that since venture capital is generally equity investment, it does not require scheduled payments. The company chooses whether it wants to declare a dividend, if it is financially able. Lastly, venture capitalists often provide management assistance to the company. Although some entrepreneurs regard this as a burden, in many cases the assistance is of very high quality.

For a company looking to raise money, venture capital has both advantages and disadvantages

Venture capital has its disadvantages. Foremost, the entrepreneur is forced to give up a considerable portion of the company. If you are considering seeking venture capital, you face this very large decision. How much of the company are you willing to give up? It is difficult to give up ownership, but remember the quote, "It is better to have a small part of something that has a chance of being successful than to own all of nothing."

Be aware that closing a venture capital deal is a long shot. Industry experts indicate that only 2 to 3 percent of all proposals are successful; roughly 60 percent of the proposals are rejected after a brief reading; some 25 percent are reviewed in some detail, then turned down; 15 percent are investigated thoroughly, and only a third of those get investment offers. Of these, only half result in venture capital financing.

Searching Out Venture Capital Firms. There are an estimated 600 private venture capital companies and SBIC's in the United States. A great number of them are concentrated in Silicon Valley near San Francisco and on Route 128 near Boston. They tend to specialize in certain stage financing and on certain types of industries. *Pratt's Guide to Venture Capital Sources* is probably the most authoritative directory of venture capital companies. It describes what type of firms the venture capital companies are looking to invest in. If you are serious about seeking venture capital, *you need to read this book.* Check your local library for this book, or contact the publisher:

Venture Economics, Inc.
40 W. 57th St.
New York, NY 10019
(201)622-4500

Like SBICs, venture capital firms tend to come and go locally, sometimes as branch offices of venture capital firms in other cities. Three associations can also provide information on sources of venture capital, and are listed on the next page:

Western Association of Venture Capitalists
3000 Sand Hill Road
Building 2, Suite 215
Menlo Park, CA 94025
(415) 854-1322

National Venture Capital Association
Suite 700
1655 North Fort Myer Drive
Arlington, VA 22209
(703) 528-4370

National Association of Small Business Investment Companies (NASBIC)
1199 North Fairfax St., Suite 200
Alexandria, VA 22314
(703)683-1601

Venture capitalists have fairly predictable criteria for evaluating funding proposals

What Venture Capitalists Evaluate. Besides considering potential growth and stage of development, each venture capital company has its own criteria for evaluating potential deals, but the following four are nearly universally considered:

Management Abilities. Potential investors look first to see who is involved in your venture and what their skills are. Venture capitalists like to back people who have had previous success in other ventures. They feel this is more important than the business opportunity itself. They usually want to see evidence of marketing, finance, and operations management experience. Review Chapter 8, Gathering Your Forces, on how to build a management team.

Nature of the Product and Industry. You need to have a unique product or service and the ability to maintain a competitive advantage because investors are looking for industries that show good growth and profit potential.

Return on Investment. The reason that investors are willing to look at risky ventures is because they believe they can obtain high returns. You will not catch much attention if you project profits to be slightly better than what the bank can guarantee. Figure 7-2 shows the rate of return that venture capitalists are typically looking for. They range from a minimum of 25 percent to greater than 60 percent. That is a bit more than the bank guarantees. Your enterprise must have the ability to generate substantial returns to investors.

Before jumping to the conclusion that venture capitalists are the newest breed of robber barons, understand that the odds are against them. Five of every ten deals backed by venture capital fail, three are marginally profitable, and two turn out to be winners. They have to win big when they do win because they don't do it frequently.

Figure 7-2. Returns on Investment Typically Sought by Venture Capitalists

Stage of Business	Expected Annual ROI	Expected Increase in Initial Investment
Startup	60%+	10-15 times
First Stage	40-60%	6-12 times
Second Stage	30-50%	4-8 times
Third Stage	25-40%	3-6 times
Turnaround	50%+	8-15 times

Schilit, 1987, p. 78.

Venture capitalists expect high rates of return on their investment

"Harvest Options". Venture capitalists do not want to own a piece of your company indefinitely. They will evaluate means of harvesting their investment. Refer to Chapter 14, Harvesting a Business, for means of cashing out of a business. You must show potential investors how they will eventually get their money out.

Approaching Venture Capitalists. The way you approach venture capitalists is important. Don't mail a business plan to every venture capital company for which you find an address. You'll have about as much success as people who mass mail resumes when they are looking for a job. Do your homework. Find out which venture capital companies consider the stage of development and type of industry that you are in. Try to get an introduction through a third party. Do you know someone who knows the investors? If someone who knows them puts in a good word for you, you can be assured that they will give some attention to your business plan.

Write a good business plan! You're tired of hearing that, but it cannot be overemphasized. You may have a great idea and opportunity, but if the business plan doesn't communicate that well, venture capitalists won't consider you. Chapter 13, The Business Plan, details the information you should include. Investors will first read the executive summary of your business plan. Often investors don't read business plans in their entirety because the summary does not capture their interest. Make sure you have a clear executive summary that grabs their attention. Since they are usually evaluating management, competitive advantages, return on investment, and harvest potential, highlight them.

The summary of your business plan needs to get investors interested

Conclusion on Venture Capital

Venture capital is not easy to get. Your company needs to display solid management, a promising competitive position, high returns, and a way of cashing out to have a chance. Make sure that you really need the money or that you can't borrow the money safely, because the venture capitalists will want a big chunk of your business. Prepare a good business plan and send it to firms that are willing to consider companies in industries like yours and that are at your stage of development.

Issuing Stock

Selling stock is another means of raising equity capital. It works similarly to venture capital in that you give up part of your company in exchange for money invested in your firm. The basic difference is that you have several or many investors instead of one venture capital company. This allows people to make smaller investments and hence reduce their risk. It can also be easier to entice many small investments than one large one.

There are two general paths for selling stock. One, called private placement, involves offering the shares to only a small number of people, such as twenty to thirty maximum. The other, known as a public offering ("going public"), involves offering the shares to a larger number. An initial public offering (IPO) is regulated by the SEC. Any company seeking to "go public" must endure a rather tortuous preparation and registration process. The hardest part, however, is to persuade people to buy the shares. After complying with securities regulations, the entrepreneur may either seek to sell shares personally or may seek selling help from a stockbroker or "underwriter". Usually the broker is in a much better position by virtue of contacts and professional experience to accomplish the selling task. A broker who agrees to market the stock may choose to do so on a "firm underwriting" basis which guarantees the sale or on a "best efforts" basis which does not. Very few startup or small companies are able to interest underwriters to handle initial public offerings on either bases, but particularly on a guaranteed basis. When a public offering is successful, it provides a substantial infusion of cash and founders usually experience a great increase in wealth as a result. Very few companies are able to attract an underwriter.

In a private placement, the stock is offered to a relatively small number of investors and the stock is not traded on a public stock exchange. Investors are assumed (and some are required) to be "sophisticated," meaning they have been involved in investing previously and are supposedly able to make sound decisions on where to put their money. The Securities and Exchange Commission (SEC) does not require as exhaustive disclosure as it does with public offerings. Companies are subject only to state securities regulations, which are called "blue sky" laws. The stock is not traded on a public exchange, which makes it considerably more difficult to resell than publicly traded stock. The pros and cons of both public offerings and private placements are described below.

In a private placement, the stock is offered to a relatively small number of investors

Initial Public Offerings

A public stock offering can be a great milestone in an entrepreneur's life. Assume that you have worked hard to build your company and are able to convince a stock underwriter that he should try to take your company public. The underwriter sells a million shares at $1 each. In negotiations with the underwriter, you keep two million shares for yourself. On paper, you suddenly have stock that is valued at $2 million, plus your company now has a million dollars with which to expand. It can be a glorious time, and yet many entrepreneurs who have gone through it regret that choice. Before the company decides to go public two basic questions should be answered: Have you exhausted other financing alternatives, and do the advantages of going public outweigh disadvantages?

Pros. Public stock offerings can raise large amounts of capital for a company. The typical IPO brings in between $500,000 and $10 million. As a company founder, you have liquidity, because you will be able to sell shares on the stock market. In general, however, you are not able to sell those original shares for at least a two-year period. Your equity in the business increases substantially. The increased equity usually allows you to raise further capital through borrowing. Having a publicly traded stock can help bring recognition to your company.

Public stock offerings can raise large amounts of capital for a company

Cons. The expenses of a public stock offering are significant. Attorney, accountant, and underwriter fees and printing costs are tremendous. These expenses can range from seven to twenty percent of the value of the offering, depending on its size. Some of these parties are willing to take some of the stock instead of being paid cash, however.

As a publicly held company, you are required to file quarterly disclosure documents to the SEC. The redtape and paperwork can be overwhelming. It can take an extra full-time person just to handle the SEC reporting requirements.

You are going to be distracted from running your business by the need to respond to stockholders

Many managers complain that they no longer have the ability to run the company as freely as they used to. Boards of directors typically take far more active roles once a company is publicly held. There is pressure on you to produce profits in the short-term, which may reduce your long term success. In general, you are going to be distracted from running your business by the need to respond to stockholders.

Can You Interest an Underwriter? Underwriters issue and promote stock. They are therefore very choosy as to whom they might underwrite. They evaluate similar factors as do venture capitalists: product potential and competitive advantage, quality of management, stage of development, and growth potential. However, they have to also consider the vagaries of the stock market. Certain industries tend to be "hot" ones in the IPO market at different points in time. Computer companies were at one time, as were genetic engineering firms at another. Underwriters also have to consider the overall market. 1983 was a good year for IPO's. More than 800 companies went public in that year. The stock market crash in October 1987 completely shut down IPO's for a period of time. People were not interested in buying newly-issued stock. Underwriters therefore are concerned not only with the viability of a company but also with the condition of the stock market.

The public equity markets remain the largest source of equity capital. In order to raise money in this way, the company must have a history of successful operations.

As a rule, the more mature a company is when it makes a public offering, the better the terms of the offering—including a higher evaluation of the company and less equity given up by the founders for the required capital. Examples of some Utah startups which have "gone public" and achieved active markets include Evans and Sutherland, Novell, Megahertz, and Dayna Communications. It is the expectation of the company's profits and future growth that governs whether the market will buy it, not the size or even existence of its profits at the time it goes public. For example, in 1993 Megahertz merged into a newly formed subsidiary of VyStar Group, Inc. while retaining the Megahertz Corporation title. Vystar facilitated the offering of common stock and provided new resources to finance capital necessary for growth. Megahertz stock is traded on the NASDAQ. One year before the merger occurred Megahertz had achieved record sales and earnings which represented an increase of 68% and 749% respectively over fiscal 1991. In 1993 the company experienced increases of 210% and 687% over fiscal 1992. Megahertz is continuing to grow. In fact, sales and earnings in the fourth quarter of fiscal 1993 were greater than the entire previous year.

As a rule, the more mature a company is when it makes a public offering, the better the terms of the offering

The Key Players. There are several key players in an initial public offering. The first is you, the lead entrepreneur. You have the most at stake and therefore will sweat the most blood. Every entrepreneur who has gone through the IPO process attests to the stress and long hours involved. You need skilled outside advisors in the process. The three main players are the attorney, the underwriter, and the accountant.

The attorney. You must have a good attorney to get through this process, and you must be willing to pay for the considerable amount of time that he puts in. Attorneys are often willing to accept stock in partial or full payment for their services. Ideally, you would like an attorney who is well acquainted with your industry and has handled previous IPO's. There have been enough public offerings by Utah firms so that many law firms have partners with experience in handling them.

You must have a good attorney to get you through the IPO process

The underwriter. An IPO can be handled either by an investment banking firm or a brokerage firm. Their task is to issue and sell the stock. They usually take a percentage of the stock as payment for their services. This percentage averages 8 percent for an IPO. If your venture shows high promise, they may purchase the stock outright from you and it is their responsibility to sell it. Otherwise, they sell as much of the issue as they can and you get the proceeds (minus fees) after it is sold.

The accountant. SEC regulations require strict accounting compliance. Your underwriter will be quite hesitant for you to hire any other than a major regional or national accounting firm experienced in SEC regulations. They fear that they may have trouble selling the issue if you have an unknown accounting firm doing the audit. Intimate knowledge of SEC and other laws and post-issue procedures by the accounting firm will be a source of comfort to both you and the underwriter.

Private Placements

An alternative to an IPO is a *private placement*. If you conform to SEC Regulation D, you are exempt from federal regulations. You are therefore freed from the enormous reporting requirements of the SEC. If you pursue a private placement, make sure you hire an attorney experienced with them. If you break the laws and accidentally get involved with a "public offering", the consequences can be severe.

Under Regulation D, you can sell stock and be an exempt issue. You qualify for this exemption through one of three means:

1. You are raising $500,000 or less. There are no federal restrictions on offerings of this size.

2. You are raising $5 million or less and you do not sell to more than thirty-five non-accredited purchasers. You can sell shares to any number of accredited purchasers (see definitions below).

3. You are raising more than $5 million and you do not sell to more than 35 non-accredited purchasers. The non-accredited purchasers must be "sophisticated" (see definitions below).

Accredited investors include:

1. Institutional investors such as banks, insurance companies, venture capital firms, registered investment companies, and SBIC's.

2. Any person who buys at least $150,000 of the offered security and whose net worth, including that of his or her spouse, is at least five times the purchase price.

3. Any person who, together with his or her spouse, has a net worth in excess of $1 million at the time of purchase.

4. Any person whose income was in excess of $200,000 in each of the last two years and who expects the same income for the current year.

5. Directors, executive officers, or general partners of the company or partnership selling the securities.

6. Certain tax-exempt organizations with more than $500,000 in assets.

Sophisticated investors are generally wealthy individuals who invest in early stage ventures on a regular basis. They attest that they are able to gauge the relative merits of the proposals they evaluate and that they are aware of the risks involved.

The benefit of a private placement is obvious—freedom from SEC filings. However, they are not without problems. First, getting brokers to sell the stock may be difficult. Even sales commissions of 15 to 20 percent may not motivate brokers to push the stock. Second, purchasers of privately placed stock may not sell the original issues for a two-year period. They are thus locked into it, which deters many investors. Third, although SEC regulations need to be observed, "blue sky" laws within the state may still be complex. Private placements do not guarantee freedom from all regulation.

The benefit of a private placement is obvious—freedom from SEC filings

The Utah Uniform Securities Act makes it unlawful for any person to offer or sell any security in the state of Utah unless the security is registered or is exempt from registration. The purpose of registration is to provide adequate information to the investing public by requiring the registrant to give complete business and financial disclosures as a part of their registration statement. For information concerning state securities registration and exemptions from registration contact the Department of Commerce.

Contact: Utah Division of Securities
Department of Commerce
160 East 300 South
P.O. Box 45808
Salt Lake City, UT 84145-0808
(801) 530-6600

Federal registration of the security may also be required. For information concerning federal regulations call or write the U.S. Securities and Exchange Commission.

Contact: U.S. Securities and Exchange Comm, SLC Branch Office
Key Bank Tower, 50 South Main #500
Salt Lake City, UT 84144 (801) 524-5796

Individuals offering or selling securities in Utah must be licensed in the state of Utah. These licensing requirements are found in the Utah Uniform Securities Act, section 61-1-3 and in Division Rule 164-4-1.

Raising capital through the public markets can be successful; however, finding an interested underwriter and the success of that underwriting depends a great deal on the mood of the investing public. In Utah's past there have been times when brokers (underwriters) were actively seeking uranium, gold, silver or oil/gas deals. At other times, nothing but a bio-tech firm seemed to succeed. So, even though you may have a very viable business concept, unless the market is receptive to the type of company being financed, you may not be able to go for a public offering.

Due to legal complexities of making a public offering, you must consult an attorney with securities expertise before making any decisions or attempting any sale of stock. Also, talking with local investment banking or brokerage firms can provide good information and can give you some indication as to whether or not your company is likely to succeed in raising money under current market conditions.

Conclusion on Stock Issues

Selling stock allows investors to own part of your company. You are not required to make set repayments to them, but they expect to share in profits and increases in stock value of the company. It is a means of raising substantial amounts of money. IPO's can result in dramatic increases in your equity in a company, and they allow you to get cash out of the business after a period of time. They are costly to undertake and require extensive reporting requirements to the SEC. Qualified private placements need not be registered with the SEC, but you may have difficulty in getting brokers to sell the stock. With either approach to issuing stock, you need an experienced attorney's assistance. Remember, too, that the guidelines presented in this chapter are subject to changes in federal and states laws as well as administrative practices of the respective government agencies.

References

1. Bloomenthal, Harold S, Cannon Y. Harvey, and Samuel E. Wing. *1985 Going Public Handbook.* New York: Clark Boardman Co., 1985.

2. Ernst & Whinney. *Going Public*. New York: Ernst & Whinney, 1984.

3. Pratt, Stanley E. *Pratt's Guide to Venture Capital Sources, 15th Edition*. Wellesley Hills, Mass.: Capital Publishing, 1991.

4. Roscow, James P. "The Venture Capital Directory." *Venture*. New York: Venture Mag. Inc. Volume 9, June 1987. pp. 71-80.

5. Schilit, W. Keith. "How to Obtain Venture Capital." *Business Horizons*. May/June, 1987, pp. 76-81.

6. Timmons, Jeffry A. *New Venture Creation*, 3rd Edition. Homewood, Illinois: Irwin, 1990.

7. U.S. Small Business Administration, 1993 Edition. *The States and Small Business, A Directory of Programs and Activities.* Washington, D.C.: U.S. Government Printing Office, 1993.

8

Gathering Your Forces

"It is better to have great people with a good idea than to have good people with a great idea"
General George Doriot

If you ask venture capitalists what they consider to be the most critical factor in the success of a high-growth venture, they will nearly always respond "management." The people behind your venture will have a large impact on its success. Sizeable companies have been built around one lead entrepreneur, but more often, several people comprise the driving force behind successful high-growth firms. Whether there is a single entrepreneur or several, a growing company requires the skills of more than one person. Successful entrepreneurs realize the limitations of their own abilities and draw upon others' talents. You can bring other people in as partners, employees, consultants, or as members of the corporate board of directors. This section describes how you identify what skills are critical to your firm's success and also how you can obtain those skills.

The success of your venture will be determined, in large part, by the quality of your management team

Determining What Skills Your Company Needs

Each company has need of different skills, and you should assess which are most critical for the survival and success of your firm. The following lists are provided as a starting point in your assessment. The lists contain skills in the general functional areas of marketing, production, finance/accounting, engineering, research and development, and general management. Go over the skills and write down which you think are critical for the success of your firm. Once you have reviewed the lists, add any other skills you think are important in your particular competitive environment-- exporting knowledge, legal expertise, connections with suppliers, for example. Add those to your list of critical skills. Your list will change as the company grows, and a key to your success will be to acquire skills before they become critical.

"Every venture needs a founder who understands the need for supporting skills and knows where to find them, when needed."

1. Marketing Skills

   a. Market research— able to identify and characterize markets
   b. Product management— able to develop sensible mix of products
   c. Distribution management— understands marketing channels and which are appropriate for firm's products
   d. Product pricing—able to competitively price products and maintain profitable margin

2. Production and Operations Skills

   a. Manufacturing— able to manage manufacturing process
   b. Quality control— able to define standards and meet them
   c. Scheduling— able to schedule people, materials, and machinery for efficient production
   d. Inventory control—able to manage system which determines what, when, and how much to buy
   e. Shop layout— able to design efficient shop layout

3. Finance/Accounting Skills

   a. Cash flow management— able to project cash requirements
   b. Raising capital—aware of different capital sources and how to approach each of them
   c. Financial analysis— able to perform breakeven and ratio analysis and interpret them, able to interpret financial statements
   d. Accounting/bookkeeping— able to set up books and keep accurate financial records
   e. Credit and collections— able to develop and enforce credit policies

4. Engineering Skills

5. Research and Development Skills

6. General Management Skills

a. Strategic planning— able to analyze competitors, internal strengths and weaknesses, and external trends and able to develop competitive strategies
b. Organization— able to structure the organization in logical units, able to delegate responsibility, able to coordinate activities of people and divisions
c. Motivation— able to inspire managers and employees to high performance
d. Controlling— able to set goals and make sure goals are being met
e. Communication— able to communicate clearly with employees, media, customer, and others
f. Teamwork— able to get individuals to work as a team
g. Cheerleading-- able to support and encourage employees

7. Other Possible Skill Areas

a. Legal expertise— knowledgeable in areas of taxes, real estate, contracts, patents, investments, etc.
b. Computer skills— able to use a computer to improve operations of firm
c. Any other skills which are critical to your particular industry

Every company requires a unique set of skills because of its competitive situation. However, many managers would support the following generalizations:

Marketing, financial, and production skills are critical to a company

- Marketing expertise is paramount at startup. Companies need to develop new markets, enter new marketing channels, and decide on marketing strategies. If the originator of the company has strong technical skills but no marketing experience, someone should be brought in with marketing skills.

- Manufacturing companies need someone with production expertise. Building a successful prototype is far different from setting up an efficient production operation. If you manufacture a product, you need someone with production skills.

- Once sales begin to increase and the size of the company grows, financial and management expertise become critical. Without cash management and financial analytical skills a firm can quickly run out of money. Management skills become increasingly important as the number of people increases.

Obtaining the Necessary Skills

Once you have decided what skills are most important for your company's success, you have the task of finding the right people and deciding how they will be affiliated with the organization. Each of the following alternatives is discussed below:

1. Forming a partnership
2. Hiring people as contractors
3. Hiring people as employees
4. Getting people to serve on your board of directors

Partnerships

Choose your partners carefully

Taking on a partner is a serious matter. You are giving up part of your ownership of the firm. It can take the form of a legal partnership or else issuance of stock in a corporation (see Chapter 2). If the partner is going to be involved in managing the company, you need to approach the relationship as carefully as you would a marriage. You'll probably be spending as much time with this person as a spouse. Incidentally, partnership divorce rates are higher than marriage divorce rates— *choose your partners carefully*!

There are obstacles to your finding a suitable managing partner. Your personalities need to be compatible, and you must trust each other. Your skills should be complementary, as stated above. Your goals for the business should be consistent. You shouldn't search out someone exactly like yourself for a partner, because you want different skills and ideas. However, you need to agree on the basics.

There are reasons why you should be willing to give up part ownership of your company and open yourself to the frustrations of a partnership. The first is a financial consideration. A partner almost always makes a financial investment in the company. The company thus has greater resources than if it were owned by a single person. The firm may forego borrowing because of the partners' investments, which reduces the risk of bankruptcy. At startup, you may not be able to guarantee anyone a salary. All you can offer is a piece of the pie. The second consideration is an issue of commitment. You do not get the same commitment from an employee that you get from a business owner. When a person's money is at stake, his perspective changes. If the skills you are seeking are absolutely critical to the success of the company, and you need a person's total commitment, a partnership makes sense. In certain cases, top-notch people will not join you without receiving some ownership of the company.

Although partnerships can bring a variety of skills to a firm, don't believe in a *leaderless democracy.* It will not work in the startup venture! You need to be the leader. Keep more ownership than anyone else to back up this point. When there are differences of opinion, someone needs to step forward and make a decision. You want people to feel a part of the organization, but you do not want them to have any question as to who is the leader.

A leaderless democracy will not work in an entrepreneurial company

Contractors

Initially, you should hire accountants or lawyers as contractors. You will not need their services on a full-time basis, so use them only as needed. Work to establish a trusting, long-term relationship with each of these. Other skills which you may need occasionally should be hired on a consulting basis — computer set-up, inventory design, etc.

Employees

Most of the people contributing to your organization will be employees. You can't expect a consultant to do a job that requires a large amount of time, nor will you be able to afford it. You don't want a large number of partners, in order to preserve your ownership position. You hire people for skills that are critical to the organization which you aren't able to or don't have the time to do. To increase their commitment and motivation, you may offer profit-sharing as opposed to ownership. If you can demonstrate the possibility of significant profits, employees may be willing to work at very modest salaries.

Board of Directors

Companies that incorporate are required by law to have a board of directors. Boards can play invaluable roles for the startup company. They include:

Advisory. If your management team lacks certain skills that are important to the company, the board can provide them. The board members become consultants, but by being on the board they are committed to the organization. Some board members may provide free consulting, but it is not something you should assume. They can also help resolve disputes in the company, set goals and objectives, and review financial statements.

A board of directors can be invaluable to the startup company

Legitimacy. The people on your board can bring legitimacy to the company. Lenders may know board members and thus look more favorably upon a loan request. Suppliers may offer you credit sooner based on board members' suggestions. You may be able to bypass certain local regulations, such as zoning requirements, if board members speak on your behalf. A startup company does not have a track record, and prominent or powerful board members can open doors.

Monitoring. Since the board reviews management decisions, it provides discipline for management. Knowing that an objective group of professional people will be reviewing your decisions, you will tend to act in a professional and ethical fashion.

Powerful board members can open doors for your company

The role of the board changes over time. At startup, the advisory and legitimacy roles are critical. As the company grows, the monitoring role becomes increasingly important. Be aware that the composition of the board should change over time. As the company requires different skills, you should seek out new board members.

Who Should You Choose? You should select first of all people whom you respect and with whom you can get along. Choose people who can effectively deal with present or future problems of the firm. Potential candidates include [1]:

- Individuals whose skills complement those of the owner-manager. If you are weak in financial matters, a person with strong financial background could be a good candidate;

- Individuals who are involved with companies that are either customers of or suppliers to the industry— but not one of your company's customers or suppliers;

- Investment or commercial bankers who are *not* your company's investment or commercial banker and who realize that they never will be bankers for the company;

- Experts in some area that is important to your company's continued growth and profitability; e.g. R&D, venture capital, labor relations, community awareness, and the like;

- Individuals with a broad perspective who can look at problems from an insightful and objective point of view; and finally and most importantly,

- Experienced executives who have been where the company wishes to go and who can help anticipate potential problems.

You should strive to keep a small board with either five or seven directors. A larger board becomes unwieldy, while a board smaller than this does not provide for sufficient interaction. You should have a mixture of both internal and external directors. Internal directors would include people actively involved in managing the company. The people described in the paragraph above would be outside directors. This mixture balances the typically shorter-term, operational orientation of insiders with the longer-term, strategic orientation of outsiders.

Strive to keep a small board of directors

Getting People to Serve as Directors. At start-up, you don't have much money to pay directors, so that should not be why they would want to serve. You want to sell them on thc fact that yours is a growing, exciting venture of which they can be a part. They will be able to work with a group of people from which they can learn. Let them know that their opinions will be listened to and that they can help shape the destiny of your company.

You should not expect board members to go without compensation. Some small companies pay several hundred dollars to each board member at each meeting, which usually lasts an entire afternoon. Stock options are also used to compensate board members. Although some board members may be willing to provide free consulting services outside of board meetings, most companies pay them normal consulting fees.

Much of the success of the board depends on you. If you view a board of directors as interfering in decisions that are rightfully yours to make, you will have a totally ineffectual board. You need to seek out board members who are committed to the organization and who know that you are willing to listen to them.

Much of the success of the board depends upon you

Conclusion

The quality of people in your venture will greatly affect its success. Assess honestly your own capabilities, and try to fill in the gaps. Don't believe that you can do it all. If you want to grow, you must bring in other skilled people.

References

1. Churchill, Neil C. and Lewis, Virginia L., "A Board for All Seasons," *Harvard Business Review*, May-June 1983.

2. Gumpert, David (ed.), "How Small Companies Can Best Choose and Involve Outside Directors," in "Growing Concerns," *Harvard Business Review*, July-August 1980.

3. Timmons, Jeffry A. *New Venture Creation*, 3rd Edition. Homewood, Illinois: Irwin, 1990.

9

Strategic Planning

"In Korea, we work for the future.
You (Americans) work for the weekend."

Two great tennis players— Ken Rosewall and Roscoe Tanner— had very different styles of play. Tanner's approach was simple and straightforward— raw power. He hit his serves well over 100 miles per hour and hit aggressively nearly every shot. Opponents feared the days when he was "on," because his power was so overwhelming it could tear the racket right out of an opponent's hand. Rosewall, on the other hand, varied his game based on whom he was playing and what type of court surface was underfoot. Sometimes aggressive, sometimes defensive, sometimes fast, sometimes deliberate, he was a master at adapting his game in order to win.

Both players had approaches that made them top players in the world. Rosewall, however, is the one who is a legend. Why? He was a master strategist. Strategy, in the long run, will win over raw power, and Rosewall demonstrated that fact. He was a formidable opponent, no matter what the court surface, no matter who the opponent, for nearly a twenty-year period.

Strategy, in the long run, will win over raw power

Although Tanner was a great player, he was not a great strategist. He was not good at adapting to different playing conditions, such as the court surface. He did not vary his game significantly depending on whom he was playing— every opponent just prepared for cannon-balls. Lastly, his career was not a long one. When the speed began to fall on his serves and other shots, which it does as players age, he did not have much to fall back on.

There are business lessons to be learned in the approaches of these two players. When you have a definite advantage over competitors, whether it be superior products or services, design skills, or marketing abilities, rely on those strengths and don't be afraid to take full advantage of them. "When you've got it, flaunt it." That is what Tanner teaches us. What Rosewall teaches us is that you need to consider the environment in deciding what competitive approach to take. He would consider court surface, wind, sun, motivation level of an opponent, and many other factors. You, as the premier strategist in your company, need to consider the economy, industry trends, changes in customers, and other environmental factors. You need to know who your competitors are, what their strengths and weaknesses are, and how they are going to react to your competitive moves. You, like Rosewall, can have a long and successful business career if you are willing to adapt to changing conditions in order to put yourself in a stronger competitive position. The purpose of this chapter is to present a "strategic" approach to managing your growing company.

You need to adapt to changing conditions

Strategic Planning

There are many different definitions of strategic planning, and most of them are vague and difficult to apply. Planning is the process of thinking about future events and taking action so that those events occur as you want them to. Strategic means nothing more than concentrating on the most critical factors affecting your company. *Strategic planning* is, therefore, the process of analyzing what opportunities and threats face your company, of assessing your company's strengths and weaknesses, and lastly of finding a fit between your company and its environment that gives your company a competitive advantage.

The process of planning doesn't stop with the initial design of the business plan

Many new strategic ventures find a formal business plan helpful in guiding them through first stages of development. However, the process of planning doesn't stop with the initial design of the plan but needs to continue throughout the life of a venture. Making consistent progress in carrying out a formal or informal business plan is usually the single most important factor in determining a successful business take-off.

There are many examples of good strategic planning. One is Megahertz, which manufactures high quality fax/modem cards for microcomputers. When Megahertz entered the microcomputer accessories market, they were one of the forerunners in credit card-size modems. Their retractable jack became quite popular and Megahertz immediately experienced enormous growth. Management was able to foresee the spread of the new standard and the firm committed itself to being a quality leader in its field.

There are also many examples of companies that have done a poor job of strategic planning at different times. J.C. Penney was the world's leading retailer of "soft" goods after World War II. The company had built its success on a strategy of cash-and-carry and selling primarily clothing. A competitor of theirs, which was much smaller, decided to start offering credit and to carry also "hard" goods, including hardware and appliances. J.C. Penney did not react to this competitive move, thinking that since their old strategy had worked a long time, why change? Penneys' smaller competitor was Sears Roebuck and Co., which is now much larger than Penneys. It took Penneys more than a decade to realize that the old strategy was no longer appropriate. Since that time, both companies have struggled with different strategic issues. In addition, both K-Mart and WalMart have intensified the competition and the struggle to come up with viable strategies.

Another example is Osborne Computer, a company that fell prey to a classic strategic mistake— poor timing. The Osborne I was the first portable microcomputer, was very affordable, and came with a full set of free software programs. Osborne was so successful with the Osborne I that they immediately began developing the Osborne II, a "new and improved" model. The company announced the II six months in advance of the anticipated shipping date. It was to be a much improved model with only a slight increase in price. After the announcement, no one wanted to buy an Osborne I, and the company couldn't survive six months without sales. It went bankrupt.

Timing is an important strategic issue

Problems in Planning

There are two types of problem planners— the over-planner and the under-planner. The over-planner has everything planned from the moment of awakening in the morning to the moment when he puts his head on the pillow at the end of the day. His days are filled with "to do" lists, appointment books, schedules, and a need for absolute order. The following line from Jackson Browne's *Reach For the Sky* illustrates the problem.

"Without dreaming of the perfect love, and holding it so high above, that if you stumbled onto somebody real, you'd never know."

An entrepreneur needs to react quickly to opportunities, many of which are difficult to foresee, and if a perfect plan blinds him to those opportunities, he'll let them pass right by. Over-planning, though a rare bird in entrepreneurial circles, will drag a company down.

Under-planning is a common visitor to entrepreneurial firms

Under-planning is a common visitor to entrepreneurial firms. The hero of this company is a pistol-toting lead entrepreneur who loves to "shoot from the hip". Most of her days are filled with pulling the trigger on a fire extinguisher, trying to put out all of the brush-fires that could have been avoided by some planning. She fails to realize that her "gut-feel," which usually is right, can lead her to disastrous decisions for the company.

Good strategic planning lies in between these two extremes. It is a formal framework of evaluating the company's position in relation to its environment on an on-going basis. However, it should not lead to "paralysis through analysis." Companies need to analyze their opportunities, gather a reasonable amount of information, and then *do something.*

The Strategic Planning Process

The strategic planning process includes six steps:

1. Define the business and develop a strategic mission
2. Formulate strategic goals
3. Analyze the external environment (including the competition)and company strengths and weaknesses
4. Formulate strategies
5. Implement strategies
6. Reevaluate strategies

You can't expect what was once a good strategy to continue being one

Generally, you should try to start with #1 and work towards #6. Be aware that in most cases you can't work straight through without going back and changing what you had previously decided. For example, after you set a strategic goal of growing by 25 percent a year, your analysis of the industry may reveal that is unlikely, so you have to go back and change your goals. Or perhaps you decide that an appropriate strategy for your company is to be an industry market share leader, producing at high volume. After assessing your production capabilities, however, you may conclude that you can't really implement that strategy, even though it is a good one. These examples illustrate the *cyclical* nature of strategic planning— you have to keep going back and reassessing previous decisions. As J.C. Penney demonstrated, you can't expect what was once a good strategy to continue being one.

Strategic Mission

Strategic mission is a basic statement of what type of business a firm is in. You need to consider what it really is that you provide to customers. For example, some companies have had to redefine what businesses they are in. AT&T decided that they were in the communication business, and not just the telephone business. Many railroad companies have redefined their business as the transportation business, since railroad was too restrictive. Many accounting firms are no longer "accounting" firms, they offer management consulting, financial analysis, and computer systems assistance. Your mission should accurately describe what it is that you provide to customers.

There are two primary advantages in having a concise, written mission statement. The first is to give direction to your company. Consider the following example:

A newly-elected president of a corporation stood before the board of directors to make an initial presentation. He had brought a board with metal arrows on it, and it appeared as below.

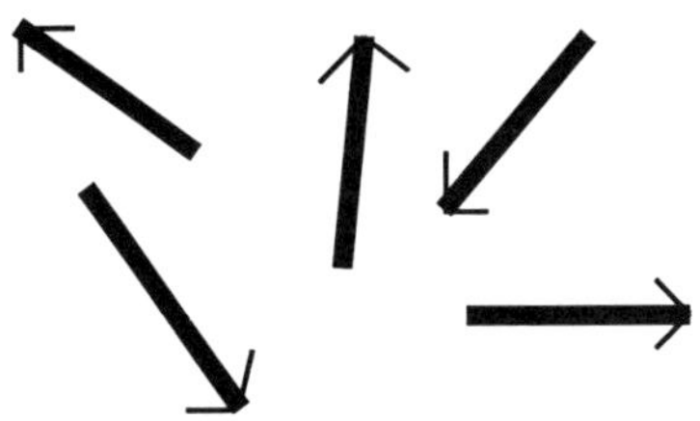

He said, "This is what the company looks like now. There are hard-working and productive people in this firm, but they're not pulling in the same direction. My intention is this," he said as he pulled a magnet from his pocket and slammed it against the top of the board. All of the arrows immediately pointed towards the magnet. "I will bring strategic purpose to this company. As a group, we will know where we are headed and we will all pull in the same direction."

A mission statement will unify people in an organization

A mission statement will unify people in an organization. The second primary advantage of a mission statement is that it reminds everyone of what the company is trying to achieve. Day-to-day pressures

A mission statement serves as a "guiding light" that helps people rise above details

require managers' and employees' attention alike. A common complaint of managers is, "I'm too busy running a company to worry about where its going." A mission statement serves as a "guiding light" that helps people rise above the many details of running a company and keeps them centered on the strategic direction of the company. Phrases portraying missions from reports of some successful Utah companies include:

Evans and Sutherland. We are providing lower-priced products. Forging strategic marketing alliances. Entering new markets.

Wordperfect (now merged with Novell). To develop, market, and support world-class applications software that meets the communication needs of our customers.

Novell. Novell is the networking company leading a transformation in our industry; a company driven by change, providing leadership in a customer-driven IT marketplace defined by change.

Franklin Quest. Our mission is to help individuals bring order to their hectic and sometimes chaotic lives. We help people identify their values, determine their goals, and then focus their time and energies on activities that lead to greater personal fulfillment.

The Huntsman Companies. We will operate safe, clean, efficient facilities in an environmentally and socially responsible manner. We are dedicated to giving our customers the finest quality and service available. We believe that ethical and moral standards are the foundation of good business policies and will operate with this integrity.

Megahertz. Megahertz is committed to developing products which are readily available, affordably priced, and solution-oriented so that mobile computer users have access to information anytime, anywhere.

Kennecott (owned by RTZ, based in Britain). RTZ's aim is to act responsibly as the steward of the resources in its charge, working for the well being of the communities and countries where they are found, adopting best contemporary practice in environmental matters, and seeking health and safety performance second to none in mining.

Strategic Goals

Strategic goals are the most important goals in your company. They bring definition and measurability to your mission statement. Listed below are typical strategic goals for companies.

- Profitability;
- Market share;
- Growth in sales;
- Quality of products or services;
- Employee relations/growth; and
- Social responsibility.

Each company will typically have some strategic goals different from these. McDonald's probably has a goal of opening a certain number of restaurants. Toyota's goal may be to attain a certain ranking on the consumer polls that evaluate quality. You should probably have no more than five to eight strategic goals. Strategic goals are the *primary* objectives in your organization. If you have too many of them, you can't concentrate on them.

Strategic goals are the primary objectives in your organization

Analyzing the External Environment

If you are like Roscoe Tanner and have overwhelming competitive strengths, you may not have to pay much attention to the environment. Just make sure your opponent is on the court and start blasting. Most businesses do not enjoy such recognizable competitive advantages; therefore, they must pay attention to what is happening in the world around them. There are three primary external areas for you to analyze:

- The general economic, legal, political, and social environment;
- The industry(s) you are in; and
- Your specific competitors.

Each of these is described below, along with suggestions on where to obtain information.

The Economic, Legal/Political, and Social Environment. Macro-economic (national and global) variables have a significant impact on both small and large companies. A small entrepreneurial firm is often affected by economic factors such as changes in the gross national product, interest rates, inflation, and currency exchange rates. That kind of data can be readily followed in the *Wall Street Journal*, one of the world's most respected business publications. Additionally, you can obtain a great deal of broad economic information published by various agencies of the United States government. This can be found at most large libraries.

If your company is involved in a local or regional market, you may need to pay even more attention to the economy in your particular area. Your daily newspaper is can be a source of data, and in-depth information on the Utah economy can be obtained free or at nominal cost from:

> The Bureau of Economic and Business Research
> David Eccles School of Business
> University of Utah
> Salt Lake City, UT 84111 or call
> (801) 581-6333

Ask to be put on the mailing list for their free monthly publication: *The Utah Economic and Business Review.* If you need special economic data on a particular part of the State, ask the Bureau what may be available.

Other useful economic publications are available from:

> Utah Division of Business and Economic Development
> 324 South State, Fifth Floor
> Salt Lake City, UT 84111
> (801) 538-8800

The legal and political environment also affects the way you run your business. There are new laws on such issues as firing an employee. Tariffs may affect how much competition you will face. Local zoning laws may restrict what you can do at your business site. New tax laws may affect your business decisions. It is wise to stay as current as possible on those legal and political changes which affect your business. Local newspapers, trade journals, and general business publications such as *Business Week* and *The Wall Street Journal* can provide valuable information.

Pay attention to social changes

Social changes are occurring constantly in this country and in your specific market area— pay attention to them. The nation is becoming a more aged population, and in fifteen years the percentage of the population over fifty years old will be dramatically higher. While this change poses threats to some businesses, such as diaper manufacturers, it presents opportunities to others, such as nursing care facilities. In the last ten years, the number of two-income households has increased dramatically. This has spawned increased demand for day-care, fast food, and home cleaning services. If your company emits pollution, community attitudes will affect how you operate. The prevailing sentiments in your community towards unionization may dictate whether you can operate a non-union shop or not.

No business operates in a vacuum. Economic, political, and social trends do affect most businesses and you cannot ignore them. Try to stay as well informed as possible about these issues and the way they might affect your company.

No business operates in a vacuum

Industry Analysis. An *industry* is a group of firms whose products are so similar that they are brought into close competition. The industry is the most important environmental factor to analyze when formulating your strategic plan. Structure of the industry determines the intensity of competition and affects which strategies work well and which don't. Analysis of the industry helps you to make two major strategic decisions:

1. Should you even be in an industry?
2. Which strategies have the best chance of success in the industry?

An assessment of the following industry structural characteristics helps to answer these two questions.

Market Size. You need to first establish that the market you are pursuing contains enough customers for you to make a profit. The greater the market size, the greater sales potential.

Market Growth Rate. A quickly growing market allows for entry of new firms, whereas stagnant markets tend to "shake out" companies. If you can establish a sizable market share in a growing industry, all you need do to grow is preserve your market share. You don't have to take away other competitors' customers.

Gross Margin. Gross margin for a firm is total sales minus direct costs (raw materials, direct labor, etc.) Although margins will differ between firms in an industry, the average margin in an industry is significant. A large gross margin allows a company to have some breathing room— to make a significant profit on individual units or to drop prices to increase sales. Industries with small margins tend to be very competitive.

A large gross margin allows a company to have some breathing room

Industry Profitability. Some companies do better than others, but still in many industries you find most companies with profits near an industry average. Some industries have traditionally been quite profitable, while others have struggled.

Entry Barriers. Entry barriers are factors which inhibit newcomers entering an industry. Examples of entry barriers include:

- High start-up costs;
- Proprietary information (patents);
- Economies of scale;
- Learning curve effects;
- Brand loyalty;
- Access to distribution channels; and
- Government regulation.

Entry barriers make it difficult for companies to enter an industry

High capital costs allow only companies that have been able to raise significant capital to enter the market. Most manufacturers who need a sizable plant and expensive equipment have high start-up costs. Patents can afford protection from potential competitors. Polaroid has been the only camera maker to have self-developing film because of a patent. You need a lot of money to enforce patents, however, and as many entrepreneurs state, "A patent is only a license to sue. If you can't afford to sue, it won't do you any good." Economies of scale allow the cost per unit to drop when larger volumes are produced. For example, the cost per unit for machinery drops as more units are produced. Large companies such as McDonalds can spend heavily on advertising and keep the cost down at individual restaurants because there are so many outlets.

Learning curve effects are quite strong in some industries. A learning curve is simply the fact that you get more efficient at doing something the longer you do it. A strong learning curve exists in high quality furniture manufacturing. The companies that have been doing it for many years have advantages over newcomers because they have skills that are not easily nor quickly learned.

Brand loyalty makes it difficult for companies to enter an industry. Some sporting goods companies develop high levels of brand loyalty, such as Rossignol in ski equipment. That loyalty makes it difficult for newcomers because they have to persuade customers to switch.

One or several firms can control access to distribution channels. A new potato chip manufacturer will have a rough time getting its products on grocery store shelves because there is a limited amount of shelving space, and that space is already taken by proven brands.

Government regulations can inhibit the entry of new competitors into an industry. Utility companies are highly controlled, as is access to that industry. There are only a limited number of micro-brewery licenses available in Utah, thus limiting newcomers.

Resist the temptation to think that entry barriers are bad. Ideally, you would like barriers to be as high as possible, but low enough for you to get in. Industries with low entry barriers, such as video rental stores, experience intense competition and usually suffer price wars. Once you get into an industry, you would like to maintain as high of barriers as possible to keep newcomers out.

Resist the temptation to think that entry barriers are bad

Power of Suppliers. If the suppliers to your industry are few, they can wield considerable power over you. Computer manufacturers recently have had problems receiving microcomputer chips from the few large manufacturers of chips. The small computer producers have been hit especially hard because they have very little leverage when dealing with the large chips producers. Ideally, you would have a large number of suppliers, none of which could wield much power over you.

Power of Customers. Selling to only a few large customers can be risky. If they stop buying your products or choose to buy them from someone else, you lose a large chunk of your sales. Granted, some companies do very well selling primarily to the government and have done it for a long time, but even that puts you in a precarious position. Ideally, you would have a large base of customers who couldn't exert much control over you.

Amount of Product Differentiation. Some industries have standard, generic-type products, such as the paper industry. Companies have a difficult time making themselves unique in the marketplace. Other industries contain products which are quite differentiated. For example, there is a multitude of shoe manufacturers who have products that vary greatly.

Overall Intensity of Competition. Some industries are extremely competitive. A variety of factors can cause intense competition. Factors already mentioned—low entry barriers, little product differentiation, low margins, low industry growth—often lead to high competition. If the main players in an industry are committed to remaining in the industry, no matter what the cost, they can make life miserable for everyone else. For example, suppose you open a hardware store in a town with two other such stores. Both of your competitors have been

A variety of factors can cause intense competition

in business for more than fifty years, are family owned, have paid off their land and building, and have no intention of doing anything except selling hardware. Do you think they are going to welcome you into the hardware community and make life easy for you? Entrenched competitors tend to be intense competitors.

Driving Forces

Entrenched competitors tend to be intense competitors

Driving forces are changes in industry structure or forces that affect the structure. They can pose threats to your company or provide opportunity. The sooner you detect these changes the easier it will be to deal with them as opportunities instead of threats. You should analyze all of the industry structural characteristics described in the previous paragraphs to determine whether changes are occurring or not. Described below are typical driving forces in many industries.

Changes in the long-term growth rate. If an industry is about to take off, and you are one of a few players in the field, you want to capture the largest portion of industry sales you can before the growth occurs. For example, Novell Incorporated in Provo sensed impending growth in the computer network industry and committed substantial resources to developing networking software in advance of competitors' moves. Novell is now a dominant player in the networking industry and is guarding its growth by expanding into global markets. If you sense early on that industry growth is leveling off, options include selling out, acquiring competitors, diversifying, or changing strategy. Novell, in a continuing effort to remain competitive, merged with WordPerfect.

Kennecott, owner of Bingham Canyon Copper Mine, the oldest and largest open-pit copper mine in North America, had been pushed into a corner by Chilean companies who drove copper prices down in the eighties. The Utah operations had high production costs, low productivity and outdated facilities. The world competition in the copper prices drove Kennecott to streamline its production, improve productivity, reduce its workforce, and make major investments to modernize facilities. The productivity improvements and modernization investments yielded outstanding results in reducing production costs. The Utah operations now produce copper at lower cost than all other U.S. producers. Major additional expansion and modernization is continuing in 1995 for the Kennecott facility.

Changes in who buys the product or how they use it. Are there new customer groups who are now beginning to use your products? The home cleaning industry used to depend on high-income customers for the majority of sales. The increase in two-income families has changed that, and now the service is purchased by a much larger group of people. Perhaps a product of yours is being used in a different fashion than it had been previously.

Product innovation. Are new products or product features being developed in the industry? Innovation can affect the competitive position of firms in the industry. Apple was on a downward slide relative to IBM until they introduced the Macintosh computer, which provided a fresh, visual approach to computing. CD-ROM disks are also shaking up the market for mass-storage devices in the microcomputer industry. The traditional hard disk storage system may become obsolete. Innovation occurs in almost all industries, and you need to stay on top of new developments and decide which have the potential to alter the strategic position of firms in your industry.

If dramatic changes are occurring in the way your industry is making products, you need to be aware of them

Process innovation. Process innovations are breakthroughs in the way products are made. Henry Ford's assembly line for cars was a process innovation. Robot usage in car factories is a process innovation. If dramatic changes are occurring in the way your industry is making products, you need to be aware of them.

Marketing Innovation. Mail order companies now sell the majority of computers and computer software. Companies like Dell and Compaq who first sensed the increasing sophistication of customers and saw the trend toward increased mail-order shopping are the companies that established themselves early in that business and have reaped the benefits.

Some companies like Utah's Lyon Design are reaping benefits of low cost manufacturing in southeast Asia. Lyon Design began operations in 1990, and since than has been growing between 40-100% every year. The company's main line of business is importing primarily from Taiwan and wholesaling novelty gift items such as sound chip devices, motion products, regular inventory, and sand pictures. The sound chip devices appear in different forms, such as key chains and paper weights devices, and when activated, vocalize humorous sayings. Products like "The Rude Cube" and "The Marriage Saver" have proven to be very successful.

The Parlant Technology company decided to focus on educational markets by providing server-based communications solutions to schools and school districts. The company's products and services provide superior results at a half to a third less than the costs of its major competitors.

Entry or exit of major firms. The air travel business is extremely competitive and there are high barriers to entry. But even in this kind of environment Morris Air was able to secure a high growth niche market. Its primary goal "was not to pull passengers from other carriers but to create a new travel market of people who would otherwise drive or not go at all" [3]. By making travel affordable they expanded market tremendously.

The company gave careful attention to expenses. An internal program called Project Six kept costs at 6 cents per seat mile—markedly below the average 10.5 cents per seat mile for all airlines' domestic service. Passengers were served inexpensive snacks rather than full meals. Before Morris Air was in the Los Angeles market, the round-trip fare from Salt Lake City was $600. After Morris Air entered, the market dropped to $118 resulting in customers benefitting from this kind of competition.

Delta Air Lines, a major provider of air service in Salt Lake City, was significantly affected by Morris Air. Delta's Salt Lake City hub is the third largest in the nation. Southwest's recent acquisition of Morris is therefore expected to have dire implications for Delta's heretofore profitable Salt Lake hub.

Diffusion of proprietary knowledge. Sometimes, instead of waiting until patents run out or trade secrets are leaked companies team up for the benefit of both sides. In the fall of 1993, Phonex, a Utah-based company, signed an exclusive marketing agreement with Thomas Consumer Electronics, the largest consumer electronics firm in America. TCE created the Digital Satellite System (DSS)—which is setting records as the highest dollar volume product ever introduced to the consumer electronics marketplace.

To meet the need for additional phone jacks in offices and homes, Phonex Corporation developed the Wireless Phonejak and Intelejak. These Phonex products create phone jacks from any electrical outlet by sending voice and data telephone signals over the AC wiring. A system can be installed by simply plugging in.

The DSS is a small 18-inch digital audio-video satellite system which hooks to a television control box. The DSS technology requires a telephone jack near a consumer's television for the modem contained in the control box. TCE was concerned that few consumers would have a jack in that location. As TCE began to research the Phonex

Intelejak as a solution, both companies realized the possibilities for other applications using this easily installed, wireless telephone jack. Beginning 1994, TCE will distribute the Intelejak under its own RCA and GE brand names.

Change from a differentiated to standardized product, or vice versa. In the last ten years, video cassette recorders have moved from being an unusual, expensive product to one that is in a majority of American households. Companies must change their strategies as this change occurs. Some products have gone in the opposite direction. Ten years ago, ice cream was basically ice cream. Now you can buy "super premium" ice cream which has more butterfat, costs twice as much, and is guaranteed to harden your arteries, or opt for "premium dietary", containing no fat or sugar. The increased differentiation in the ice cream business has changed manufacturers' approaches.

Regulatory influences and government policy changes. Deregulation has turned the airline industry upside down. Removing limits on exporting logs has shaken the logging and wood mill industries. Government legislation can affect competition in an industry and should not be ignored.

Competitor Analysis

America's capitalistic system is based on the theory of free competition. Without competition, the system would collapse. From an individual company's perspective, however, the major strategic goal should be to reduce or to control the competition the firm has to face. This goal is not un-American; it strictly makes good business sense. To deal with competitors, you must know who they are, what their strengths and weaknesses are, and what their strategies are.

You should try to reduce or control the amount of competition you face

Determining Who Your Competitors Are. For a company new to an industry, the competitors are not always obvious. Go to a major trade show and you will probably discover most of them. Some companies will not feel threatened by you and will tell you about themselves and other firms in the industry. If you are aware of customers who have purchased the type of product you have, ask them who the major producers are. Talk to suppliers in your industry. Since they sell to similar firms, they can tell you about them. Customers, suppliers, and non-threatened competitors to your industry can provide you a wealth of information.

Analyzing Your Competitors' Strengths and Weaknesses. Your success will be determined in large part by your company's strengths and weaknesses relative to competitors. There are many factors to consider. On the next page is a grid which allows you to compare your company to competitors. Some of the factors may not be relevant to your industry and can be overlooked.

Understanding Your Competitors' Strategies. You must look beyond strengths and weaknesses of competitors and seek to understand their basic strategies and assumptions about the industry. Try to answer the following questions about your major competitors:

How long have they been in the industry and how committed are they to staying in it?

What is their basic approach to competing? Have they changed that approach much over the years?

How do they react to strategic moves of other firms? Do they respond strongly, or do they ignore what other companies do?

Assessing Your Company's Strengths and Weaknesses

Your strengths and weaknesses are relative to your competitors'

Your strengths and weaknesses are relative to your competitors. Therefore, you should analyze your capabilities at the same time you assess your competitors. The grid in Figure 9-1 allows you to make the comparisons. You may want to develop some type of scoring system, such as on a scale of one to ten. Be aware that some of the factors will not be relevant in your industry.

Figure 9-1. Evaluation of Company's Strengths and Weaknesses

1. Products or Services
    - Quality
    - Reputation
    - Breadth & depth of product line
    - Warranty

2. Distribution
    - Channel coverage
    - Distributors' loyalty to firm

3. Marketing & Selling
    - Market share
    - Marketing skills
    - Training and skills of sales force

4. Operations
   Quality of plant & equipment
   Quality control
   Labor force climate; unionization situation
   Access to raw materials
   Ability to manufacture efficiently

5. Research & Development
   Patents and trade secrets
   Quality of research equipment
   Quality of research staff

6. Overall Costs
   Overall efficiency
   Ability to raise equity capital

7. Financial Strength
   Cash flow
   Borrowing capacity
   Ability to raise equity capital

8. General Management Skills
   Leadership of top management
   Experience of top management
   Entrepreneurial savvy

Distinctive Competencies. A distinctive competence is a skill or activity that you do especially well compared to your competitors. Having completed the strengths and weaknesses grid above, you should be able to determine your distinctive competencies. You usually build your strategy around these, so this assessment is important. Described below are some common distinctive competencies along with Utah companies that reflect them.

A distinctive competence is a skill or activity that you do especially well compared to your competitors

Technology. Lithocad excels at extremely small tolerance manufacturing software for the semiconductor industry.

Quality. Digitran of Logan designs and builds training simulators for drilling and production procedures in the petroleum industry as well as crane operator simulators. The company employs a highly educated workforce, most of them engineers, and is able to produce top quality products which gives them control of 95 percent of the international simulator's market in the petroleum industry and a stunning 100 percent of the simulator's market in the crane industry.

Megahertz of Salt Lake City is the largest worldwide manufacturer of modems for mobile computers. All products are fully produced within the United States. Megahertz stands behind its entire product line by providing a five-year warranty and superior technical support via a toll-free support line and an electronic bulletin board service.

Service. The core of the Franklin Quest's success is customer satisfaction. The Franklin System combines the most effective time management training curriculum with the popular Franklin Day Planner. Franklin Quest offers superb customer service and has greatly simplified the ordering of its products. Its friendly and experienced representatives are on hand to answer customer's questions and help with product selection Monday through Saturday, 24 hours a day.

Location. In 1994, a segment of Packard Bell moved its operation based in Chatsworth, California, to Utah—a move that created 600 new jobs. The Company is the nation's fourth largest maker of personal computers. Its Technical Support Operation for the computer division moved to a 35,000-square-foot building in Magna's Arbor Park commercial development. The service center provides customer support 24 hours a day, seven days a week in more than 30 languages. The center has a natural geographic fit in Utah where many residents are bilingual, largely due to The Church of Jesus Christ of Latter-day Saints' missionary training program. The program provides training in more than 60 languages.

Utah is famous for its ski resorts, parks, and recreation areas. Many recreation equipment companies prefer being located closer to environments where the equipment is used. For example, Black Diamond, a company which moved to Salt Lake City in August of 1991 from Ventura, California, makes back-country skis, boots and bindings as well as climbing gear. There are several other outdoor equipment firms operating in Utah: Evolution Ski Co., a tiny ski manufacturer with bold graphics; DaleBoot, which manufactures the only alpine ski boot made in America; Marker International, parent company to one of the ski industry's leading binding and soft goods manufacturers; and the Cant Co., maker of tiny plastic wedges that fit under ski boots to increase ski performance.

Filling a Special Niche. Dynix, the world's leading supplier of library automation systems, conceived Dynix Automated Library Systems a decade ago. The firm created affordable and improved computerized library systems for small-to mid-sized libraries—a niche which had been largely ignored by existing library automation companies.

Flexibility and Adaptability. Flexibility played a big part in Novell's ability to recognize in 1983 that computer hardware production would be a bloodied battlefield. After joining Novell in 1983, Roy Noorda transformed the company into a software giant with about 5,000 workers in Utah and elsewhere. The need for flexibility in the ways Novell organizes its expanding networks is counterbalanced by the desire for consistency in the way the company is able to manage them.

Reputation and Image. Franklin Quest is listed #12 on the recent *Forbes'* ranking of Best Small Companies in the world; #5 on the *Business Week* list of 100 Best Small Companies in America; #2 on the *Equities Magazine* list of Fastest Growing Companies on the New York Stock Exchange. Started in a basement with three people in 1984, the company now employs about 1,500 people and ships products to over 150 countries. Franklin Quest is regarded as having the highest quality products in the industry. Customer satisfaction is the key to their success, and as a result they have very high customer retention.

Personnel. "A former Brigham Young University professor, Ashton and his ex-student Bruce Bastian founded WordPerfect in an Orem basement 15 years ago. As it merged with Novell in 1994, the company was the world's fourth-largest software publisher, employing more almost 4,000 people."[(4)] The amazing growth of the company is often attributed to the utilization of graduates from two outstanding Utah universities and access to a fine labor force. Nearly 40 percent of WordPerfect's personnel are at least bilingual.

Personnel are considered valuable assets at WordPerfect. Recent layoffs at Wordperfect have shown that even when hard times come the company is able to treat employees with dignity. In order to generate more revenues and improve sales per employee which were lower than the industry's averages, the company decided to prune its workforce by 17 percent. The company gave the laid off employees two months of salary and benefits and provided them with an outplacement center and outplacement search firm hired from New York.

Value. Regardless of the quality of products, some companies are known for giving exceptional value. Smith's takes much pride for having and attempting to maintain the best total grocery prices in the state.

Evaluating Your Own Personal Desires. One last factor has to be evaluated before you launch into setting your company's strategy—what are *your* desires for the company? Up until this point, you have done your analysis in an objective fashion, as if your personal motivations made no difference. In a small, privately-held company, strategy *cannot* be separated from the lead entrepreneur's personal motivations. Where do you want the company to go? What type of products do you think you should have? Where do *you* want to be in five years? Ten years? An objective analysis may point to a certain strategy making sense; however, if that strategy does not fit with your aspirations, it obviously won't work. Before formulating the firm's strategies, write down your personal goals for the company.

Strategy cannot be separated from your personal desires

Formulating Strategy

Once you have analyzed the economy, the industry, your competitors, your firm's strengths and weaknesses, and your personal motivations, you need to look at strategic alternatives. The first decision you need to make is *what business to be in*. This may sound silly to you if you have already made that decision, but if you are not heavily committed at this point in your business you should question if this is a good one to be in. The industry analysis will help you decide if this line of business is a good one to be in. Each industry usually has some attractive and some unattractive features. Consider both and evaluate the overall attractiveness. Ideally, you would like to see industry characteristics as described below.

The first decision you need to make is *what business to be in*

Size of the market. Bigger is not always better, but you want to ensure there are enough customers to allow you to have substantial growth.

Growth of the market. A growing market allows you to grow without taking away from other companies' market shares, which helps to avoid fierce competition. Typically there is more opportunity in an industry that is earlier in its life cycle.

Gross margin. A large gross margin allows you generate a considerable gross profit with low sales. Since you will probably not have high sales for a period of time, this reduces your risk. Granted, Wal-Mart makes a lot of money selling low-margin items, but small companies cannot generate the sales volume that Wal-Mart does.

Overall profitability. Don't try to fight the current. Get into an industry that has shown profits. You may, through product differentiation, be able to enjoy higher profits than the industry average.

Entry barriers. You would like to have entry barriers as high as possible, but low enough for you to enter, if you are not already in the industry. You want to be able to protect your competitive position once you have chosen a particular strategy, and entry barriers make it difficult for newcomers to copy you. Look over the list of entry barriers described previously and consider how you can protect your position.

Power of customers. The broader the customer base is, the better. There is danger is relying on only a few customers, who then are in strong bargaining positions against you.

Power of suppliers. The same principle applies to suppliers. If you are small and there are only a few suppliers, they will almost always favor your larger competitors. A diversity of suppliers is an advantage.

To succeed in industries with little differentiation, companies usually need to achieve high market share

Amount of product differentiation. In general, smaller companies can prosper more easily in an industry that has differentiated products. For example, there are many styles of ladies clothing. This allows companies to focus on selective types and carve out niches. Contrast that to the manufacture of pencils, which is a standardized, non-differentiated industry. To succeed in that setting, firms usually need large market share. New companies can start off small more easily in differentiated markets.

Overall intensity of competition. Some industries are less hostile than others. Competitors have learned to live with each other or perhaps tend to ignore each other. Other industries are competitive blood-baths. The pizza restaurant/delivery business has been saturated with competitors, resulting in price wars and low profitability for most companies.

Driving forces affect the attractiveness of an industry. Change is a threat to those companies which are prospering under current conditions, but change also provides opportunity to newcomers. Young, entrepreneurial firms should look at change as a potential blessing. Look over the list of potential driving forces below. Are any of the following changes occurring?

- Is the industry growth rate increasing?
- Are new customers entering the market? Are current customers beginning to use the products in new and different ways?
- Are new products being developed?

- Are new ways of manufacturing products being developed?
- Are new ways of marketing products being used?
- Are some major players leaving the industry?
- Have some patents run out? Are new patents being filed?
- Are products becoming more differentiated? The interest in premium ice creams opened the door for small companies such as Salt Lake's own local brand, Snelgrove.
- Have regulations changed? Airline deregulation opened the door for discount competitors. Changes in banking laws allowed banks to become quite entrepreneurial.

Look for changes in the industry and analyze how they affect the attractiveness of that type of business.

You need to assess your capabilities of competing in the industry. The microcomputer industry is a thriving one, but not everyone should try to enter it. Try to determine what the *critical success factors* are in the industry. They are capabilities that firms must have in order to compete in the industry. Is it quality? Service? Unique products? Low prices? Look over the strengths and weaknesses grid for your company and see how well they match up with the critical success factors.

There are three primary competitive strategies— cost leadership, differentiation, and focus

Competitive Strategy

Having looked at industry structural characteristics, driving forces, and internal strengths and weaknesses, you should be able to decide if you are in or are about to enter an attractive industry. These factors can do more than help you decide if you are in a good industry; they can give you clues about how to compete against other companies. There are three primary competitive strategies— cost leadership, differentiation, and focus— and each is described below.

Cost Leadership. Cost leadership is at the opposite end of the spectrum to differentiation. Cost leadership emphasizes keeping the costs down in making a product. The advantages of such a strategy are that you have higher margins than competitors and you are better able to compete on price. To have a cost advantage, you usually need high market share. High market share allows you to have economies of scale— you buy raw materials for less, you spread equipment costs over more units, you spread advertising costs over more units, among other savings. This strategy leaves you with lower unit costs than competitors.

A cost leadership strategy is usually characterized by several of the following features:

- High volume and market share;
- Competitive or discount pricing;
- An emphasis on cost reduction, i.e. tight budgets, low overhead, etc.;
- Little money spent on research and development (if any is spent, it is to make the production process more efficient); or
- No-frills products.

In most industries, you can pick out one or several firms which stand out as cost leaders. Wal-Mart is an obvious cost leader in the general department store industry. PayLess Shoe Source has a definite cost advantage in the retail shoe industry. Bonanza restaurants compete with a few-frills, low price strategy. Recognize the difference between *cost* and *price*. Cost is the cost to you of making a product, whereas price is what you charge. Having a low price alone will not bring you success— competitors can match the price and you have a very thin gross margin. Having a lower cost is the basis of the strategy. If you have it, you can drop below competitors' prices and still have a decent margin, or else you can match their prices and have a larger margin.

Cost* is not the same as *price

Differentiation. Differentiation is a much different means of competing. You make your product better or unique in some fashion so that customers purchase your product because of its superiority. There is a great variety of ways of differentiating a product, and Chapter 2 describes quite a few of them. Design and engineering is one means. BMW takes this approach in making "driving machines." Superior technology is another, which Sun Computers employs in making high performance computer workstations. Unique features can differentiate a product, such as goretex fabric. It keeps rain off a hiker, but allows the fabric to breathe so that sweat evaporates. A unique means of distribution can differentiate companies, as Mary Kay and Avon have done with cosmetics. A differentiation strategy is usually characterized by some of the following factors:

- Large emphasis on superior quality and/or service;
- Significant R&D expenditures;
- Premium pricing;
- Lower market share (than cost leaders); and
- An emphasis on creativity, customization, and being different.

A differentiation strategy allows you to maintain high margins because people are willing to pay premium prices for high quality. Typically, you also develop a strong reputation and brand loyalty, thus erecting entry barriers to other companies.

A focus strategy is based on choosing a product line or target market which is more narrow than competitors'

Focus. A focus strategy is based on choosing a product line or target market which is more narrow than competitors'. In concentrating on fewer products, you can usually differentiate yourself because you are not spread so thinly. Consider a golf pro shop. It carries exclusively golf equipment and apparel, and if you have questions about either, a golf pro is happy to help you. Compare the pro shop to a sporting goods store, which carries baseball, basketball, football, tennis, weight-lifting, a multitude of other sports, and of course, golf equipment and apparel. If you ask the salesperson about what length club you should have, he'll say he doesn't know but he'll ask his weight-lifting buddy. By being more narrowly focused, you are better able to understand and meet customers' needs.

In certain cases, a focus strategy can provide cost advantages. Consider the earth drilling business. A certain segment of this market needs portable drilling equipment. The large drill manufacturers produce the portable drills using their standard production facility, which is large and capital intensive. The portable drill can be produced, however, in a small warehouse using relatively inexpensive equipment. A company that focuses on the portable line of drills is able to forego large capital expenditures, and therefore has a lower cost.

Different means of focusing exist. The first is by product or target market. Delorean concentrated on a type of automobile— the sports car. If the company had received a chance to get its feet on the ground and had its president stayed out of drug trafficking, it may have done well. Another type of focus is by geographic area. If you can offer products which are better suited to people in your particular area, you have an advantage over more widespread competitors. D.A. Davidson offers securities of regional companies that the nationally-based investment houses do not carry, for example. You can also focus by size of order. You may have large competitors who do not consider small, custom orders because they don't feel that they are worth the time. Small companies can capitalize on such niches. The key is to find a niche that is large enough to satisfy your growth expectation, but small enough to remain uninteresting to your large competitors.

To be focused, you must be more narrowly oriented than your competitors. For example, a restaurant owner stated, "I am quite focused in my business. I am in the restaurant business, and that's it. We don't try to get into anything else." Interestingly enough, 90 percent of his competitors were involved only in the restaurant business. Focus is *relative to competitors*. You must be in a more narrow market segment or serve a smaller geogaphic area than competitors to be truly focused.

Focus *alone* is not a strategic advantage. Once you have chosen a particular segment, you must either have a better product or else be able to produce more cheaply than competitors. Focusing often allows you to do this because of your concentration on a particular market or geographical area. But if you can't excel in either quality or cost, focusing won't do you any good.

A focus strategy is usually differentiated

Be aware that most companies don't have strategies that drop cleanly into one of these strategic slots. In retail clothing, K-Mart has positioned itself pretty much as a cost leader. Recently the company has begun carrying many more brand name items, such as Nike and Converse in shoes. They discount them also, but they are definitely departing from a "no-frills" posture. Penney's and Sears seem to be somewhere in the middle ground between differentiation and cost leadership. They carry medium quality products at medium prices. The strategy is no accident— that segment purchases more clothing than either the high end or the low end. Therefore, variations in between cost leadership and differentiation are possibilities.

There can be a danger in this middle ground, however. It is called "stuck in the middle." Being "stuck" means that customers view you neither as a place to go to purchase quality items, nor as a place to go to get a good deal. If the market is such that one segment insists on quality, and the other is concerned with price, companies in the middle ground do not do well. Analyze the industry and determine if there seems to be this polarization of the market. Avoid middle ground in this case.

Determining Which Generic Strategy to Pursue. Unfortunately, there are no unbreakable principles in choosing the best strategy. The choice depends on the analysis that you have done up to this point. One of the best approaches is to apply the principles of industry and competitor analysis to *strategic groups* within the industry. In any industry, there tend to be clusters of companies that have strategies similar to each other, but differing with other clusters. Each of these clusters is considered a strategic group. Looking again at retail clothing, the cost leadership end is comprised of WalMart, K-Mart, Fred Meyer, Target, and others which are generally viewed as discounters. In the middle are J.C. Penney, Sears, ZCMI (locally), Dillards, among others. There are quite a few highly focused retailers: big and tall, petite, maternity, outdoor sports, and others. List all of the strategic groups that you see and the firms in them. The strategies you assign to each group may or may not be variations of the three generic strategies described above.

There are no unbreakable principles in choosing the best strategy

Assess the attractiveness of each strategic group through industry and competitive analysis. Assume that you intend to open a single discount clothing store in Salt Lake City. First consider the cost leadership group. The market is large and is growing, although not as fast as several years ago. The gross margins are relatively thin, since discounting is prevalent. Industry profitability is high— K-Mart and WalMart do extremely well. Large entry barriers exist. K-Mart experiences large economies of scale by being able to purchase in quantity and spread many costs over their large number of stores. They have a strong reputation that newcomers would have to overcome (which can be an advantage if you are able to overcome the barriers yourself). The power of suppliers is significant. Many of the suppliers are companies such as Osh Kosh and Nike. They will definitely give preference in order-filling and pricing to the larger companies. The customer group is broad-based, and therefore the risk of one or a few customers wielding much power is small. Product differentiation is not great. You tend to see a lot of the same merchandise in all of the discount stores. This typically leads to competitive pricing. Overall intensity of competition is great. Some of the large discounters will accept advertised prices of any of their competitors, which lets you know that competition is *intense* in this industry.

Assess the attractiveness of each strategic group in your industry

Some of the industry features are attractive and some unattractive. Two of them are probably overriding. The entry barriers to this strategic group are enormous. If you hope to be able to compete on a large-scale basis with the likes of K-Mart, you have enter the market in a big way. Small companies don't have such resources. Competing with K-Mart would tax the resources of even the largest competitors. The other striking industry feature is the intensity of competition. This industry is cut-throat. If you pose a threat to these companies, they will retaliate.

If you try to compete with K-Mart head-on, you will lose. But what about a focused approach to the cost leadership strategy? You see occasional "warehouse liquidation" sales by local, smaller companies. They buy quantities of goods at bankruptcy auctions, rent an abandoned retail spot, and advertise it as "below cost" prices. By focusing on this one approach, the companies are able to compete on price. They must do all right, because you continue to see them. The key to their success is to avoid direct competition and find a few niches where they can compete on price.

The market is not nearly as large as the cost leadership market, but that is almost always the case. Market growth is small. Gross margins are usually better in this segment since discounting is not normally used extensively. Some entry barriers exist, but not near the size in the cost leadership segment. Reputations for quality of the other stores pose perhaps the largest barrier. There are not large economies of scale. Power of suppliers is not great, since there are a large number of high-quality clothing manufacturers who can sell to you. Power of customers is not great, either, since you still will have a fairly large base of customers to sell to. There is a large amount of product differentiation, since many types of quality clothing are produced. Lastly, competition is moderate to high. Although many premium stores have closed, competition is still high for the now smaller number of customers. It still is probably not as fierce as in the cost leadership segment.

In general, a differentiation strategy is better suited to the entrepreneurial company than is a cost leadership approach

The differentiation segment has its pros and cons. Although the industry is not growing and competition is stiff, margins are good and the entry barriers are not so formidable. This strategic group probably offers more opportunity than does cost leadership for the start-up company. A key strategic issue here is timing. Companies that can survive the hard economic times and the inevitable wash-out of companies will be in a good position when better economic times return. In general, a differentiation strategy is better suited to the entrepreneurial company than is a cost leadership approach.

A focus strategy often makes sense for the start-up company. The "big & tall" segment is a focus example in the retail clothing market. It is not an exceptionally large market, but it has been growing. Entry barriers are not great, although reputation and store location may provide some protection from new competitors. Gross margins are good— definitely higher than in the discount stores. Industry profitability has been good on a national basis. Power of suppliers and customers is small, since there are a large number of each and no one or few wield much power. The overall intensity of competition is moderate. There are only a couple of big & tall stores in town, and the discounters and premium retailers do not compete much in this market. The local big & tall market is not affected by the local recession as much as is the premium segment. The market is fairly differentiated, with a wide variety of products that allow firms to differentiate themselves.

You need to assess whether you have the skills and resources to compete in each of the strategic groups that you have identified. To compete with K-Mart in the cost leadership group, you need to match their buying power, which is enormous. It appears that nothing other than a huge company with large financial resources could successfully compete in this segment (other than the focused "warehouse liquidation" approach described previously).

To compete in the differentiated or focused segment, you need to be better or unusual in some fashion. Can you get apparel that is truly unique? Do you have buying skills that surpass your competitors? Do you have ideas for merchandising that are unique? Do you have enough money to stock a premium line of clothing? Do you have quality salespeople that know how to sell the clothing you have? Is your location better than competitors'? The point is this:

"Having a good strategy is one thing.
Being able to make it work is another."

You need to be sure that you can implement a strategy before you charge ahead.

Assess whether you have the skills and resources to compete in the strategic groups that you have identified

If you have found a strategy that seems sound and you feel that you can make it work, you have one last question to consider: "Is this a strategy that I *personally* can be committed to?" There can be a mismatch between the personality of the lead entrepreneur and the strategy she has chosen. The strategy won't work if she isn't personally committed to it. A cost leadership strategy requires strict attention to cost reductions, budgets, and few frills. The basic "spirit" of the strategy is get the product out to as many customers as possible, and don't worry about selling them something "special." The differentiation strategy requires creativity and ingenuity on your part. You need to have the desire to be the best, and a touch of perfectionism might be helpful. You have to be committed to quality.

With a focus strategy, you need to be absolutely committed to meeting the needs of the whatever niche you have chosen. The CEO of the most prosperous waste management firm in San Francisco explained his success quite simply, "I love garbage." If you have a big & tall store, you need to know your customers inside out to be able to meet their needs. With a focus strategy, you need to be driven to be a "big fish in a small pond." By focusing, you are choosing to be in a smaller pond.

The Strategic Plan

Once that you have gone through the steps in formulating strategy, you are ready to write a strategic plan. Having the plan in your head is not sufficient. Until you get it on paper, review it, and have others review it, it will not be organized. The following outline shows the typical elements in a strategic plan.

A. Analysis of the Business and Its Environment

- The economic, regulatory, and social environment
- Industry structure
- Industry driving forces
- Competitors
- Internal strengths and weaknesses

B. The Strategic Plan

- Mission statement
- Strategic goals
- Corporate level strategy
- Business level strategy

C. Implementing the Plan

- Marketing strategy
- Financial strategy
- Personnel strategy

The elements in (C) are each discussed in other chapters of this book. The marketing strategy is covered in Chapters 4 and 10, the financial strategy is covered in chapters 7, 11, and 12, and personnel strategy is covered is Chapter 8.

Conclusion

Strategic planning is critical to your business. Don't expect that "shooting from the hip" is going to get you by. You need to continually scan the environment and assess your own strengths and weaknesses. Follow the outline in this chapter, write down your strategic plan, and then get after it.

References

1. Porter, Michael. *Competitive Strategy: Techniques for Analyzing Industries and Competitors*. New York: Free Press, 1980.

2. Thompson, Arthur A. and Strickland, A. J. *Strategic Management*, Sixth Edition. Plano, Texas: Business Publications, Inc., 1991.

3. Denalli, Jacquelyn. *An Airline of Her Own.* Nation's Business, August 1993.

4. Impoco, Jim. *How Utah Created a Mountain of Jobs: A Pro-Business Climate Lures High-Tech Industry.* U.S. News & World Report, Feb. 22, 1993, page 43.

10

The Marketing Plan

The purpose of marketing is to *produce long-term, profitable sales*. You do this by meeting the needs of your customers. Too many businesses are run with an internal orientation, focusing on what is good for the company. Such an orientation is dangerous. You tend to forget that customers ultimately pay the bills for your company. Don't assume that you know what your customers want because you're an expert. Take the time to listen to them and understand what they are looking for in the type of product or service that you offer. Tom Peters, in *A Passion for Excellence*, states, "If you concentrate on the customer and meeting his needs, the other stuff, like market share, profits, etc,. will take care of itself."

Commitment and consistency are critical to a marketing plan

There are two themes that you must incorporate to develop a good marketing strategy— *commitment* and *consistency*. No matter what strategy you decide on, you must be willing to "stay the course." Marketing efforts rarely produce instant results; only hyped-up sales promotions do that. Don't become discouraged if you spend money on a promotional campaign and sales only increase slightly. If you *commit* yourself to a sound marketing strategy, it will eventually bear fruit. Moreover, you must remain *consistent* in your message. Sears has suffered over the years from a lack of a consistent theme. The company has wavered back and forth from being a discounter, to a quality retailer, to somewhere in between. As a consequence, no one is quite sure what the company is now. Try to choose a solid strategy and stay with it.

Choosing a Marketing Strategy

The process of formulating a marketing strategy is depicted in Figure 10-1. The goal of this process is to decide what product features and services to offer, how to distribute products, how to price, and how to promote products for each target market. The illustration makes the process look well-defined and sequential. *It is not.* Very often you will get to one stage of the process, decide that a previous decision was incorrect, and skip back to that stage. For example, assume that you own a ski resort and have chosen as a target market families just beginning to ski. As you research this market (see "2. Characterize Markets" below) you find that they spend a lot of time in the lodge drying off and trying to warm up. You only have a small lodge and don't have the money to expand it. Having done the customer characterization, you realize that you chose the wrong target market and must go back to that step and redefine your market. Or perhaps you had defined your market as intermediate skiers. After analyzing competitors, however, you realize that the competing ski resorts in your area all cater to this group and you would have no real advantage over them. You need to abandon that ship and again go back to choosing a new target market. You usually change your marketing strategy several times before you get through the whole process. This process allows you to refine and focus your marketing strategy. Each of the steps in the process is described below.

The process of setting a marketing strategy requires continuous revision

Figure 10-1. The Process of Setting a Marketing Strategy

1. Select Target Markets
2. Characterize Markets
3. Evaluate Competition
4. Formulate Marketing Strategy

Select Target Market(s)

You will be tempted to try to sell your products to a wide variety of customers. Resist that temptation. Most successful smaller businesses focus on a few *market segments* and try to meet the specific needs of those customer groups. Every market usually has several distinct segments whose needs differ somewhat from each other. Those which you choose to appeal to are called your *target markets*. The first step in the marketing process is to decide what target market(s) you will pursue. Each of them requires a distinct marketing strategy.

A quick way to fail is to try to sell to everyone

The landscaping business has several distinct market segments. One includes general contractors who build new homes, another includes homeowners, and another includes commercial establishments. Each one of these has needs different from the others' and requires a distinct marketing strategy. Each of these target markets could be further segmented. For example, you could divide homeowners into two groups: one that wants major landscaping work done and another that needs only grass mowing and tree trimming. The more narrowly you define markets, the better you will understand and be able to appeal to their specific needs. Of course you can carry this process too far. You could define markets so narrowly that there are only a few customers in each one. However, most small businesses suffer the opposite problem: they are not focused enough.

Most small businesses are not focused enough

Characterize Markets

After you have selected a target market(s), you seek to thoroughly understand the needs of those customers. This is termed *characterizing the market.* Marketing research, described in Chapter 4, provides this information. Expert interviews, focus groups, secondary data, surveys, and experiments are all possible means of gathering information about customers. You want to know who buys products like yours, what motivates them to buy, what features they are looking for, what they are willing to pay, and what type of promotions they pay attention to. Analyze the customers in each of your target markets.

Analyze Competition

Customers can buy from you or from your competitors. If you do not know what your competitors are doing, you may be losing sales without a clue as to why. Many startup business owners claim that they have "the best product on the market." And yet they have not looked closely at competitors' products to make a valid judgment. You need to put consistent efforts into assessing what your competitors are selling and what they are charging. Chapter 4, Marketing Research, and Chapter 9, Strategic Planning, describe the process of analyzing competitors. Since each of your target markets may have different competitors, be sure to evaluate competitors in all market segments.

Formulate Marketing Strategy

Once you have selected target markets and evaluated customers and competitors in each, you need to develop a marketing strategy for each. This is the fun part! This is why you have knocked yourself out doing all of the research described above. In fact, you need to keep reminding yourself of this goal. Otherwise, it is easy to get wrapped up in the research and lose track of what you really want to accomplish. The purpose of this whole process is to develop a good marketing strategy, not to conduct good research. There are four primary elements of a marketing strategy:

- Products, product features, and services offered.
- Type(s) of distribution.
- Pricing.
- Promotion.

These elements together comprise your *marketing mix*. Each of them should be consistent with the others. For example, if you are selling a no-frills product, you typically have discount pricing, mass distribution, and widespread promotion. On the other hand, if you are selling premium quality products, you usually need to charge premium prices and use select distribution channels. Your promotions should be high class. A *consistent theme* is important.

Products, Product Features, and Services Offered

Your choice of target market together with the products and services you choose to meet customers' needs is called *positioning*. David Ogilvy, who has placed several billion dollars worth of advertising through his ad agency and who is considered one of America's marketing authorities, states that positioning is the most critical marketing decision to be made. He says that the quality of advertising is much less important than the basic positioning of the product or service in the first place. If you can select the best market niches, and offer products and services that meet customers' needs better than competitors, you are well on your way to a solid marketing strategy.

Product positioning is more important than quality of advertising

Customers buy benefits, not products. People don't want shampoo— they want silky hair that smells nice. They don't want an old used car— they want cheap, reliable transportation. A Kirby vacuum cleaner salesman can't convince you to spend $1000 on a vacuum cleaner. However, he can convince you to spend that kind of money because you won't have to replace your $5000 carpet. Or, you won't have to live in a house with the awful dirt your old vacuum leaves behind (he'll show it to you). You must be able to clearly identify what benefits your products offer to customers. If you consistently think in terms of customer benefits and not product features, you will sell a whole lot more.

Most smaller businesses need to *differentiate* their products. You typically will not win a cost game with larger companies. Your products or services have to be better in some way. Chapter 2, Developing Business Ideas, discusses a variety of ways of differentiating products and services. Tom Peters, in *A Passion for Excellence*, states, "Nothing is a commodity. *Anything* can be differentiated." The following are only a few means of differentiating products.

***Anything* can be differentiated**

1. Higher quality product;
2. Quicker response to customers;
3. Less maintenance to customers;
4. Better warranty;
5. Better service;
6. Better trade-in policy;
7. Better compatibility with other products;
8. More flexible product usage;
9. Safer product;
10. Healthier product;
11. More compact or portable product;
12. More attractive product;
13. More status appeal;
14. Better service to dealers;
15. More convenient hours;
16. More fun for the customer; or a
17. Friendlier environment.

Try to differentiate your products or services in more than one way. Also try to differentiate in a way that is not easily copied. For example, Domino's Pizza was the original "fast delivery" pizza outlet— thirty minutes or less. They built their reputation on quick delivery. Unfortunately, the new high-speed pizza ovens allow just about anyone to meet that deadline. Domino's no longer enjoys that advantage, and about the only competitive tool they have left is discount pricing. That hurts them. You *may not* be able to differentiate in ways that are enduring. In that case, you have to be a constant innovator. You have to always be searching for a new way to stay ahead of the pack. Don't be a stationary target, keep moving.

Don't be a stationary target

You may be selling a product, but the service you offer may be what closes the deal. This is true of car dealerships. Many customers stay loyal to one dealership, regardless of the brands of cars offered. People trust that any car they buy will be well serviced and that the salespeople are giving them a fair deal. A copy shop is a copy shop, but certain ones develop a reputation for quick, error-free work and a willingness to bend over backwards to meet customers' needs.

These are the ones that stay busy. One of the best marketing weapons a small business has is *good service*. You can beat most larger companies on customer service. This may be the most important feature of the products that you sell.

Distribution Channels

Distribution channels are the means by which products get from the manufacturer to the customer. In every industry, there are usually several different channels that are possibilities. For many manufacturers, the standard distribution channel is to sell to retailers who sell products to the public. There is a variety of alternatives, however. Some industries have distributors who buy, warehouse, and resell products from many different manufacturers and resell to retailers. The automobile parts industry has such distributors. Some manufacturers use independent sales representatives, who promote their products to retailers. Although they neither own nor take possession of merchandise, they are the selling arm for many companies and thus can be considered part of the distribution channel. A few companies sell their products directly to consumers through a mail catalog. Some manufacturers sell products through catalog companies that promote a large number of companies' products, usually under a central theme. These catalog companies, such as Franklin Quest of Salt Lake City, are direct mail retailers.

In every industry, several distribution channels may exist

The channels described above are not the only means of distributing, but they are the most common. Each of them is depicted in Figure 10-2.

Figure 10-2. Common Distribution Channels

- Mfger — Retailer — Consumer
- Mfger — Distributor — Retailer — Consumer
- Mfger — Sales Rep — Retailer — Consumer
- Mfger — Consumer
- Mfger — Catalog Co. — Consumer

You need to understand which distribution channels exist in your industry. In many cases, the manufacturer's dilemma is not to convince the consumer that a product is worth purchasing, it is gaining access to the distribution channels so that the product can be presented to the customer. Find out from whom retailers purchase in your industry. Do they buy from manufacturers, from independent sales reps, from distributors, or from a combination of sources? Once you have established what the channels are, talk to businesses at every step in them. Find out what products they are willing to carry and what type of companies they want to deal with.

You will be tempted to "skirt around" established distribution channels because of the margins that they cost you. Of your final selling price, retailers may take up to 40 percent, sales reps 5-20 percent, and distributors another 10-15 percent. Compared to direct marketing, you may receive only 25-50 percent of the selling price of the product. It's hard to give up that kind of margin.

In spite of the fact they lose margins, there are several good reasons to consider going through established channels instead of attempting direct marketing. Direct marketing may not be easy for a startup company, plus sales may develop only very slowly. Established distribution channels allow you to get your products to a large number of retail establishments quickly. And although you may have to do a fair amount of marketing to get your products into channels, once they are in you are relieved of a lot of the marketing pressure. *Others* sell your products, while you can concentrate on meeting orders. Players in the channels also buy in quantity, relieving you of processing and filling small orders. If, in spite of these compelling reasons to go through established marketing channels, you are still tempted to market directly, refer to the subsection below on direct marketing.

There are good reasons to go through established distribution channels

Tradeshows and Consumer Shows. Tradeshows are a form of promotion (which is discussed in a separate section later in this chapter). Yet they are so valuable in getting into distribution channels that they need to be discussed here. Tradeshows bring players from all stages of distribution channels in an industry together under one roof and thus are helpful in penetrating those channels. Other advantages include your being able to show products to many buyers in a short period of time. They also relieve you of having to travel all over to meet with potential buyers. Compared to sending a salesperson out on the road to make individual visits to buyers, tradeshows are much cheaper. You can also contact distributors, sales reps, and catalog companies and check out your competition in just a few days.

Trade shows are valuable in getting into distribution channels

One of the largest tradeshows in the world is the annual COMDEX (Computer Dealers' Exposition) show. Approximately 2,000 manufacturers of computer products display their wares to approximately 80,000 resellers (mostly retail stores, but also distributors and sales reps). Each of the manufacturers has a booth with one or more salespeople who tell resellers about their products and try to get them to place orders for their products. The tradeshow benefits both the people who display and the buyers. The companies displaying get exposure to a large number of buyers in a short period of time. For the buyers, they get to evaluate a large number of competitive products under one roof. Most tradeshows are nowhere near this large. However, the activities in most tradeshows are about the same.

A consumer show is different from a tradeshow

A *consumer show* is different from a trade show. In a tradeshow, the buyers are not buying for their own usage. Instead, they resell the products they purchase. At a consumer show, individual consumers are shopping for themselves. Consumer shows are often held at the Convention Center, Expo Mart, or State Fairgrounds, including themes such as boat, ski, auto, and Christmas shows.

The advantage of this type of show is you can sell at full retail and receive cash on the spot. They provide a means of showing your product to consumers and gaining some sales. However, the disadvantages include the cost of buying selling space and renting materials needed for booth set-up, the absence of a regular circuit of shows to attend in the area, sales not being significant, and few follow-up sales after the shows.

The Salt Lake Area Chamber of Commerce sponsors annually a *Business to Business Expo*, usually held in March. Many start-up and service-oriented companies use this opportunity for PR and presenting themselves to the business community.

For a list of various Utah consumer shows, contact:

Salt Lake Convention & Visitors Bureau
180 South West Temple
Salt Lake City, UT 84101
(801) 521-2822
Fax (801) 355-9323

State Fair Grounds
(801) 262-0812

Expo Mart
(801) 531-6699

Finding Out About Tradeshows. How do you find out about tradeshows that would be suitable for you? First, talk to people. Visit or call retail stores that carry the types of products that you make. Ask them if they attend tradeshows, and which ones. Seek information from competitors who are not threatened by you, perhaps in other locales. Talk to people in the same general industry who make different types of products than yours. For example, if you sell trout flies, talk to someone who makes lures. You would probably be attending the same tradeshows.

There are other sources of information on tradeshows. Industry associations almost always announce major tradeshows. If you don't know which associations represent your industry, consult *The Encyclopedia of Associations*, which is in the reference sections in many libraries in the state. *The Tradeshow Week Data Book*, is the most complete listing of tradeshows in America. It is published annually and describes major national shows broken down in seven different ways, including industry and geographical area. It provides information such as exhibit space cost, number of exhibitors and attendees at the previous show, profiles of exhibitors and attendees, number of years in existence, and the show manager's address and phone number. Both of these can be good sources of information on tradeshows in specific industries.

Deciding Which Shows to Attend. The people you contact to find out about shows can tell you how good they are. If retailers, other manufacturers, and industry associations tell you which tradeshows exist, they will probably also tell which ones are the best. In most industries, as you talk to more and more people, the names of certain shows will tend to be mentioned over and over. Listen to people who have attended certain shows and find out how they view them.

You should contact tradeshow managers and have them send you a packet about their shows. They will usually give you information such as how many people attend, what type of people attend, the price of a booth, and how many years the show has been put on. You want to find a show which caters to resellers of the type of product that you make. Therefore, a smaller show may be better for you than a larger show, if the smaller one has a higher percentage of the type of buyers you are trying to reach. For example, a ski manufacturer has the choice of attending a ski show or an outdoor sports show. Although more people may attend the outdoor sports show, there may be more *qualified* buyers for her product at the ski show.

You don't want to take more orders than you can fill

Be aware that you don't want to attend a show that may generate more orders than you can fill. Although the order-taking will feel wonderful, you will have very unhappy customers if they cannot receive your products quickly. As a small manufacturer, you may want to exhibit in a smaller, regional show to test the waters before attending the larger shows.

You must prepare carefully for a tradeshow

You must prepare carefully for a tradeshow. Once you are there and the doors open, you must be ready for the onslaught of people. Several sources are listed in the reference section at the end of this chapter on preparing for tradeshows.

Independent Sales Representatives. Independent sales representatives, commonly referred to as "sales reps," can help a startup business penetrate markets. A sales rep is a business person who makes commissions by selling products of two or more different manufacturers. They sell primarily to retailers. They are not employees of the manufacturers, rather they work under contract. Independent sales reps are also called manufacturers' agents or manufacturers' reps. An agent oversees an office with multiple reps working in it. Therefore, if a company works with a manufacturer's agency, a group of people will be promoting the product, whereas a rep is an individual salesperson. In most cases the rep is restricted contractually to a certain geographic area. She does not take title to the goods, is paid on a straight commission basis, and has little or no control over prices, credit, or other terms of sale. Although the rep is not a collection agent, manufacturers sometimes ask him to remind buyers of overdue accounts. Very importantly, the rep is an *independent* business person and is not an employee of a manufacturer.

A sales rep is an independent business person

There is a significant number of agents in the outdoor equipment industry, representing a large number of relatively small producers. These agents visit retail stores in their region, attempting to sell a variety of outdoor products, such as tents, backpacks, snowshoes, etc. The agent seeks to carry a broad enough line to generate satisfactory sales at each retail store. They are inhibited from carrying too many lines because they may not be able to adequately promote too large of a variety. Industries that have a large number of smaller producers tend to foster the use of independent sales reps. The outdoor equipment industry is only one of many industries that incorporates independent reps.

There are some good reasons to use sales reps, including:

- Your sales volume is not sufficient to attract full-time salespeople. For smaller manufacturers, this is often the case. By using an independent salesperson, however, you can contract with a rep who is already in targeted retail establishments selling other manufacturers' products. The rep draws a portion of her sales commission from each manufacturer, and therefore need not rely on only one for her income.

- You want to concentrate on manufacturing, not marketing. Many manufacturers have a strong production focus and have either no background or no desire to be involved in marketing. The independent agent can alleviate some, but not all, of the marketing pressure on your firm.

- You want to penetrate a market quickly. An established independent rep already has contacts and is selling to retail establishments. She knows the buyers, knows their preferences, and has already established a relationship of trust with them. These reps are in a better position to introduce your product than someone who does not know the buyers.

- You want to gain significant market share in a certain area. An independent rep in many cases can have a smaller geographic territory than a hired salesperson because of the variety of lines that she carries. She sells more per store, therefore she can concentrate on fewer stores. This concentration allows her to visit stores more often in a certain territory and gain greater market penetration for the products that she is selling.

The advantages in using sales reps are significant, but there are some disadvantages

- You want to reduce marketing costs. You pay an independent rep nothing if no product is sold. This reduces the financial risk to you by not requiring up front training and salary costs to salespeople. Reps also pay their own expenses.

- You want to gather information about competitors and customers. Independent sales reps are excellent sources of competitor information, since they are exposed to them often. They are not associated as closely with individual companies, and therefore can obtain information more easily. They are also in constant contact with buyers, and can get more objective information about customers than a person representing a particular company.

- You don't want to worry about hiring and training new salespeople. If an agency is hired, it hires salespeople and oversees training, removing that burden from you.

Problems Associated with Sales Reps. The list of potential problems is shorter than the list of reasons to work with reps, but almost every manufacturer who has used reps has had problems. They include:

1. Inability to find and work with good reps. The list of advantages of using reps is long, but there is one overriding challenge: *it is hard to find good people*. Manufacturers will tell you war stories about the difficulties of finding good reps and how difficult it is to tell in advance how well a rep will sell their products.

2. Inability to closely control reps' activities. Reps are their own bosses, and therefore are difficult to control. Since they carry a variety of products, you cannot ensure how much they are going to push yours. Their knowledge of your product and expertise in promoting it may not be as great as you would like. What controls independent reps more than anything else is that their goal is the same as the manufacturer: to sell product.

3. Reps under contract who are not selling up to expectations. A contract can make it difficult for a manufacturer to quickly drop one rep and pick up another.

How to Find Sales Reps. Finding good reps is not an easy task, and there is no one best way to look for them. Listed below are different means of searching for reps.

1. Talk to retailers. Since reps are selling to retailers, you should contact retailers and ask them from which reps they buy and with which they are impressed. Contact retailers not only in your immediate area, but also ones in larger metropolitan areas where there is higher sales potential. Once you have the names of reps with a good reputation, then you must sell them on your products. Even if they are not willing to take your lines, they can probably give you names of other reps to contact.

2. Talk to manufacturers who make similar products. If they don't view you as a direct competitor, they may be very willing to give you names of people whom they feel are good. For example, if you produce computer forms, you may want to talk to producers of computer furniture, whose reps would also be selling to office supply stores.

3. Tradeshows often are good places to contact reps. If you have a booth in the show, put up a sign that you are looking for reps. In the show guide, you can place a want ad for reps, or look at the listings of reps seeking lines. In large tradeshows, there is

frequently a booth set up by the industry rep organization to facilitate reps and manufacturers meeting each other. Retailers and producers of similar products are in large attendance at shows, so if you have the time to get away from your booth to talk to these people they can give you leads on good reps.

4. Manufacturers' Agents National Association (MANA) is the largest trade association of manufacturers' agents and reps, with membership of approximately 8,000. Manufacturers can join the organization as associate members for a fee of about $200 and have access to the *Directory of Manufacturers' Sales Agencies* and also receive a monthly magazine entitled *Agency Sales*. Pages from both the directory and the magazine show listings of agents looking for lines and manufacturers looking for agents.

5. Industry associations exist in just about every industry, and they are an excellent source of information. You may have to join the association to get access to their information, but membership fees are usually under $200 per year. Membership usually entitles you to a directory of all members, an industry publication, and access to back issues of their publication. One often finds classified ads in the publications for reps looking for lines, and vice versa. The section of this chapter that deals with tradeshows discusses how to find out about industry associations. The primary source is *The Encyclopedia of Associations*.

Finding good sales reps can be a trial-and-error process

6. Trade publications are published both by industry associations and other private groups. For example, in the log home industry there is no strong industry association but there are two trade journals that are widely read. They usually have want ads with listings of reps seeking lines and vice versa. *The Encyclopedia of Business Information Sources* is a good source of information about trade publications.

7. Yellow Page Directories in larger cities carry fairly large listings of reps under the heading *Manufacturers' Agents and Reps*. Most libraries carry phone books of major U.S. cities, or you can contact your local telephone company to obtain directories.

8. Want ads can be placed in major cities' newspapers, usually under "Help Wanted, Sales Positions."

How to Screen and Select Sales Reps. Manufacturers who use reps will attest to the difficulty in foreseeing which reps will work out well.

Producers will humbly admit that reps that they thought would be tremendous have fizzled, and ones they had little confidence in sometimes ended up being winners. You try to screen as thoroughly as possible, but you are going to have to expect some turnover of people who just don't perform. Realize also that the nature of recruiting reps changes as you grow in sales and reputation. At first, you have to do all of the pursuing because no one knows about you. As you become more established, reps usually seek you out because they have heard that you have products that move.

Orders with catalog companies tend to be large

Catalog Companies. The catalog industry has experienced a period of explosive growth in recent years, and the success of the industry is based primarily on the fact that people enjoy the convenience of shopping at home. "Independent" cataloguers produce no products themselves; rather, they market different manufacturers' merchandise through direct mail. The cataloguers purchase certain amounts of goods from the manufacturers and try to sell it all. There is a large number of mailing lists that the cataloguers have access to.

For you, the manufacturer, the opportunity to sell to catalog companies can have advantages. First, order sizes tend to be large. If you sign a contract with a cataloguer, you usually sell at least several hundred units of a product. Secondly, you are able to order inventory and produce the goods knowing that they are already sold. This reduces the risk you typically have of overproducing and not being able to sell all of the finished goods. Thirdly, if you have a contract with one or more cataloguers, the amount of marketing work can be reduced in your firm. The contracts are usually substantial, and if they can be maintained, there is less of a need for brochures, sales calls, etc.

There can be disadvantages in trying to get cataloguers to carry your products. First, for most manufacturers it is not easy to find a *quality* cataloguer interested in carrying their products. There is an overabundance of catalog companies, with many going out of business every year. You should strive to get your products in reputable, established catalogs. Second, catalog companies will typically carry only one or a few of your products. If you have a broad product line, you will not be able to push them all through catalogs. Another drawback of selling to catalog companies is that they usually expect a price that is 5-10 percent below your normal wholesale price. Lastly, a disadvantage of catalog selling is that so many of your eggs are lumped in one or a few baskets. If a major portion of your business is through catalogs and only one catalog drops your product, your sales may plummet. The large catalog accounts are wonderful, but don't be lulled to sleep and forget about all marketing efforts.

How to Find Out About Catalog Companies. As mentioned above, finding good independent catalog companies is not easy and requires research. The first step is to talk to people, including:

1. Consumers who like your type of product. For example, if you manufacture reproduction antique furniture, people who have antiques could probably tell you if they receive any catalogs with that type of product.

2. Trade associations. They can be good sources of information on cataloguers. Find out which associations represent your industry and ask them if they are aware which cataloguers carry merchandise from your industry.

3. Retailers. They may tell you which catalogs carry products in their industries. Be aware that the cataloguers are direct competitors to the retailers, hence the retailers may not want to tell you about them. In other words, if the retailers tell you that there are no cataloguers, don't be too quick to believe them.

4. Tradeshows. They often are attended by cataloguers. Typically, the catalog buyers would be attending the larger shows in the industry. Your presence in these tradeshows may provide you with contacts with them. Put up a sign in your booth or place an ad in the tradeshow program. Many of the other people selling at the tradeshow may be willing to give you their advice on catalogs. Don't be afraid to approach other merchants and talk to them about what works for them.

There are several directories of catalog companies. The most comprehensive is *The Directory of Mail Order Catalogs*, which is in the reference section of the several Utah libraries. This book provides information on not only catalog companies, but on companies that publish their own catalogs. A recent edition of the book contains 6,800 entries, which are indexed by product and by company name. The following information is provided for each entry: name, address, and phone number; a brief description of the types of products it carries; the credit cards it accepts; names of the marketing or sales manager, buyers, production manager, and list manager; frequency of publication; catalog price; whether a mailing list is available; size of its mailing list; length of its catalog; its sales volume; and, whether it sells books related to its area of specialty. Another book entitled *The Great Book of Catalogs* contains only 2,000 catalog listings.

There are several directories of catalog companies

To locate potential cataloguers, you search by product section for companies that catalog the type of products you make. Phone numbers and addresses are given for the companies in the directory. Distinctions are not made between those cataloguers that carry other people's products and those that market only their own. A mailing list of catalog companies can be obtained from the publisher of the directory at the rate of $85 for 1000 names. They will also print the labels.

Another source for contacting cataloguers is through the *Catalog Product News*. This quarterly publication that began in March of 1988 shows pictures of and describes a variety of products. You pay to have your products listed in the publication. The magazine is mailed to 23,000 buyers at over 6,000 catalog companies and showrooms, direct marketing firms, and home television shopping companies. In other words, it is a catalog for direct-order merchandisers.

Direct Marketing. The American public has grown to trust direct marketers. More than 90 percent of all Americans have purchased some product as a result of direct marketing. Its use is continuing to grow at over 10 percent per year, in spite of the fact that over 50 billion direct marketing pieces are already mailed each year. A variety of directing marketing means exist, including:

90 percent of all Americans have purchased some product as a result of direct marketing

1. Direct mail
2. Telemarketing
3. Direct response television
4. Direct response radio
5. Inserts
6. Want ads
7. Coupons in newspapers and magazines
8. Catalogs
9. Postcard decks
10. Bulletin boards

In 1982, telemarketing surpassed direct mail in dollar expenditures. The fastest growing segment is postcard decks, wherein a marketer mails a stack of approximately fifty promotional postcards. The customer flips through the deck and either calls or mails in the postcards for products that interest her.

Advantages of Direct Marketing. The dramatic increase in direct marketing is no fluke. There are compelling reasons to use it, including:

1. You sell at retail price and don't give up margins to "middlemen".
2. You can easily track the success of your marketing program. When you run other ad campaigns, it is difficult to know what effect advertising has. With direct mail, you know immediately.
3. Your costs can be kept low. Many companies using exclusively direct marketing operate out of a garage or warehouse. As long as your promotional piece looks nice and the person answering the phone is polite, the customer doesn't know the difference. You can direct your campaign to small segments and keep your promotional costs down also.
4. Society is moving in a direction of relying more on direct marketing. People are rushed these days. They enjoy being able to shop from their home or office and not have to "go out shopping".
5. You can be selective in choosing the group to which you will market. Mailing lists are becoming more and more refined and you are able to concentrate on specific market segments. Because of this selectivity, you can personalize your approach to different groups, even to different customers.
6. You can test your approach on a small sample of potential customers and refine or abandon it without spending a large amount of money.

Direct marketing does have some drawbacks

Disadvantages of Direct Marketing. If, after reading the list of advantages of direct marketing, you have begun to believe it is a panacea, understand that it is not. It does have disadvantages, including:

1. People are being bombarded with more and more direct marketing promotions. Your approach has to stand out to be noticed in the barrage.
2. Some products do not lend themselves well to direct marketing (see below).
3. You may not be able to reach nearly as many customers compared to other distribution channels.
4. It may be slower in producing sales than other channels.

Who Should Use Direct Marketing. Direct marketing works better in certain situations. Some of them include:

1. When products are standardized and customers are educated about what they are getting. Customers feel that they don't need explanations of product features, they just want to know which are offered. Office supply products are sold directly through

catalogs, and customers feel comfortable that they know what they are getting.

2. When you are having difficulty getting into established distribution channels. You may have no choice but to try direct marketing.
3. When you are selling products that people are embarrassed to buy in public. A significant portion of society has bladder problems. These people would probably appreciate being able to purchase "diapers" through the mail.
4. When your target market is small and focused. More conventional approaches, such as newspaper or television advertising, would be wasteful since your buying group is so small.
5. When your potential customers have difficulty shopping for the products that you sell, including elderly people or people living in remote areas.
6. When your industry is more mature. When an industry is young, customers are not very knowledgeable nor have they developed a "trust" for it. When it matures and people are used to buying products, they are more willing to order without seeing the product in person.

Who Should Be Cautious in Using Direct Marketing. Companies who are in the situations described below should carefully analyze whether they should attempt direct marketing.

1. Companies in young, emerging industries. Customers are not knowledgeable nor have they grown to "trust" the industry.
2. Firms with customized, highly-differentiated products. When people are shopping for highly-customized products, they usually want to see directly what they will be getting and want to deal face-to-face with someone.
3. Firms with large and/or heavy products. Freight charges may make these products non-competitive.
4. Businesses whose customers are more service-oriented than price-conscious.
5. Companies whose products are often purchased on an impulse basis. If you are selling blank audio cassette tapes, you may have a tough time direct marketing them. People usually buy them when they need them, and they can purchase them in a grocery store.
6. Companies selling products for which customers are not willing to wait. If a customer runs out of toilet paper, he's not going to wait a week for his order to arrive.

A variety of quality books on direct marketing is available. Some are listed in the reference section at the end of the chapter. They teach you how to implement direct marketing programs for each of the approaches mentioned in this section.

Strategy for Marketing Channels. If you can get your products into established marketing channels, your sales should increase dramatically. However, it usually takes time. In the interim, you need to make *some* sales to survive. Direct marketing to customers and retailers is usually a necessity in the early stages of product distribution. If there are any consumer shows in your area, they can produce good sales for you. Visit retailers in your region and try to get them to carry your products. Tradeshows will allow you to sell directly to retailers outside of your local area. Through these means, you will gradually build up a group of retailers carrying your products.

Once you are selling enough to prove the saleability of your products, you can concentrate on expanding your distribution. You need to be patient and persistent in seeking to break into distribution channels. If sales reps service your industry, you are better off in early stages to use them than to try to hire your own salespeople. If distributors serve your industry, find out who are the best ones and work on getting them to carry your products. Reps and distributors can gain *widespread* distribution for your products. As they grow in importance, you will probably rely less on selling directly to retailers and stop selling in consumer shows.

Reps and distributors can gain widespread distribution for your products

Some companies who become solidly established in distribution channels and whose products become well known consider drawing back somewhat from the channels and doing more of the marketing themselves. The firms grow large enough to afford their own salespeople and they drop their independent reps. Retailers want their products enough that they will purchase directly from the manufacturer instead of through distributors. The manufacturer, therefore, retains the margin that the distributor used to take. The company often times can pay more attention to individual accounts than could a distributor. In certain cases, product recognition becomes high enough that consumers will buy directly from the manufacturer. Once you are established in marketing channels, you might consider drawing back somewhat and doing more of the marketing yourself.

In general, the strategy for market channels is:

1. In early stages, do some direct marketing and sell directly to retailers to generate initial sales.

2. Work persistently to get into established channels, through sales reps and distributors.
3. Once you are established, you can increase your margins and your control of the marketing process by selling directly to retailers with your own sales force.

Promoting through Channels. To gain access to any distribution channel, you must first have a product that customers want and are willing to pay for. But there are other factors that can help you to get your products into channels.

1. Provide display cases or racks to resellers.
2. Offer good payment terms to resellers.
3. Provide prompt, reliable delivery of products.
4. Offer a good return policy.
5. *Service* resellers. Listen to their problems. Work with them.
6. Price products at prices that will sell but allow distributors and resellers good margins.
7. Package products appropriately.
8. Offer "co-op" advertising to resellers, wherein you pay part of the costs they incur in promoting your products.

Once you are established in marketing channels, you might consider drawing back somewhat and doing more of the marketing yourself

Generally, you need to meet personally with distributors or sales reps to get them to carry your products. You can meet either at your or their place of business or else at a tradeshow. You need to have some type of printed material about your products, whether it be a flier, a brochure, or a catalog. You will need to decide which is most appropriate (and what you can afford). You should also have product samples available for them to look at. In many cases, it may take several visits and phone calls before any type of agreement is reached. Advertisements in industry journals and newsletters may put you in touch with interested distributors.

Most manufacturers use the promotion methods mentioned above in a "push" strategy. They put their efforts into "pushing" products into marketing channels and allowing the retailers to promote the products to the buying public. If you are a retailer, you need to use another approach—a "pull" promotion strategy. You promote products so as to "pull" customers in to buy them. Some manufacturers have well established products and also use a "pull" strategy to increase demand for products. Oshkosh B'Gosh products are pushed through distribution channels, but the company also does a fair amount of promotion directly to the buying public. You usually need considerable financial resources as a manufacturer to undertake a large-scale "pull" strategy.

Pricing

Price according to the market and not according to what a product costs you. Some businesses under price their products because they base it on their costs. For example, a manufacturer may be able to produce a new chemical formulation for dog deodorant. The direct chemical and filling costs are only $1.50. The owner believes that a 50 percent gross margin on retail sales is fair, so he charges $3. His competitors charge $5. If he stays at $3, he may be making a mistake. He needs to analyze his positioning of the product. Does he want to be a discounter? Is that the image he wants? Will competitors drop their prices right down to his level if he sells for $3? He should base his decision on the market, and not on his costs. If he wants to be a discounter, he should analyze the market and determine how much he should drop his price below the industry standard $5 to be considered "a bargain." Perhaps his product is good enough to be considered "premium," and he could charge $7 for it. A healthy margin never hurt anyone. And besides, his formula may be copied and then he may have to start dropping his price.

Most manufacturers use a "push" strategy

Sometimes a small manufacturer's costs are high relative to the industry. You can't charge a higher price just because your costs are higher. You have to have a better product to do it. The only point at which your costs become a factor in pricing is when you decide whether you can afford to make a product at all. If your product is not highly differentiated and the market price leaves you with a thin margin, you may have to decide not to produce it at all. Once again, *price according to the market.* If you find you can't survive at the price you have to charge, consider getting out of it.

Price according to the market

Price your products in a manner consistent with your product positioning. If you have premium products, you should be able to charge premium prices. Part of your entry strategy with a product may be to offer a lower price than competitive products in the premium segment, and that is fine. Or, to reinforce the image that your product is better than others', you may consistently need to be priced above the competition. The important point is that your pricing strategy should be consistent with the rest of your marketing strategy.

There is a variety of unique pricing strategies. For new products being introduced, a short-term deep price discount strategy sometimes works. That is what Bernstein's did with its salad dressings. When they first came out, they priced their dressings well below the industry average. People bought them because they were cheap. Once they tried them, they said, "this stuff is great.", and continued buying because it "tastes great, but is less costly." Several months later, those faithful customers were shocked to see that Bernstein's salad dressing was no longer less expensive than the market, but was considerably higher. They bought it anyway, though, because they liked it so much. Their strategy was a good one. Get people to try the product by discounting it, and once they realize how good it is, raise the price. You have to have a very good quality product to make this strategy work.

There is a variety of unique pricing strategies

Another unique pricing strategy is to charge a low, competitive price for the main product, but keep a healthy margin on accessories or replacement parts. This is done with electric razors. You can buy a good quality electric razor for less than $40, and pricing is competitive between the major manufacturers. If you tear a hole in the thin metal screen, which you will in a short period of time, you find that the screen alone costs nearly $10. That is where they make their money. You're not going to purchase another new razor just because the replacement screen is expensive. Automobile dealers make much better margins on replacement parts than they do on new cars. For this strategy to work, you obviously must sell accessories or replacement parts besides your primary product.

Some companies make money on accessories and not on the main product

Most smaller businesses should try to keep a decent margin on their products. Product differentiation and high customer service should allow you to gain sales without slashing prices. Again, the basic marketing strategy for most small businesses should be:

- Focus on a few markets; and
- Differentiate your products to those markets.

If you do this, you should be able to maintain healthy margins.

Promotion

Promotion is the fourth and final component of your marketing mix. Its purpose is to educate customers about your products, create in them an interest in your products, and prompt them to buy. Promotion is also used to create an image of your company in customers' minds. With these critical goals, promotion is obviously very important. Four elements make up your promotional strategy—personal selling, publicity, sales promotion, and advertising. Each is briefly described below. You need to learn more about each of them, however, and references are listed at the end of the chapter.

Personal Selling. Personal selling is asking customers for business, eye-to-eye. It is the oldest form of promotion. There are three critical steps to personal selling. The first is *contact.* Those first few moments that you have with a potential customers are incredibly important. Try to *establish a relationship.* Make sure that you are dressed appropriately. Be warm and honest with people. The best approach is to talk to customers *about themselves.*

The second step is *presentation.* You are describing the features of your offering and the benefits to the customer. Remember, *people buy benefits and not products.* Therefore, focus on how your product will meet a customer's needs. Describe what is *unique* about your product. Try to *show them something,* rather than just talking to them.

Four elements make up your promotional strategy—personal selling, publicity, sales promotion, and advertising

The third step is *closing,* which is when the sale is made. In some cases you may present your products and close at a later date. But in many cases you must close while the customer is present or else lose them. Remember one overriding principle—*people like to buy.* They may be choosy and terribly tight with their money, but they still enjoy buying something new. Therefore, don't be afraid of closing. You're *doing your customers a service!* And besides, if they don't buy from you they will buy from someone else. You need to develop a sixth sense about when a customer is ready to purchase, and then you need to ask for the sale.

Publicity. Publicity can be the cheapest, and possibly the best, form of promotion. You can't control it precisely, but you can certainly take steps to affect it.

Kennecott prides itself in investing in resources that strengthen Utah's future. The company is praised by media for its commitment to a clean environment. It has been emphasized that Kennecott was the first U.S. copper company to comply with the 1970 Clean Air Act when its existing smelter was retrofitted between 1974-1977. Nowadays the company is committed to restore old mining properties after they have extracted the useful minerals. As part of Kennecott's environmental master plan, Kennecott Utah Copper has 13 cleanup projects completed or underway. All work is being done within government standards. All of their cleanup work is open to public scrutiny and gets a lot of attention in local newspapers and media.

Publicity works well because someone else makes a testimony on your part. This carries weight. However, to get this publicity, you need to aggressively write and distribute the information you want the media to use. Short, interesting articles should be written and distributed to newspapers, trade magazines, radio talk shows and to any other appropriate source. Advertising keyed to the same issues can be combined with PR for further impact. For example, Kennecott state in an advertisement in the Salt Lake Tribune (March 16, 1994) "While we make a living here, we live here too. We want our environment protected as much as you do."

Think about new products, new employees, new markets, or anything interesting about your company that media might consider worthy of publication. Write it up as an interesting, fun article and make sure that the appropriate media receive copies of it.

Sales Promotions. Sales promotions catch customers' attention and encourage immediate sales. They include such items as coupons, samplings, rebates, contests and sweepstakes, and point of purchase displays. They include whacky approaches such as camping on top of your business until a certain amount of sales occurs. The purpose is to draw attention to your products and encourage a prompt sale.

Advertising. Advertising is the most frequently used form of promotion. There are many ways to advertise your products. Listed below are the most common forms. Read books on advertising and learn the relative advantages and disadvantages of one medium compared to the others. Some companies hire ad agencies to put together all of their advertising and public relations, while others do a very respectable job in-house. Whichever way you go, it is still important for you to know as much about advertising as possible. Consider each of the following forms of advertising and how cost effectively it will reach your customers:

1. Newspaper
2. Television
3. Radio
4. Magazine layout ads
5. Want ads
6. Yellow pages
7. Billboards
8. Transit (such as busses)
9. Personal letters
10. Handbills/flyers
11. Posters
12. Newsletters
13. Postcard decks
14. Gimmicks, including calendars, bags, notepads, matchbooks, pens, buttons, T-shirts, hats, actors, etc.

Conclusion

Marketing is the key to success for most businesses. Finance, accounting, and management are all important, but they take a backseat to marketing. Why? Because marketing is *your contact with customers*. And meeting their needs is why your business exists. A good marketing strategy needs to be top priority in your venture.

Learn as much as you can about marketing. This chapter covers only general strategy issues. You need to learn the details. Don't assume that an ad agency can do it all for you. Read books and magazines and go to instructional seminars. The following reference section and Chapter 16, Business Resources, describe marketing resources. Make marketing a high priority.

References

1. Chapman, Edward A. *Exhibit Marketing*. New York: McGraw-Hill Book Company, 1987.

2. Gottlieb, Richard. *Directory of Mail Order Catalogs*, Third Edition. New York: Grey House Publishing, 1987.

3. Pinkerton, Betsy and Pinkerton, Steve. *The Great Book of Catalogs*, Fourth Edition. Pinkerton Marketing, 1988.

4. Porter, Michael. *Competitive Strategy: Techniques for Analyzing Industries and Competitors*. New York: Free Press, 1980.

5. Thompson, Arthur A. and Strickland, A. J. *Strategic Management*, Sixth Edition. Plano, Texas: Business Publications, Inc., 1991.

6. *1992 Tradeshow Week Data Book*. New York: Tradeshow Week, 1992.

7. *Catalog Product News*, premiere issue. New York, Catalog Age Publishing Corporation, 1988.

8. *Directory of Manufacturers' Sales Agencies*. Laguna Hills, California: Manufacturers' Agents National Association, 1991.

11

Cash Management

"Happiness Is a Positive Cash Flow" ©
Stan Rich

Cash flow is the *single most important* financial consideration of a business. In the short term, you need cash to pay your bills, purchase inventory, buy equipment, pay employees and yourself. You can't pay your employees with income off of your income statement; you must pay them with cash. A business doesn't go bankrupt because of a loss on an income statement; it goes bankrupt because it doesn't have the cash to pay the people to whom it owes money. Some people think that their bank and creditors will be lenient if they show them an encouraging income statement, even though they have no cash to pay their immediate bills. There are bankruptcy notices every week for people who believe that.

There can be some dramatic differences between net income and net cash flow in the short term. Accountants can calculate your financial statements by using different means, and your net income can vary greatly, depending on what means they use. Depreciation can be changed, inventory methods varied and other manipulations made, all of which change your income. An income statement can be manipulated to show just about anything you want to. You can't do that with a cash flow statement— you either have the cash or you don't.

There can be dramatic differences between net income and net cash flow

In the long term, cash flow is also critical. Some business owners state, "Cash flow right now isn't important. We want to build the business up and sell down the road." Well, perhaps cash flow is not critical at this point in time, since they can pay their bills and have enough cash to live on. However, when they go to sell the business, cash flow will mean everything. It will make little difference at selling time how much profit they will have earned over the years—only the

IRS is concerned with profits. What will make a difference to them is how much CASH they put in their pockets when they sell the business. They won't be able to buy a house, take a trip or buy a boat with profits, but they can with cash from the sale of it. Cash flow is *the* ultimate measure of the long term success of a business.

In summary, put more emphasis on the cash flow statement than on the income statement, and take steps to manage the cash in your business. The cash in a business will not "take care of itself." You have to manage it.

The symptoms of cash flow problems are not pleasant ones

Almost every business manager has experienced cash flow problems, and the symptoms are not pleasant ones. You can't pay bills on time, checks bounce, creditors call, you rob Peter to pay Paul, and spend large amounts of time with bankers trying to get money, all of which consume huge amounts of your time and your energy and force you to run the business in a very inefficient manner. There are a number of causes of cash flow problems:

- Lack of profitability for an extended period of time;
- Seasonality of sales;
- A lack of planning; and surprisingly enough,
- Fast growth in sales.

The symptoms and possible solutions to each of these causes of cash flow problems are discussed below.

Breakeven Analysis

Many companies go through periods of losses and continue to pay their bills; however, a long-term lack of profits will cause cash flow problems. You can stay afloat by selling assets, borrowing to cover losses, or by other means, but they all tend to erode your equity in the business. A breakeven analysis allows you to predict what profits will be, based on a sales projection.

The breakeven analysis tells you what level of sales you need in order to pay your expenses. At the breakeven point you are not showing any income, rather you are just covering your expenses. Be aware that a calculated breakeven point is *only an estimate*. It does, however, give you a ballpark estimate of whether or not the company will be profitable at a given sales level.

The first step of the analysis is to label all of your expenses as either fixed, variable, or a combination of the two. Fixed costs are those expenses that tend not to change with the level of sales of the firm. For example, rent and insurance costs do not generally fluctuate with sales. Whether you have a good month or a bad month, these areas are not affected. It doesn't mean they never change--your landlord can raise the rent, you can change locations and hence rent, or your insurance agent can certainly raise your premiums, but these are still considered fixed costs in the sense that sales levels do not affect them.

Variable costs are those expenses which fluctuate directly with sales. For example, sales commissions are variable costs, as is cost of goods sold. If you sell twice as much, your expense is twice as much. Some operating costs are a combination of fixed and variable expenses. Utilities can be a combination of the two expenses— you have to pay a certain amount to keep the lights on and the building heated, but if you have a good month, you spend more on electricity for your manufacturing process. Your payroll may be a combination of fixed and variable costs: if your salespeople are guaranteed a base, which is a fixed cost; plus commission, which is a variable cost.

Some expenses may be a combination of both fixed and variable costs

You can calculate the breakeven level of sales for either a month's or a year's time. If you are in a highly seasonal business, do a breakeven on an annual basis. If your business is not highly seasonal, a monthly breakeven is often easier to interpret than an annual one. If you are doing a monthly analysis, project costs for a "typical" month. Realize that a breakeven analysis is an *estimate*, and you need not be overly precise in your figures.

Figure 11-1 shows how one company classified all of their monthly expenses as either fixed or variable, or a combination of the two. For fixed costs, the total monthly amount is written in the "FIXED" column. The company shown pays $1000 per month in rent. Variable costs are written as a proportion of sales. Raw materials average 30 percent of sales, while direct labor averages 20 percent. The total fixed costs per month are $15,000, while variable costs add to .50.

The breakeven formula is:

BEP = FC / (1 - VC)

BEP is the breakeven point in dollars
FC is total fixed costs
VC is variable costs expressed in decimal form

Therefore, in order to cover expenses the firm must sell

BEP = 15,000 / (1 - .50) = $30,000 per month.

Figure 13-1. Sample Breakeven Analysis

COSTS	FIXED AMOUNT	VARIABLE %
Raw materials		0.30
Direct Labor		0.20
Merchandise		
Wages & Salaries	9000	
Payroll Expenses	1800	
Supplies	500	
Repairs & Maintenance	0	
Advertising	500	
Car, Delivery, Travel	300	
Accounting & Legal	200	
Rent/Lease	1000	
Telephone	150	
Insurance	100	
Utilities	150	
Taxes, Real Estate, Etc.	200	
Depreciation	400	
Other Expenses	700	
TOTALS	15,000	0.50

BREAKEVEN POINT = 30,000
PRICE/UNIT = 75.00
BREAKEVEN POINT IN UNITS = 400

Realize that at this sales level, the company is only meeting expenses. Most people are in business to be able to take some money home. That amount can be added to fixed expenses. For example, if the owner wants to draw $3,000 a month, it is added to fixed expenses, which then total $18,000 per month. Plugging the numbers in the same formula yields a new breakeven point: $36,000 per month. This is how much the company will have to sell per month to pay all expenses and allow the owner to draw $3,000.

Figure 11-2. Sample Breakeven Graph

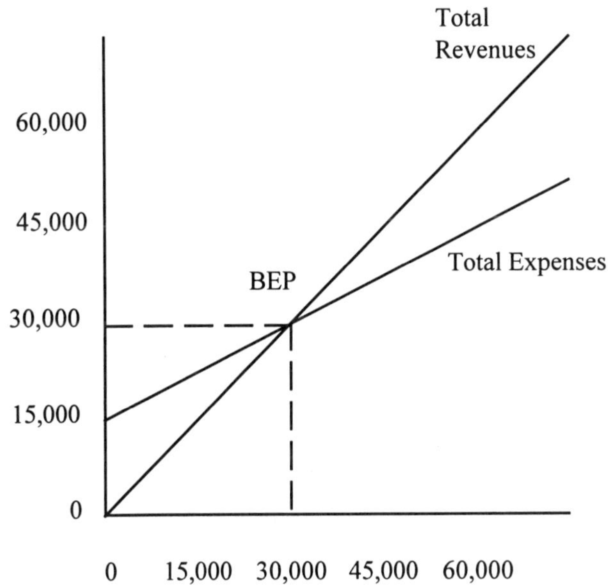

Figure 11-2 illustrates a breakeven graph based on the original calculated breakeven point of $30,000. Both axes are in terms of dollars. The breakeven point (BEP) is where the revenue and total expense lines cross. The vertical distance between these two lines is the amount of profit or loss that the company is experiencing. Naturally, at the breakeven point of $30,000 there is neither a profit nor a loss. At sales of $20,000, however, the company would have a $5000 loss, which is the vertical distance between the two lines at that point. If the company sold $40,000, it would earn a profit of $5000.

If a business is not above the breakeven point, the main source of its cash flow problems is simple—a lack of profits. The firm needs to increase revenues, cut expenses, or both before it will make much headway in solving its cash flow problems.

Cash Management Principles

If your business is profitable, but you still experience cash flow problems, you are not alone. In fact, it is a very common problem, especially in growing or seasonal businesses. There are three fundamentals to effectively manage the cash in a profitable business:

- Planning
- Timing
- Frugality

Planning

The single most important thing you can do to avoid cash shortages is to plan

Probably the single most important thing you can do to avoid cash shortages is plan. Unfortunately, planning does not come naturally to many people. In fact, it is amazing the extent to which people go to avoid planning. Nevertheless, if you are going to control your cash, you must predict what your revenues and your expenses will be. Many people resist forecasting revenues and expenses because they are afraid the numbers will look bad, and that can be really depressing. In this case, ignorance is bliss. So what happens? A cash shortage occurs, which was foreseeable, but no one bothered to predict, and then the manager arranges a short notice meeting with the banker to see the business through the cash crunch.

Bankers do not like these kinds of meetings. Bankers do not like to be surprised, even on their birthdays. This business owner would have been much better off if three months previously he had taken a cash flow projection to the bank, showed the amount and timing of the cash shortage, showed how down the road the bank would be repaid, and made arrangements in advance. Bankers much prefer this type of setting for approving a loan—after all, they are in business of loaning money.

Figure 11-3 illustrates a cash flow planning sheet. The Small Business Administration has sheets such as this, as well as workbooks on preparing business plans for general types of enterprises such as retail, service, construction and manufacturing, and makes them available at low cost. General microcomputer spreadsheet programs, such as Microsoft Excel, are extremely helpful for allowing exploration of "what if" questions in such financial programs. More specialized (and expensive) programs, such as Ronstadt's Financials, provide extensive guidance for such forecasting and business planning. A spreadsheet template of this same worksheet is provided on the diskette included with this book. Here is how you use the sheet. In the

Figure 11-3. Projected Cash Flow Statement

	Jan Proj	Jan Act	Feb Proj	Feb Act
Beg Cash on Hand				
Cash Receipts				
(A)Collections				
(B)Int & Misc				
(C)Loan, Contrib				
Tot Cash Rcpts				
Tot Cash Avail				
Expenses				
Purchases				
Payroll				
Payroll Expenses				
Outside Expenses				
Supplies				
Repairs/Maintnce				
Advertising				
Auto & Travel				
Accounting, Legal				
Rent				
Telephone				
Utilities				
Insurance				
Taxes				
Interest				
Other Expenses				
Subtotal				
Loan Prin Payment				
Capital Purchase				
Start-up Costs				
Reserve/Escrow				
Owner Withdrawal				
Tot Cash Pd Out				
Cash Position				

"Estimate" column, forecast revenues and expenses for at least three months, and do it in pencil. Try to be as accurate as possible in the timing of your figures. For example, if you pay insurance every six months, get the figure in the correct month, and don't average it across all twelve months. If you can forecast for more than three months, that's all the better. If you can't project at least three months, this forecast will be of little value.

After a month has passed, write in the actual figures, compare them to your projection and if necessary, revise your ensuing projections (that's why they should be in pencil). You should then be able to forecast another month's figures. In this way, you make a "rolling" forecast as time passes, and you are constantly revising the forecast.

If you are going to implement only one portion of this whole cash management program, make sure it is this cash flow projection. It is absolutely the most critical step in avoiding cash flow problems, and that is to know in advance when a cash shortage is coming.

Timing

Many cash flow shortages are caused when "everything hits at once," in other words when timing is terrible. Some you can't avoid, many you can. Figure 11-4 shows a cash flow diagram. The basic strategy for resolving cash shortages is to speed up conversion of assets into cash and slow down the flow of cash out of the business.

Many cash flow shortages are caused when "everything hits at once"

Consider the circular part of the cash flow diagram. Cash is used to purchase inventory, which turns into sales, which turns into receivables, which turns back into cash. The strategy: slow down the flow of cash into inventory, but once you have bought merchandise, speed up the cycle of turning that into sales —> receivables —> back into cash.

You slow down cash outflows into inventory but speed inventory turns through good inventory control. The two primary types of inventory control systems are a bin and a perpetual inventory system. Either system tells you what, when, and how much to buy. Loose inventory control can be a terrible cash drain on a business. While you are scrapping to pay your bills, there may be a tremendous amount of cash tied up on your shelves that is either overstocked or is not moving. You must know what products are moving in your business, how much you will be selling, and how long it takes you to get those products once you have ordered them. Many Japanese companies are expert at timing the arrival of raw materials so that they don't end up being stored for any lengthy period of time, and hence they tie up very little cash.

If you've got old merchandise sitting on your shelves, mark it down and get rid of it. It's freezing your cash. If you don't know which merchandise moves and which doesn't, you must learn it. Purchase the products that move, and don't overbuy. Without risking stockouts, minimize how much merchandise you carry and try to time getting merchandise in with when you will be selling (and get good suppliers!).

Be very careful about paying bills late as a strategy to improve your cash flow (although it is probably the most commonly used). Very few people are foolish enough to pay bills early, unless discounts are given. The discounts, by the way, can be significant. A 2/10 net 30 discount is the same as putting the money away for twenty days in an account bearing 36 percent, which is tough to find these days. Unless you have an understanding supplier or other creditor, your paying late will upset them (and will probably cost you dearly in interest). If you are going to rely on them for prompt and consistent delivery so that you trim your inventory, you'd better be prompt in paying them. Do not pay late as a strategy to improve your cash flow. Pay when your bills are due.

The next portion of the cash cycle is converting inventory into sales. Again, you are attempting to speed the flow of other assets into cash. You need good marketing to do this. Chapter 10 explains the steps in formulating a sound marketing strategy.

Accounts receivable are in many cases the cause of cash flow problems. Make sure that you are not offering credit to the wrong people. For a fee, credit bureaus will check on applicants' credit histories. Standard credit forms are available at office supply stores. For smaller firms, calls to other creditors are a less expensive way of checking credit. Don't believe everything on a credit application form. Check it out. It takes time and some money, but may really save you headaches in the long run. A clear, written credit policy must be adopted and adhered to. The policies will vary between industries, in some cases dictated by what is standard in the industry. Don't let your customers *ever* give you the excuse that you hadn't told them what your credit policy was.

Let your customers know up front what your credit terms are

Even the most careful credit checks will still result in accounts that are overdue. Careful attention to those accounts will help keep them to a minimum. The fairest assumption is that customers want to pay as agreed. The majority will, when reminded, pay in a timely manner. However, a customer's situation may change from that which existed when the agreement was made. Restructuring a debt is usually better than turning the account over to a collection agency.

Standard collection letters are available from a variety of sources. The key to good collections is *diligence*. Do you remember the parable Jesus told about the man who woke his neighbor in the middle of the night to borrow a loaf of bread? Well, the neighbor was very upset and didn't want to give him anything, and so told him to go away. The man kept knocking, and even though the neighbor didn't want to give him any bread, he did so just to be rid of him. The best bill collectors operate under the same principle. Don't bully the people who owe you money, just be persistent. They may not want

Figure 11-4. The Cash Flow Cycle

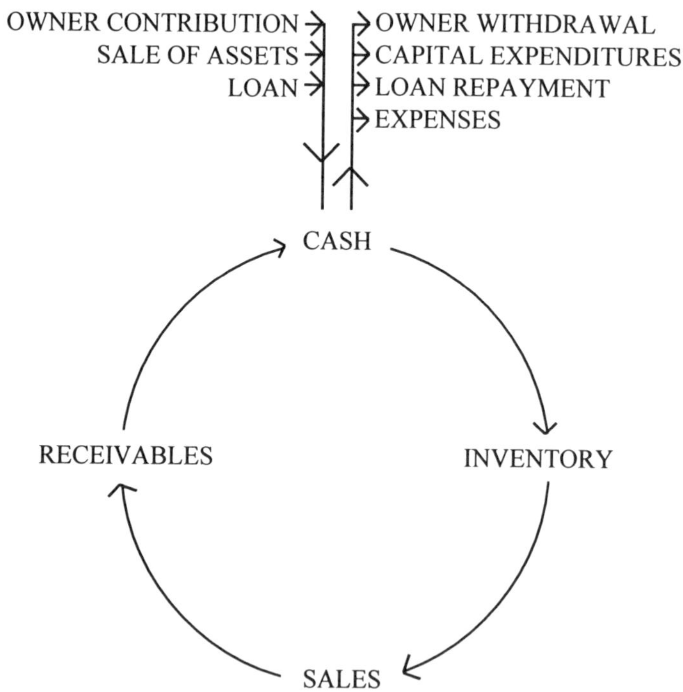

to give you any bread either; but if they have any money, they'll pay you just to get you out of their hair. On the other hand, if you sit back and don't do or say anything, you'll go right to the bottom of their list to be paid.

Consistency must be used in enforcing credit policy. If terms are "net thirty," customers must be notified immediately if they are overdue. If late payment interest charges are written in the policy, they must be enforced. Some business owners who pay after the discount date and still take the discount. Why? Because the company they buy from never clamps down on them. All you need do is let a customer slide once on a late payment or not paying interest, and chances are they will continue to do so. Even if it costs you more to send the notice than what you will collect, you need to do so. Good credit control requires diligence.

Good credit control requires diligence

Other Cash Flow Timing Issues. For seasonal businesses, there are approaches you can take to spread your expenses to more cash-rich times. Look at all of your expense accounts: can you arrange to pay them when you have more cash available? Start with suppliers. Are they willing to extend longer credit terms so that you are able to pay once your heavy selling season is over? What about people from whom you purchase equipment? Can they wait also? Can you arrange to pay your insurance at different times? What about your accountant? Some of these may not be possibilities, but they are certainly worth a try, and you may be surprised how willing some of these people would be to accommodate you.

Non-cyclic Cash Considerations. Referring back to the cash flow diagram, you will see that there are cash inflows and outflows outside of the circular part of the diagram. These represent steps that you can take on an occasional basis to improve cash flow. You can obtain additional cash by selling assets. Many times you can sell non-productive assets when cash shortages are foreseen. Foresight is important, because rarely can you immediately liquidate assets. For example, Bill once owned a golf pro shop and taught golf. He owned a $3000 video camera system which helped him to analyze students' strokes. He loved the system, and that was the problem. The business it generated couldn't justify the expense, yet he had to have it. When cash got really tight, he sold the system and at quite a loss. The moral of that story is that the asset was not critical; it froze a lot of cash and he waited to try to sell it until he had to. Don't make the same mistake. Get rid of marginal assets when you can get a reasonable price, and don't wait until you absolutely need the cash.

Many businesses are continually strapped for cash because they are undercapitalized and need further investment to provide a working capital cushion. You can obtain additional funds through loans or equity investment. To get either, you probably need to present a business plan to a banker or investor. An outline and description of a business plan is presented in Chapter 13. A line of credit is the "ultimate" bank loan, whereby the bank puts money into your account as needed, up to a certain limit. This takes enormous pressure off you as a cash manager, but bankers are hesitant to give this type of loan. Another possibility of easing cash pressures is to refinance current debt, borrowing a larger amount, and thereby providing an immediate chunk of cash to work with.

Many businesses are continually strapped for cash because they are undercapitalized

Other possibilities for improving cash flow are found on the right side of the cash flow diagram, and they involve slowing down the non-cyclic outflows of cash. Foremost is cutting expenses. Can you reduce your expenses without significantly reducing the quality of your product or service? Can you remove any "fat" that may exist in the firm? This will increase both profitability and cash flow.

Slowing capital expenditures is another means of improving cash flow. Are projected capital expenditures really needed? Have you thoroughly analyzed the purchase's impact? Will purchase of the equipment cause cash shortages in ensuing months? These are questions you should ask before every capital purchase. Avoid buying equipment on an "emotional" basis.

Increasing owners' contribution to the business or decreasing owners' withdrawals are often "last resorts" to resolving cash flow problems. Many owners take small withdrawals and have already invested most of what they have. In some cases, however, owners can postpone withdrawals during cash-tight periods, or else invest extra funds during those same periods, if they can see the crunch coming.

Frugality

Frugality is the last cash management principle, and the concept is simple: When times are good, don't think they will last forever. When there is cash in the till, don't run out and buy new equipment, give bonuses, or take that long-postponed trip until you have completed a cash flow projection and made sure that you will have enough cash to survive the tough times. Even if tough times are not on the horizon, why not put a chunk away just in case things don't go as expected? The Japanese save three times per capita as much as Americans do,

When times are good, don't think they will last forever

and it provides them with a real advantage—they have something to fall back on. That cushion, even if never used, may provide you with a tremendous peace of mind.

Conclusion

In summary, these are the steps you should take in managing your cash:

- First, do a breakeven analysis and make sure you know how much in sales you need to meet expenses. If you are below that level consistently, you will not avoid cash flow problems. You need to increase revenues and/or decrease expenses.

- Next, if you are above the breakeven point but still experience cash flow problems, follow these guidelines:

- Project your cash inflows and outflows on a cash planning sheet. This will help you to foresee when you might have shortages.

- Work to speed up your cash inflows and slow down your cash outflows in the cyclic part of the cash flow diagram.

- Talk to people to whom you pay money, and try to arrange payment schedules that fit the cash flow pattern in your business. If approached *in advanc*e, most people are reasonable in working with you.

- If necessary, consider steps to increase cash flow in the non-cyclic portion of the cash flow diagram.

- When times are good, save some of the money, and don't believe that the good times will last forever.

12

Financial Management

"I've always found that making money is easy.
Keepin' it's the hard part."
Bill Gallagher

Cash flow management, as explained in the previous section, is the most critical financial concern of a growing company. Financial statement analysis is a process which is also important to the growing venture. At the start-up stage of a company, the entrepreneur can typically keep a firm grasp on the finances of the business from the checkbook and simple financial statements. As the company grows quickly, however, many entrepreneurs begin to lose financial control of the business. Since sales are increasing dramatically, it seems natural to pump money into inventory, buy new equipment, and sustain sales growth through liberal credit policies. The combined effect of such decisions can be disastrous for a company. At this point, it is no longer easy for the entrepreneur to "keep the train on the tracks" without a clear understanding of the financial statements and the ability to understand the implications of the numbers shown there. Good financial statement analysis allows the entrepreneur to make sound financial decisions.

Financial management is a balancing act

The definition of *finance* is the process of maximizing profits without jeopardizing the firm's ability to pay its bills. These two elements often oppose each other— what maximizes profits may reduce the amount of cash available in the business. Therefore, financial management is a balancing act. *Financial analysis* helps you make decisions which increase the profitability of your company while ensuring that it has enough cash to pay its bills.

Most entrepreneurs are not fond of the task of financial management. It is a technical procedure. Nonetheless, they usually grow to appreciate its importance. A series of cashflow crises or a sudden drop in profits makes you realize how important it is to maintain close financial control of your company. You probably won't conduct a financial analysis yourself— that is usually the job of a financial manager or an accountant. However, *you need to be able to understand what they tell you, because you are the one who can enforce financial controls.* This chapter gives you an understanding of basic financial management so that you can communicate with the people who perform the financial analysis.

The two financial statements typically generated for a business are an income statement and a balance sheet (even though you know that a cash flow statement is more important). The income statement shows revenues, expenses, and the difference between them, which is profit. It can cover any period of time. Many businesses generate it monthly, all should generate it quarterly, and all *must* generate it on an annual basis to comply with IRS regulations. An example of an income statement is shown in Figure 12-1.

The balance sheet shows a firm's assets, liabilities, and owners' equity. Whereas an income statement covers a span of time, the balance sheet is a "snap-shot" picture of what the company owns, what it owes, and the difference between the two, which is the net worth of the firm at any point in time. A balance sheet is shown in Figure 12-2.

Verifying Financial Statement Information

You need to assess the accuracy of the accounts on your financial statements

Analysis of financial statements will have little value if the figures on which it is based are not representative of the company's position. You need to look at every account on your income statement and balance sheet and assess their accuracy before running the analysis. Don't use the financial statements that you took in to impress the banker, use the ones that portray reality. Most of the distortions that may occur show up in assets (which then distort net worth). The following accounts are those that are most suspect.

Accounts Receivable are often overstated. Are all of the receivables collectable? Many firms avoid writing off bad debts because of the negative effect on the balance sheet. Make sure that all receivables listed can be collected, and as a general rule, anything over 120 days should probably be written off or discounted significantly.

Inventory is often misstated. Since it has a direct effect on reported profits and thus taxes, it can be manipulated (legally and illegally) to reduce taxes. To do a proper analysis, you need a *realistic* assessment of the inventory value. It is important to know whether a last-in, first-out (LIFO) or first-in, first-out (FIFO) system has been used. In times of inflation (none of us can remember anything else) the FIFO system will value inventory at a higher level. You don't have to change your inventory valuation system to do the analysis, but be aware that the system you have chosen may account for some variation from industry standards.

Notes Receivable need to be verified. Are there loans to owners or managers which realistically will not be repaid in the near future? If these notes are not removed from the statements, they will distort the analysis.

Fixed Assets need to be examined to ensure their representativeness. Have assets been depreciated, and yet still have considerable value? Or conversely, are assets shown on the statements which are now obsolete? Do real estate values approximate their true worth? Don't break accounting rules to change the statements; however, when you do the analyses, consider the differences that exist here in drawing conclusions.

Asset values on a balance sheet can be misleading

Industry Averages of Financial Ratios

Ratio analyis is the process of comparing the values of two accounts on the financial statements. For example, a commonly cited ratio is return on equity, which is net profit divided by net worth. You typically compare the ratios to published industry averages to get indications of potential problems within your company. There are two major sources of industry financial ratios, and the companies and their addresses are shown below. For a subscription fee, you can obtain their publications. Many local and university libraries in the state carry these reference materials.

Robert Morris Associates	Dun & Bradstreet
P.O. Box 8500, S-1140	99 Church Street
Philadephia, PA 19178	New York, NY 10007

Each of these publishers of financial information must make decisions on which industries to include in their books, since there are thousands of industries. They tend to choose the largest, most visible industries in America. If you are in an unusual industry, you may find industries in the publications which only remotely resemble yours, or else you may find none which are similar. In this case, you should seek industry financial statistics from an industry association, if one exists. Chapter 4, Marketing Research, discusses how to find out about industry associations.

The ratios provided by Robert Morris Associates (RMA) and Dun & Bradstreet (D&B) are given in three groups: upper quartile, median, and lower quartile. For any given ratio, these figures are calculated by first computing the value of the ratio for each financial statement in the sample. These values are then arranged in order from strongest to weakest (although in many cases either extreme may indicate a problem) with general banking guidelines used in determining which end of the spectrum is "strong." In such an array of values, the figure which falls in the middle between the strongest and weakest ratio is the median. The figure that falls halfway between the median and the weakest ratio is the lower quartile, while the upper quartile is computed in the same fashion on the other end of the spectrum. Quartiles allow the reader to understand the amount of variation in the ratio in a particular industry. In certain industries there is a wide spread of values of particular ratios, indicating that a substantial variance from the median may not indicate a problem.

Computing and Interpreting the Ratios

Computing the ratios is a science; however, interpreting them is an art. Calculating one ratio and trying to draw conclusions from it alone is usually not of much value. The ratio needs to be compared to other ratios and also to industry averages. Ratios are comparisons of two values: if a ratio is high, it could be because the numerator is unusually high, or the denominator is unusually low. Assume that a business has a high return on equity: is that good or bad? It is good if the business has a substantial net worth. It could be bad if losses in other years have reduced net worth to dangerously low levels, and therefore even a small profit results in a high return on equity. Therefore, look at ratios in groups. If there is a problem in some area of a company, it will be signalled by several different ratios, not just one.

Interpreting financial ratios is an art

Common Size Income Statements and Balance Sheets

The first step of financial analysis is to divide every account on the income statement by net sales and divide every account on the balance sheet by total assets, and then compare those ratios to industry averages. In a common-size income statement, all accounts are expressed as a percentage of total sales. Figure 12-1 shows a common-size income statement. Comparing the percentages to industry averages might reveal that the firm has a lower gross margin, lower operating expenses, or higher net profit than is typical for competing firms. This information helps the entrepreneur understand what the major expenses in the business are and how well she is controlling them compared to other firms.

Figure 12-2 shows a common-size balance sheet. All accounts are expressed as a percentage of total assets. Comparison to industry norms might show if a firm has higher debt or less liquidity than competitors. This information helps the entrepreneur control the assets and debts of his company. Common-size statements are good starting points for ratio analysis. The ratios are easy to compute and often give an early indication of potential problems, which ensuing ratios may support.

Key Business Ratios Analysis

You can calculate dozens of different ratios from financial statements, some having more importance in certain industries. Some entrepreneurs prefer that their accountants calculate the ratios. Accountants are very good at this, and they can save you time. If you do not have a *basic* knowledge of ratio analysis, however, you probably won't understand what the accountant says to you about the ratios. In that case, he may as well have not given you the ratios. Whether you do the analysis yourself or not, it is important to know the basic concepts presented in this section.

You need to have a basic knowledge of ratio analysis

There are five major groups of ratios:

Solvency ratios measure the quality and adequacy of current assets to meet current obligations as they come due.

Coverage ratios measure a firm's ability to service debt.

Leverage ratios measure the amount of debt that companies have, and hence their vulnerability to business downturns.

Operating ratios assist in evaluating management performance.

Profitability ratios show how successfully a business is earning a return to its owners.

Solvency Ratios

Quick ratio is computed by dividing cash plus accounts receivable by total current liabilities. Current liabilities are all liabilities that fall due within one year. This ratio reveals your ability to meet short-term obligations. It shows the number of dollars of liquid assets available to cover each dollar of current debt. Any time this ratio is as much as one to one, your business is said to be in a liquid condition. The larger the ratio, the greater the liquidity.

Current ratio is current assets divided by current liabilities. Current assets include cash, accounts and notes receivable (less reserves for bad debts), merchandise inventories, and marketable securities. This ratio measures the degree to which your current assets cover your current liabilities. The higher the ratio the greater ability you have to pay your current debts. A rule of thumb (which is often broken) is that the current ratio should be greater than two to one.

Coverage Ratios

Earnings Before Interest & Tax to Interest ratio measures your firm's ability to meet interest payments. A high ratio may indicate that you would have little difficulty in paying off your current loan(s) and could possibly take on more debt.

Leverage Ratios

Total Liabilities to Net Worth ratio is obtained by dividing total current plus long-term liabilities by net worth. The ratio measures the extent to which your company is financed by creditors. A ratio greater than one indicates that creditors have provided more funds than you and other investors.

Fixed Assets to Net Worth ratio reveals what proportion of your net worth has been used to finance fixed assets. This ratio tend to fluctuate greatly among industries. As a general rule of thumb, a ratio of over 75 percent indicates possible over-investment in fixed assets.

Efficiency Ratios

Collection Period is calculated by dividing your accounts receivable by sales and then multiplying by 365. The quality of the receivables of a company can be determined by this ratio when compared with selling terms and industry norms. It *does not* measure the average number of days required to collect an account; you would need to divide by credit sales to do so. Generally, when most sales are on credit, any collection period more than one-third over normal selling terms (forty days for thirty-day terms) indicates slow turning receivables. When comparing the collection period of one firm with another's, you should allow for possible variations in selling terms. Be aware that the ratio can fluctuate appreciably in seasonable businesses, in which case accounts receivable aging would be more appropriate.

Net Sales to Inventory ratio is a guide to the rate at which your merchandise is being moved. This ratio varies widely between industries and is meaningful only when compared with industry averages. The ratio does not tell how many times inventory "turns." You would have to divide cost of goods sold by inventory to arrive at that. For seasonal businesses, inventory will fluctuate, and thus timing is an issue when calculating this ratio. An unusually high or low ratio may signal problems. A low ratio is the most common problem, indicating possible overstockage. However, an unusually high ratio may reflect insufficient merchandise to meet customer demand and could result in lost sales.

Sales to Net Working Capital ratio is calculated by dividing annual net sales by the difference between current assets and current liabilities. This relationship indicates whether a company might have too little working capital for the amount of sales, which can cause a shortage of cash, or a low ratio indicates potential waste in having too much working capital for the amount of sales.

Profitability Ratios

Return on Sales is calculated by dividing your net profit after taxes by annual net sales. This reveals the percentage of sales that ends up as profit. The ratio indicates your firm's ability to withstand adverse conditions such as falling prices, rising costs, and declining sales. When calculating this ratio for partnerships and proprietorships, it should be calculated after a realistic salary is deducted from net profits for the owner of the business (presuming the owner manages the business).

Return on Assets is your net profit after taxes divided by total assets. This is the prime measure of the efficiency of the firm, as it measures the profits generated as a percentage of the assets used to generate those profits.

Return on Net Worth is obtained by dividing your net profit after tax by your net worth (owner's equity). It is used to analyze your ability to realize an adequate return on the capital invested in the company.

How to Analyze Your Financial Statements

Once you have confirmed the numbers on your financial statements, you need to compute the ratios. If you don't feel confident doing it, have your accountant do it. Start by first generating the common-size income statements and balance sheets, and then compute the above ratios. Besides these fourteen ratios, other ratios may have importance in your particular industry. Compute them, and you are ready to begin the analysis.

Look for *groups of ratios* which may indicate a problem

Look for groups of ratios which may indicate a problem. The example was given previously of a company which had a very high return on equity, and the managers couldn't tell if it was good or bad. They have to look at other ratios to tell. In this example, they should look at the common-size balance sheet and see what percentage of total assets that owners' equity comprises. They should then look at the debt/net worth ratio to see if it is out of line. If these two ratios are not out of line, they can feel certain the company is indeed earning a very nice return for its investors.

Perhaps the owners of the firm believe that they have an inventory problem. There are ratios they can study to assess that. Again, they should first look at the common-size balance sheet and see how their inventory/assets ratio compares with the industry. They could then compare their sales/inventory ratio to the industry to see if there is a significant difference. Invariably, a problem in a certain area of the company will show up in a *group of ratios, and not just in one.* Problems are also usually signalled by *large deviations* from industry norms, not slight ones.

Beware of jumping to quick conclusions when a group of ratios is out of line with the average. After all, who wants to be average? Many Japanese companies are expert at timing arrival of inventory just before production begins, therefore they would show very low inventory ratios. Some firms have excellent cash managers who keep just enough cash around to pay bills and invest the excess in income-producing assets. Their liquidity ratios would probably be way out of whack with industry standards. What first appears to be a financial problem may actually be an indication of the strength of a company. Therefore, look beneath the numbers when your firm's ratios are not near the industry average.

The last step in financial analysis is to perform a *trend analysis.* Often times it is not the values of ratios themselves which indicate financial problems, rather it is the *changes* in them. For example, a company's current sales/accounts receivable ratio may be near the industry average, which would not signal a problem. However, if the company had previously had an above-average ratio, this would signal that its efficiency in collecting receivables could be slipping. Conversely, a company's gross margin percentage may be below the industry average, but when compared to last year's percentage, it has improved. Therefore, trend analysis can uncover problems that do not show up in ratio analysis for only one period, or else the trend may serve to show that problems areas are improving.

If you have past financial statements, do the trend analysis. Common-size statements for several years can be compared and can indicate changes for the good or bad. Figures 11-1 and 11-2 show comparative common-size statements, and trends are easy to see.

Conclusion

You may never become adept at performing a financial analysis. That's okay. However, make sure you can understand one when it is set in front of you. Work with your financial manager or accountant to ensure that your business has proper financial controls. Know the danger signals when finances are becoming a problem so you can take immediate steps to bring them back into line.

Figure 12-1. Comparative Income Statements

	Year 1	%	Year 2	%
Revenues	1,500,000	100	2,000,000	100
Cost of Sales	1,000,000	67	1,300,000	65
Gross Profit	500,000	33	700,000	35
Expenses				
Payroll	100,000	07	150,000	08
Payroll Expenses	18,000	01	25,000	01
Supplies	3,000	00	3,500	00
Outside Expenses	0	00	0	00
Repairs & Maintenance	6,500	00	10,000	00
Advertising	50,000	03	75,000	04
Auto & Travel	45,000	03	80,000	04
Accounting,Legal	8,000	01	10,000	01
Rent	24,000	02	24,000	01
Telephone	6,000	00	6,000	00
Utilities	4,500	00	5,000	00
Insurance	2,500	00	3,000	00
Taxes	6,000	01	6,000	00
Interest	55,000	04	50,000	03
Other Expenses	0	00	0	00
Depreciation	150,000	10	150,000	08
Total Expenses	478,500	32	601,500	30
Net Profit	21,500	01	98,500	05

Figure 12-2. Comparative Balance Sheets

	Year 1	%	Year 2	%
ASSETS				
Current Assets				
Cash	15,000	01	50,000	04
Accounts Rec	225,000	16	275,000	20
Inventory	350,000	25	400,000	29
Tot Current Assets	590,000	42	725,000	53
Fixed Assets				
Land	200,000	14	200,000	15
Building	500,000	36	500,000	36
Less Dep	-100,000	-07	-200,000	-15
Equipment	200,000	14	200,000	15
Less Dep	-40,000	-03	-80,000	-06
Furn & Fixtures	50,000	04	50,000	04
Less Dep	-10,000	-01	-20,000	-01
Total Fixed Assets	800,000	58	650,000	47
Total Assets	1,390,000	100	1,375,000	100
LIABILITIES				
Current Debt				
Accounts Payable	340,000	24	354,000	26
Notes Payable				
Taxes Payable				
Total Current Debt	340,000	24	354,000	26
Longterm Debt				
Loan	550,000	40	500,000	36
Notes Payable				
Total Longterm Debt	550,000	40	500,000	36
Total Debt	890,000	64	854,000	62
Equity	500,000	36	521,000	38
Total Debt + Equity	1,390,000	100	1,375,000	100

13

The Business Plan

The term *business plan* has become very popular in the last decade. Bankers and venture capitalists want to see one before they make an investment decision. Business schools are putting increased emphasis on the need to write one for any business, whether new or existing. Experienced business people encourage aspiring entrepreneurs to "write the business plan." Their advice is sound. Writing a business plan forces you to think about all aspects of running your new venture. You may spend up to two hundred hours researching and writing the plan at a time when you are already incredibly busy. However, you have to find the time. You need to know what you are getting into before you forge ahead.

There are rewards for developing a business plan. If you are seeking investors, it allows them to critically evaluate your venture. Most of them will not even talk to you if you have not prepared it. A written plan allows others to give you suggestions. The financial section of the plan may open your eyes. You may discover that there is little chance of a profitable business and stop your plans before investing a lot of money. In certain cases, the information uncovered in researching the market may steer you to change your product or the way it is marketed.

You have to find the time to write the business plan

You need to be involved in writing the plan *yourself.* If you hire someone else to do all of it, it's not the same. You need to have a solid understanding of your business and its environment. Granted, hiring others to do some research or to edit the plan makes sense, but you need to be intimately involved yourself.

You can't write a business plan without knowledge of a broad spectrum of business principles

A business plan is a comprehensive description of your business, the environment in which it operates, and how you will run it. Most plans describe three years into the future, although some project for five or more years. Nearly every section of this book needs to be incorporated into the plan. You can't write a business plan without knowledge of a broad spectrum of business principles. The plan is larger in scope but includes all the sections of a strategic plan. The business plan adds information to the strategic plan and includes more detail. There are numerous outlines for business plans, but all are quite similar. The outline below describes the major sections of a typical business plan.

- Executive Summary
- The Company and Its Overall Strategy
- The Market and Competitors
- Marketing Strategy
- Design and Development Plans
- Manufacturing and Operations Plan
- Management Team
- Overall Schedule
- Critical Risks and Problems
- The Financial Plan
- Proposed Company Offering
- Financial Exhibits
- Appendices

Don't be afraid to adapt the business plan outline

Each of these sections is described below, along with the questions you should try to answer in each. Be aware that some questions will not be pertinent to your business and can be disregarded. Conversely, each business has certain unique operating circumstances that need to be described but cannot be included in a general outline like the one above. The outline presented is a general, well-accepted one. Don't be afraid to adapt it to convey any unique aspects of your business.

Business plans should contain enough detail to allow an expert to assess the venture as well as sufficient explanation, possibly in an appendix, to let a non-expert clearly understand how the business is supposed to work. Pictures and diagrams are typically quite helpful. Libraries usually carry books on how to write business plans that include worksheets and sample business plans.

The Utah Small Business Development Center periodically runs courses on creating a business plan. You receive weekly feedback on the progress of your plan and a final evaluation at the end of the course.

The registration fee is usually $95. For information and/or registration call the Utah SBDC at (801) 581-7905.

Executive Summary

The executive summary, in one to two pages, should catch the reader's attention and give an overview of the plan. Three elements are of critical interest to a potential investor—the market opportunity, the management team, and the financial returns. These need to be described in this section. If you are trying to raise money, you need to describe the terms of investments that you are seeking. Potential investors always read the summary first to determine if the plan merits a complete reading. If you don't make a good presentation up front, you will probably lose the investor. If you aren't seeking to raise capital, the summary is still important because you need to clarify the basics of your business.

The executive summary, in one to two pages, should catch the reader's attention and give an overview of the plan

The Company and Its Overall Strategy

You have to start the plan somewhere, and a short history of the company (or idea of the company) and backgrounds of the people involved make sense. Keep the backgrounds short, since you will be describing management in detail later on in the plan. The following questions are typically addressed:

- How and when did the company (or idea) get started?
- What has been the development process? What stage is the company at now-- still working on prototype, patent approved, sales achieved, etc.?
- How did major players in the company get involved?
- Briefly, what are the firm's products and services?
- What is the current opportunity?

In this first section, you must describe the opportunity the company faces

Next, you want to describe your company's general strategy. The analysis supporting your choice of strategy will be included in the following sections in the plan. Review Chapter 9, Strategic Planning, in writing this section. Answers to the following questions can be included:

- What growth stages do you foresee in the next three years? Will you be opening other branches, expanding sales to other areas, vertically integrating, adding people, etc.?
- What industry(s) will you compete in? Will that change over time?
- What are your primary advantages over competitors?
- Which of the following strategies will you follow-- cost leadership, differentiation, focus, or a combination? How will you make that

strategy work?
- If you need to raise money, how do you intend to do it?
- What are your (and any partners') personal goals for the business?

The Market and Competitors

In this section, you must establish that markets exist for your products and that you are able to enter those markets and successfully compete. There are three primary components of this section—industry analysis, competitor analysis, and customer analysis. Each is described below.

Industry Structure. The structure of an industry has a large impact on the success of firms in it. You should thoroughly understand this structure before deciding on your company's strategy. Industry structural analysis is described in detail in Chapter 9. Answers to the following questions may be important to convey in this section of the business plan:

- What are total sales in the industry?
- What is the growth in the industry?
- What are typical gross margins?
- What is the average profitability in the industry?
- What entry barriers exist?
- What industry driving forces exist?
- What strategic groups exist in the industry? What are the characteristics of the strategic groups? (answer the questions above for each group)
- What do firms have to do well to succeed in the industry?

Competitor Analysis. To survive and succeed, you must compete with other companies in the marketplace. Very few firms need not monitor nor react to competitors' moves. Chapter 9, Strategic Planning, discusses competitor analysis. Review that chapter before writing this section. First, decide what is important to do to be successful in your industry, then evaluate how other companies in your industry rate on those factors. What are the strengths and weaknesses of major competitors? A table is often the best way to present your evaluation. You need to evaluate companies against each other. Several firms in your industry may have high-quality products, but which one(s) is known as the quality leader? Which is (are) the most efficient and can keep costs below others? Answers to the following questions can be used in your Competitor Analysis section:

The structure of an industry has a large impact on the success of firms in it

For all major competitors, evaluate:

- What is the quality of their products and services?
- What is their reputation?
- Are their customers brand loyal?
- How wide is their product line?
- What type of warranty do they offer?
- How do they distribute their products?
- How large is their market share?
- How well do they market their products?
- How efficient is their manufacturing operation?
- Do they have good research and development skills?
- Do they have patents which give them an advantage?
- Do they have strong financial resources?
- Do they have good managers?

Again, what is important is comparison of competitors, not merely a description of each.

You need to understand customers and what motivates them to buy a product like yours

Customer Analysis. To be successful, you must sell to customers. If you understand customers and what motivates them to buy a product like yours, you will be better able to design your product and present it to them so that they will buy. In this section of the plan, you are trying to describe in detail who your customers are. If you are not able to answer most of the questions posed below, you need to do some marketing research. Chapter 4 describes means of obtaining information about customers.

A very important point made in Chapter 10 is that you may be selling to several different target markets. For example, an all-terrain-vehicle (ATV) manufacturer may be selling to farmers, recreationalists, the Forest Service, and other groups. Each of them has somewhat distinct needs, and each certainly needs to be approached in a different fashion. Each of these groups requires a different marketing strategy. Therefore, if you are selling to more than one target market, you must describe each in this Customer Analysis section. Answers to the following questions can be used in this section:

For each target market:

- What type of people purchase your products?
- What ages?
- Sex?
- Income groups?
- Married vs. single?

- Where do they live?
- How often do they usually buy?
- How much do they usually spend?
- How price sensitive are they?
- How quality conscious are they?
- What features do they want?
- How much service do they need (and are willing to pay for)?
- Where do they shop for this type of product?
- Do they do much comparison shopping?
- What types of promotion reach them?
- What TV programs do they watch?
- What radio stations do they listen to?
- Do they read a newspaper?
- What trade journals do they read?
- How brand loyal are they?
- How satisfied are they with current products?

Analyze customers in *each* of your target markets

There are many other questions that could be asked concerning customers. The key in this section is to relate who customers are and what their thought processes are when they buy products like yours.

Talk to the "middle people" that you will need to deal with and understand what motivations they have in choosing suppliers

Analysis of "middle people." Many businesses do not sell directly to customers. Rather, they sell products to distributors and/or retailers who in turn resell the products. It is just as critical to know what is important to these people in their buying decisions as what the final consumers want. A good example of this is the grocery business. Grocers have the ability to carry a large number of products that they can obtain from many distributors, but they have limited shelf space. The grocers evaluate more than just the products when deciding which ones to carry. They want to know what type of packaging will be used, how often products will be delivered, if display racks will be provided, what type of payment terms are offered, what type of return policy is provided, etc. Talk to the "middle people" that you will need to deal with and understand what motivations they have in choosing suppliers. The characterization of these people should be included in this Customer Analysis subsection.

Marketing Strategy

Marketing is more than selling, it includes your decisions on target markets, product features, how you will service products, pricing, promotion, and distribution. Your marketing strategy should directly support your overall competitive strategy. If you have chosen a differentiation strategy, your marketing strategy should detail how you will implement that strategy in the marketing area. Consider

Nordstroms'. It is differentiatied by quality of clothing, customer service, and the ease and fun in shopping there. Its marketing plan supports that strategy. The store charges premium prices for its clothing and its promotion is targeted to people who can afford the prices. It promotes its products as very high quality and differentiates itself with a no-questions-asked return policy. Its promotional materials reflect this quality. Its compensation system is geared to individual performance of sales people, allowing them to earn incomes that are exceptionally high compared to sales clerks of most stores, thereby motivating them to work very hard at serving customers effectively. That is not to say Nordstroms' is the only "right system." Other stores succeed with different strategies. But the pieces of any system should fit together logically. You should seek consistency such as this in your marketing stategy.

Your marketing strategy should directly support your overall competitive strategy

You need a marketing strategy for each target market that you select. Nordstroms' probably targets several groups. One is the affluent person who wants quality products with the Nordstroms name. Another is the customer who is willing to pay more for the personalized service and no hassle return policy. Each of these groups may require a different marketing strategy. You may not be able to attract both with one strategy. Review Chapter 10, Marketing Strategies, before writing this section of the business plan. For each of the markets that you target, try to answer the following questions:

You need a marketing strategy for each target market that you select

- What features of your product make it better or unique?
- How will it be packaged?
- What type of warranty will be offered?
- What services will be offered along with the products?
- How will products be priced?
- Will prices be changed over time?
- Will quantity discounts be offered?
- How will products be advertised?
- Will you attend trade shows? Which ones?
- Will you print a catalog?
- If you use "middle people," how will you "sell" them on your products?
- Will you use direct marketing? Telemarketing?
- Will you need to offer an "800" number?
- What credit policies will you offer? Will you accept MasterCard, VISA, and other credit cards for payment?
- Will you employ multi-level marketing?
- Will you use your own sales force? How will you train them?
- Will you use manufacturers' reps?

- Will you use distributors?
- If you sell overseas, how will you do it?
- Will you use any other means of distributing your products?

Design and Development Plans

If you have a product or service which needs further design work before it can be put on the market, those plans need to be described in this section. If you are looking to raise money, investors will want to know the state of product development and what needs to be completed. If product development is completed, but you foresee continued product redesign in the next several years, describe those plans. If you have no further product development plans, this section can be omitted. If you do have them, answers to the following questions can be included in this section:

- What is the current status of product development?
- What remains to be finished, and when will it be completed? How much will it cost?
- What product improvements or further design work will be undertaken in the next three years?
- What patents are currently applied for or secured? Are there any others that will be pursued in the future?

Manufacturing and Operations Plan

If you are a manufacturer, this section should first describe how you make your products. Next, you describe how business is to be conducted on a day-to-day basis. If you are not a manufacturer, you will describe just the latter. You show that you know how to "run the business," and are not just theorizing on how the business should operate. Answers to the following questions can be included in this section:

The Operations section describes how your business is run on a more day-to-day basis

- Where will your facility(ies) be located? What advantages does the location hold— labor availability, visibility, proximity to customers, proximity to suppliers, low cost, etc.?
- What type of plant or store facility will you have?
- What type of machinery and equipment will be used?
- Will equipment be purchased or leased?
- Is there room for expansion?
- How much manufacturing will be done on-site, and how much will be subcontracted?
- Will manufacturing be done on a continual, assembly-line process, or will it be a job shop?
- Will inventory be stocked? If so, what inventory control system

will be used?
- How will the business be run on a day-to-day basis?

Management Team

The management team is critical to the success of your business. Be sure to read Chapter 8, Gathering Your Forces, before writing this section of the business plan. As mentioned in that chapter, make sure that your company has skills in the areas of marketing, finance, and production (if you are manufacturing), showing a blend of good technical and managerial skills. You would also like to show that people are experienced in the roles they are filling. Answers to the following questions can be included in this section:

Try to show a balance of skills in your venture

- What is the organizational structure (draw it) of the company?
- What are the general responsibilities of each of the major people in the firm?
- For key management personnel, what is each person's educational background, job experience, or other abilities that suit them for the position they have in the company?
- Which people will be owning partners, and which will be hired employees?
- Who will be on the board of directors? What are their backgrounds?
- Will outside consultants be hired? What are their skills?
- Will profit-sharing or employee stock ownership be offered?

Overall Schedule

In this section, you are writing a schedule of major events to launch your new enterprise. It is important that you project the order and timing of major events in your company's development. Each firm will have a unique set of events to schedule, but the following questions relate to what are major milestones for many businesses. If some of them have already occurred, list them and state when it took place.

- When will the company be incorporated?
- When will design and development be completed?
- When will patents be secured?
- When will prototypes be completed?
- When will the plant/store be completed?
- When will sales first occur?
- What will be the trend in sales growth?
- When will additional people be brought in?
- When and where will sales be expanded geographically?

Critical Risks and Problems

Describe how you would deal with potential problems

Every business has its risks. The purpose of this section is to force you to think about the major risks in your undertaking and to plan how you will address those potential problems. If you are trying to raise money, you might wonder how wise it is to point out potential problems to investors. They are going to think of them, anyway, so you may as well come right out and show that you have thought about them and have some kind of game plan for dealing with them. The following list of questions is by no means exhaustive of the types of risks that businesses face, but they are fairly common ones.

- What if competitors react by dropping prices?
- What happens if sales projections are not met?
- Can costs be substantially higher than projected?
- Is there a good chance that supplies will be hard to come by?
- Will it be difficult to get good people to join the organization?
- What if a patent is not obtained?

Describe the three or four most critical risks in your proposed venture, and state what you will do if each occurs. Try to state how you would deal with each potential problem and survive and succeed in spite of it.

The Financial Plan

You need to describe your financial projections and not just grind out pages of numbers

You need to determine that your venture will be a profitable one and that cash flows are sufficient to pay all bills. This section of the business plan needs to describe the major conclusions from four financial statements— breakeven analysis, cash flow statement, income statement, and balance sheet. Review Chapter 11, Cash Management, and Chapter 12, Financial Management, before writing this section. This section should be the *description* of the financial worksheets. The worksheets themselves are included in the section entitled Financial Exhibits. You want to write this section without overwhelming readers with numbers; rather, you want to describe your *general conclusions* of what all the numbers in the financial exhibits mean. A one to two paragraph analysis of each of the four financial statements is appropriate. Your underlying assumptions for generating the worksheets belong with the worksheets themselves, and not in this section.

Lotus 1-2-3 templates for each of these financial analyses are included on the diskette provided with this book. You can generate these financial statements by hand, but with only a beginner's understanding of a computer spreadsheet program you can do it on a computer and greatly speed your work. You can use any spreadsheet program (there are many) that reads 1-2-3 files to work on these templates. A description of the financial templates and instruction in their usage is included in Appendix B, Computer Financial Templates.

Breakeven Analysis. Breakeven analysis lets you know how much you have to sell in order to pay your bills (see Chapter 11 for a detailed description of breakeven analysis). It also tells you what profit or loss you would have at different sales levels. It is only a general estimate. You want to show early in the financial section that you will have enough sales to reach breakeven in a reasonable period of time after startup. Most businesses are not immediately profitable. It may take several months, in some businesses several years. Your cash flow analysis will show how you will survive until your business reaches a breakeven point. State what the breakeven point in sales dollars is and how soon the firm will reach it. If your sales projections grow quite larger than breakeven volume, state how much profit would be generated at those sales levels. If it is very difficult for you to accurately predict sales levels for your company, relate how much profit or loss would occur at several different possible sales levels.

Use the computer financial templates in Appendix B to generate your financial projections

Cashflow Analysis. Cash is the lifeblood of a business. You don't necessarily go broke by not making a profit. You go broke by not having enough cash to pay your bills. In the early years of a business, you should pay more attention to the cash flow statement than the income statement.

In this section of the plan, you are describing the cash position of the company for the next three years. The first year is usually broken down by months, and years two and three are broken down by quarter. You want to state the beginning cash position, the general trends in cash position, and causes of any major fluctuations in cash flow. These could include seasonal sales, capital purchases, taking out or paying off of a loan, owner withdrawal or cash infusion, or any major expenses. If the cash balance becomes low at some point, describe why it happens and how the company will address the problem.

Income Statement. The income statement subtracts expenses from revenues, yielding net profit. Profits provide returns to investors and are a source of capital to build your company. In this section of the business plan, you want to describe the trend in profits over a three-year projected period and also the major determinants of profits. Describe trends in sales, gross margin, major expenses, and net profit.

Explain any major fluctuations in profits over the three-year period. Several financial ratios are important to relate. Return on sales, return on equity, return on assets, and gross margin percentage should be stated.

Pay more attention to the cash flow statement than the income statement

Balance Sheet. The balance sheet shows what your company owns, what it owes, and the difference between them— which is called net worth. You should project a balance sheet at startup and after one, two, and three years. In this section of the plan, you should describe your major observations of trends in the balance sheets. Growth in assets, debt, and equity should be cited. A few financial ratios and their trends should be stated. The current ratio gives an indication of the liquidity of the firm. Debt/equity measures the amount of borrowing that supports the company. Inventory turnover and days receivable indicate how well those current assets are managed. You would like to be able to compare the ratios to industry standards and demonstrate the financial soundness of your company.

Proposed Company Offering

This section is included only if you are trying to raise capital by borrowing or by getting people to invest on an equity basis. Chapter 7, Raising Capital, discusses strategies for raising money. If you want to borrow money, state how much you need, when it will be paid back, and what you will use it for. If you know what you intend to offer for collateral, state that.

Be aware that investment terms are usually negotiable

If you are seeking equity investments, you need to describe what you are proposing. Be aware that investment terms are negotiable, hence your proposed offering is only a starting point. State how many shares you are selling, what the selling price is, and what owners' resultant percentage of ownership would be. Equity investors are typically looking to cash out of the investment in a three to ten year period, and you should describe how that will be a possibility for them. Chapter 14, Harvesting a Business, describes different means of getting cash out of an investment in a company.

Financial Exhibits

The financial exhibits in your business plan should include a breakeven analysis and graph, pro forma cash flow statements, pro forma income statements, and pro forma balance sheets. The breakeven analysis is usually done only for the first year. A sample breakeven analysis is shown Exhibit 13-1 with corresponding graph in Exhibit 13-2. The cash flow and income statement projections are done on a monthly basis in the first year and by quarter in years two and three. Sample pro forma cash flow statements, income statements, and balance sheets are shown in Figures 13-3 through 13-7. The major assumptions you use to arrive at your projections should be included with the financial exhibits and *not* in the financial section of the plan.

Conclusion

Writing a business plan is a formidable task. You have noticed in this chapter references to almost every other chapter in the book. If you write a thorough business plan, you know the business inside and out. Take the time to research and write the business plan. Once you have done it, continue to update it and keep it current. There is a tendency to forego continued planning once your venture is started because you get too busy to keep up with it. Believe the experts— continue to refine your plan. A sample business plan is shown in Appendix B. Listed below are a list of "Do's and Don'ts" from Timmons' *New Venture Creation*. [2].

1. Do keep the business plan as short as you can without compromising the description of your venture and its potential. Cover the key issues that will interest an investor, and leave the details of secondary importance for a meeting with an investor. Remember, venture capitalists are not patient readers.

2. Don't overdiversify your venture. Focus your attention on one or two product lines and markets. A new or young venture does not have the management depth to pursue a number of opportunities.

3. Don't have unnamed, mysterious people on your management team, such as Mr. G., who is currently a financial vice president but will join you later. The investor will want to know early on exactly who Mr. G. is and what his commitment is to your venture.

4. Don't describe technical products or manufacturing processes in a way and with a jargon that only an expert can understand. A venture capitalist does not like to invest in what he doesn't understand or what he thinks you don't understand because you can't explain it to a smart fellow like himself.

5. Don't estimate your sales on the basis of what you can or would like to produce. Do estimate carefully your potential sales, and from these determine the production facility you need.

6. Don't make ambiguous, vague, or unsubstantiated statements. They make you look like a shallow and fuzzy thinker. For example, don't merely say that your markets are growing rapidly. Determine and delineate past, present, and projected growth rates and market size.

7. Do disclose and discuss any current or potential problems in your venture. If you fail to do this and the venture capitalist discovers them, your credibility will be badly damaged.

8. Do involve all of your management team in the preparation of the business plan, as well as any special legal, accounting, or financial help that you may need.

9. Don't claim that you have no competition, or indicate that you expect to "get rich quick." Both are good ways to turn off investors and others who know better.

References

1. Rich, Stanley R. and Gumpert, David E. *Business Plans That Win $$*. New York: Harper and Row, 1985.

2. Timmons, Jeffry A. *New Venture Creation*, 2nd Edition. Homewood, Illinois: Irwin, 1985.

Business Plan Financial Projection Templates

Pages 190-196

Figure 13-1. Sample Breakeven Analysis

COSTS	FIXED AMOUNT	VARIABLE %
RAW MATERIALS		0.30
DIRECT LABOR		0.20
MERCHANDISE		
WAGES & SALARIES	9000	
PAYROLL EXPENSES	1800	
SUPPLIES	500	
REPAIRS & MAINTENANCE		
ADVERTISING	500	
CAR, DELIVERY, TRAVEL	300	
ACCOUNTING & LEGAL	200	
RENT/LEASE	1000	
TELEPHONE	150	
INSURANCE	100	
UTILITIES	150	
TAXES-REAL ESTATE, ETC	200	
DEPRECIATION	400	
OTHER EXPENSES	700	
TOTALS	15000	0.50

BREAKEVEN POINT =	30,000
PRICE/UNIT =	75.00
BREAKEVEN POINT IN UNITS =	400

Figure 13-2. Sample Breakeven Graph

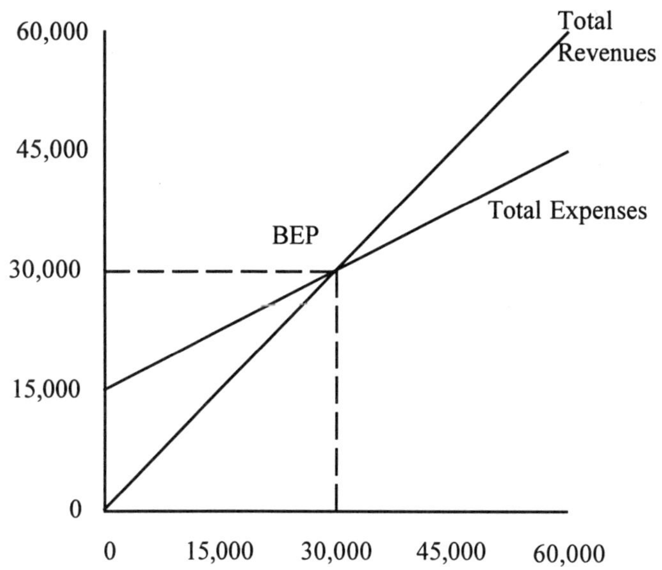

Figure 13-3. One Year Cash Flow Projection

Period	Jan	Feb	Nov	Dec	Total
Cash on Hand (Beg of Month)					
Cash Receipts					
(A)Collections					
(B)Int & Misc					
(C)Loan, Contrib					
Tot Cash Rcpts					
Tot Cash Avail					
Expenses					
Purchases					
Payroll					
Payroll Expenses					
Outside Expenses					
Supplies					
Repairs/Maintnce					
Advertising					
Auto & Travel					
Accounting, Legal					
Rent					
Telephone					
Utilities					
Insurance					
Taxes					
Interest					
Other Expenses					
Subtotal					
Loan Prin Payment					
Capital Purchase					
Start-up Costs					
Reserve/Escrow					
Owner Withdrawal					
Tot Cash Pd Out					
Cash Position					

Figure 13-4. Cash Flow Projection for Years 2 & 3

Period	Qtr 1	Qtr 2	Qtr 3	Qtr 4	Tot Yr2	Qtr1	Tot Yr3
Cash on Hand (Beg of Month)							
Cash Receipts							
(A)Collections							
(B)Int & Misc							
(C)Loan, Contrib							
Tot Cash Rcpts							
Tot Cash Avail							
Expenses							
Purchases							
Payroll							
Payroll Expenses							
Outside Expenses							
Supplies							
Repairs/Maintnce							
Advertising							
Auto & Travel							
Accounting, Legal							
Rent							
Telephone							
Utilities							
Insurance							
Taxes							
Interest							
Other Expenses							
Subtotal							
Loan Prin Payment							
Capital Purchase							
Start-up Costs							
Reserve/Escrow							
Owner Withdrawal							
Tot Cash Pd Out							
Cash Position							

Figure 13-5. One Year Income Statement Projection

Period	Jan	Feb	Nov	Dec	Total
Revenues					
Cost of Sales					
Gross Profit					
Expenses					
Payroll					
Payroll Expenses					
Supplies					
Outside Expenses					
Repairs & Maintence					
Advertising					
Auto & Travel					
Accounting, Legal					
Rent					
Telephone					
Utilities					
Insurance					
Taxes					
Interest					
Other Expenses					
Depreciation					
Total Expenses					
Net Profit					

Figure 13-6. Income Statement Projection for Years 2 & 3

	Qtr 1	Qtr 2	Qtr 3	Qtr 4	Tot Yr2	Qtr1	Tot Yr3
Revenues							
Cost of Sales							
Gross Profit							
Expenses							
Payroll							
Payroll Expenses							
Supplies							
Outside Expenses							
Repairs & Maintence							
Advertising							
Auto & Travel							
Accounting, Legal							
Rent							
Telephone							
Utilities							
Insurance							
Taxes							
Interest							
Other Expenses							
Depreciation							
Total Expenses							
Net Profit							

Figure 13-7. Projected Balance Sheets for 3 Years

ASSETS	Startup	End Year 1	End Year 2	End Year 3
Current Assets				
Cash				
Accounts Rec				
Inventory				
Tot Current Assets				
Fixed Assets				
Land				
Building				
Less Dep				
Equipment				
Less Dep				
Furn & Fixtures				
Less Dep				
Total Fixed Assets				
Total Assets				
LIABILITIES				
Current Debt				
Accounts Payable				
Notes Payable				
Taxes Payable				
Total Current Liabilities				
Longterm Debt				
Mortgage				
Notes Payable				
Total Longterm Debt				
Total Debt				
Equity				
Total Debt + Equity				

14

Harvesting a Business

The sign of a true entrepreneur is his ability to plan how to get out of a business at some point with cash in his pocket. This requires building value in the enterprise. In general, most entrepreneurs do not intend to run one business all of their lives. The thrill lies in undertaking new ventures. To have this liberty, you must be able to *harvest* the old business. Harvesting is simply drawing cash from the business and need not necessarily involve selling it. Six harvest strategies are described in this chapter:

1. The outright sale of the business
2. The cash cow
3. The management buyout
4. The merger
5. The employee stock ownership plan (ESOP)
6. The public offering

Most entrepreneurs do not intend to run one business all of their lives

The Outright Sale

This option leaves you the most freedom of pursuing other ventures. Ideally, you would like the entire sale price in cash up front. In many cases, the potential buyer will offer a package that is less attractive. It may include balloon payments, carrying a contract, stock ownership, and/or stock options for you. You need to decide how badly you want to sell the business. Each of these options means less liquidity for you. There are thousands of business owners in this country running firms that they had sold on contract and later received back because the new owners could not make it.

How much is your business worth? There are a variety of methods to quantitatively calculate the value of your business, and two are discussed below. But don't forget, *your business is worth what someone is willing to pay for it.* You may have a great business selling caribou hides out of northern Alaska, but when it comes time to sell the business you may have trouble finding someone willing to live at 70 degrees North Latitude. Conversely, you may be able to sell a professional baseball team at a far higher price than its cash flow could justify because people find it glamorous to own such a business. Three commonly used methods of calculating the value of a business are described below.

Your business is worth what someone is willing to pay for it

The Net Worth of Your Business. The most straightforward means of calculating the value of your business is to subtract the amount of debt you have from the value of your assets, which results in your net worth. Calculating debt is easy. Calculating *accurate* asset values is not. For example, if you own a restaurant you will show kitchen equipment as assets on your balance sheet. If you tried to sell the equipment, you probably couldn't get much for used equipment. Therefore, the listed value on the balance sheet may be much different than its true value. The same principle applies to real estate. Accounting rules state that you must list it at its original purchase price. If you have owned the property for a few years, chances are that it has appreciated. When you use this method, try to list assets at their true value, instead of at their book value.

Many business sellers will put "goodwill" as an asset on their balance sheet. Goodwill is the added value of a business beyond what assets are worth. Accountants shudder at the term, and in some cases the extra value does not exist, while in others it truly does. As an example, a software company may have value far beyond the worth of its assets if its software has significant sales potential. Yes, the company is worth more than its net worth, and goodwill definitely exists. Its value is difficult to calculate. Ironically, "badwill" has never been listed on a seller's balance sheet. Certainly it exists also.

Valuations of your business are only estimates

Discounted Cash Flows. This method of business valuation assumes that buying a business is no different than investing in other assets, such as stocks and bonds. You need to look at the stream of cash flows that the asset generates and then *discount* the amount of the cash to present day values. For example, the value of $1000 given to you five years from now is not nearly the value of $1000 given to you today. If you invested the $1000 today in a bond yielding 8 percent and let it sit for five years, it would be worth $1469 in five years. Clearly, you have to adjust for the timing of cash flows to make them comparable. What is the current value of receiving $1000 five years from now? If 8 percent is the rate you can earn, $681 today would be worth $1000 in five years. Therefore, $681 is the *present value* of the future cash flow. It is calculated by discounting the future cash flow.

To determine the present value of a business, you discount its future cash flows. Review Chapter 11, Cash Management, on the differences between profits and cash flow. You may wonder how far into the future to project cash flows, since theoretically the business could exist infinitely. Discounting reduces to almost nothing the value of cash flows far in the future. Fifteen to twenty-five years is reasonable. Included on the diskette provided with this book is a Lotus 1-2-3 template entitled NPV (for net present value). The template steps you through the process of calculating the net present value of future cash flows.

The final selling price of your business will probably be between the discounted cash flow value and the net worth of the business

Projecting future cash flows is not easy, especially when you try to do it fifteen to twenty-five years into the future. If you look at current cash flow, project inflation and a growth rate, you will come up with a reasonable cash flow projection. You and your potential buyer will have to argue over how reasonable the numbers are. If you plug those numbers into the NPV program, it determines a net present value for you. For example, a business that shows a positive cash flow of $10,000 in each of the next ten years and then a positive cash flow of $15,000 in each of years 11 through 15 has a calculated net present value of approximately $105,000 if the discount rate is 8 percent. The *discount rate* is somewhere between what you can get if you invest your money in a fairly safe investment and what the bank lending rate is to you.

Calculate the worth of your business using both the net worth and net present value methods. The value of your business is *probably* in between the values each of these methods generates. Again, the *real value* of your business is the price that you and a buyer agree upon. Remember also that the *terms* of the deal are just as important as the selling price. If you are able to get cash up front, a lower price may be a far better deal than one which you have to finance a large part of and/or accept part ownership.

Multiple of Earnings

Multiple of earnings method assumes that the worth of your business should be based on its income, and not on its net worth. The value of the business is its current income times a certain multiplier. The multiplier varies by industry and by region. For example, a bakery at St. George may sell at a multiple of three times earnings, while a software company in Provo may sell at twenty times earnings.

There are experienced brokers who can derive the value of your business from its potential growth, strategic direction, estimate of future net income, and intangible assets like goodwill. Since, you will obviously get more out of your business if you have several or many people bidding for it, it makes very good sense to get a reputable business broker involved. While they will charge a fee (sometimes even an up-front fee to make a valuation as well as a presentation booklet), they also will expose your business to many more potential buyers than you might do by attempting to sell the firm yourself. Before dealing with a specific broker, get particulars on how many companies they sold last year, what their total sales volume was, and who specifically they worked with.

Business brokers usually can expose your business to far more potential buyers than you would be able to

The Cash Cow

A *cash cow* is a business which generates cash flows beyond what it needs to operate and grow. This excess cash is at the owners' disposal to invest in other ventures (or vacation homes or whatever). Not a lot of businesses are in this enviable position. Usually the opposite is true. Even succcessful, growing businesses frequently run short of cash. Nonetheless, some firms can become cash cows and allow their owners to either use the cash or the borrowing capacity of the business to start other companies.

Cash cows are usually established high-margin businesses. Growth is not significant, and the firm usually has either high market share or a very strong reputation. The past efforts that went into designing products and/or creating markets can be curtailed and the rewards of previous hard work are reaped.

The Management Buyout

Many managers dream of owning the company where they work. They know the business. The problem in selling to them is that they usually do not have a lot of cash to purchase the business. As a result, most management buyouts are done with small amounts of cash down and a large note with the old owner. If you are selling to a manager or managers of your business, try to get as much cash down as possible. When settling on a selling price, use the methods outlined in the section above.

The problem in selling to management is that they don't usually have a lot of cash in their pockets

If you do sell the business on contract, at least you know the management skills of the new owners. Some management buyout contracts have provisions that pay a portion of profits to the former owners. These can be advantageous to you if the company prospers, but you need to be careful. As mentioned many times in this book, accountants can legally change the profits of a company by using different accounting conventions. Profits of the company can be manipulated to avoid having to pay you. Consult a good business attorney and write in the contract how profits are to be calculated. Some management buyouts are done gradually. For several years, managers buy in gradually to the business. You and the managers can see how it is working before deciding on a final buy-out contract.

Some management buyouts are done gradually

The Merger or Acquisition

Being bought by or merging with another company is a special type of "outright sale." Several companies in Utah have been acquired by larger firms. The most distinctive merger in 1993 was Southwest Airlines' acquisition of Morris Air in a stock deal worth some $130 million. Morris Air had a strategy similar to Southwest Airlines—that of targeting low-budget passengers who would not ordinarily fly the higher-priced major carriers. The linkage of the two airline systems, which do not compete with one another, enables Southwest to provide even lower-fare competition, more quickly, to an expanded geographic area and to more American consumers. There is no question that this is a pro-competitive, pro-consumer joinder between the two companies.

In June 1993 Megahertz Corporation merged into a newly formed subsidiary of VyStar Group, Inc. while retaining the Megahertz Corporation title. This merger has simplified corporate structure, facilitated the offering of common stock, and provided new resources to finance capital necessary for growth.

The announcement of Novell Inc. on March 21, 1994, that the company agreed to acquire WordPerfect for $1.4 billion in stock and Borland International's spreadsheet business for $145 million will create a stronger competition against its archirival Microsoft. It will enable Novell to compete virtually on all fronts with a Washington based company. The acquisition by Novell is considered by many analysts the best way for WordPerfect to go public.

Mergers and acquisitions bring insiders from Utah home-grown industries major financial rewards. The founders and other significant insiders are (will be) the prime benefactors of these deals.

Buyouts usually have special terms. In many cases, the acquiring company will want you to stay on as a manager of the company and will expect you to sign non-competing clauses, making it illegal for you to start another company in the same industry. You usually retain some ownership in the company as an incentive to have the firm prosper. In some cases you may exchange stock with the larger company. In doing so, its more liquid stock is easier to sell and provides the "harvest."

The Employee Stock Ownership Plan (ESOP)

ESOP's have become increasingly popular in small and mid-size companies. They allow employees to purchase shares of the business. From a motivational standpoint, it gets employees committed to the long-term success of the firm. From a harvest standpoint, it allows owners to achieve liquidity through sales of stock to the plan and to employees. Although such a plan does not provide for a total sale of the business, it can provide some liquidity to current owners.

The Public Offering

Public stock offerings are complicated and expensive. Few companies do it. In 1983, the best year for small company new stock offerings, only 888 companies "went public." For a company that is able to do it, however, relatively large amounts of money can be raised and owners can achieve a high level of liquidity. Chapter 7, Raising Capital, discusses the public offering process in detail.

Conclusion

The most important aspect of a harvest strategy is to plan it in advance

The most important aspect of a harvest strategy is to plan it in advance. Granted, in the early years of your venture you are too busy building it to worry about harvesting it. But after year three, if you are interested at all in eventually harvesting, you should begin to think about how it will be done. Nearly all of the six approaches to harvesting described above take considerable time to orchestrate. You might consider a plan that allows you to cash out of the business in years seven through ten.

Even though you may not be able to conceive getting out of the business after a few years, realize that your feelings may change over time. After many years in a business, people burn out or get bored and then want a change badly. You should *not want to sell badly* when you go to sell. Buyers sense this and will offer you less. Be patient.

Industry and economic conditions greatly affect what price you can get for your company. If you are in a rush, you will probably make some foolish mistakes.

If you get an offer, try to evaluate it objectively. Your emotions are so tied up in your business that this may be difficult to do; however, realize that most people believe their businesses are worth far more than they truly are. Don't be greedy. Many entrepreneurs have turned down initial offers condescendingly and later accepted lower offers out of desperation.

Lastly, do a thorough job in seeking out advice on harvesting. Most business brokers, like real estate agents, are motivated by the commission on the sale. They would rather get a sale, at a lower price, than no sale at all. Plus, they are sometimes not involved in long-term planning for a harvest— they would like to see a sale in the next six months. This is not a criticism of brokers, but it is the reality of the system in which they work. Ask around about who might be able to give advice on harvesting. Be persistent and patient in finding them. Wise counsel is important.

References

1. Timmons, Jeffry A. *New Venture Creation*, 3rd Edition. Homewood, Illinois: Irwin, 1990.

2. *Growing Concerns*, ed. David Gumpert. New York: John Wiley & Sons, 1984.

15

The Utah Economy

In Chapter 9— Strategic Planning— location factors affecting a new enterprise were discussed as well as the importance of national and local economic matters. Utah remains a relatively small state population-wise (approximately 2 million people) with low per capita income and only average household income. Both factors may constitute a drawback for certain types of retail or distribution businesses. Nonetheless, the general economic climate for business as of early 1995 is good— very good— and will be addressed in this final chapter.

The Utah economy is currently one of the most vigorous in the nation, and state and local government seem dedicated to sustaining this growth, even accelerating it in order to provide a higher standard of living for all Utahns. However, many believe careful planning will be required to make sure that growth does not impinge unfavorably on the quality environment which is nurturing this job growth. Utah's sustainable advantages for economic development fall into the following five categories: workforce, education, technology development, quality of life, and favorable business climate.

Workforce

Utah is one of the fastest growing labor markets

Utah currently has the fastest growth rate in the United States. Salt Lake City's labor force, ranked first in the nation by *Fortune* magazine, is large and well-educated. Utah has one of the strongest economies in the country, with its job base in 1994 expanding over 3 percent for the 7th consecutive year.

During 1994 Utah businesses added a record 50,000 new non-farm jobs, business bankruptcies for the final nine months of 1994 were down 5 percent over the same period in 1993, personal income grew 8.7 percent and unemployment remained at a low 3.7 percent. Economists are predicting a continued increase in personal income of about 7.4 percent in 1995. Employment for 1995 is forecasted to increase about 4.3 percent. The only areas of decline have been in defense and defense-related manufacturing, and mining. The sharp job growth is closely related to improvements in information technology, construction and service sectors of the Utah economy.

Since 1986, the number of jobs in Utah's information technology sector has doubled

The number of jobs in Utah's information technology sector is now estimated to be 44,500, while the number of computer and telecommunications companies along the "info-tech corridor", as officials dub the 100-mile stretch from Provo to Logan, has jumped from about 450 to some 1,500. These companies developing, producing and selling computer hardware, software and communications products and services, had $5.3 billion in revenue in 1992, an 8 percent increase over 1991. In 1993, the information technology industry in Utah had about $6 billion in sales. Workers in these industries earned an average of $35,136, 57 percent higher than the average of the state's non-agriculture wage of $22,400. Industry leaders are projecting 10,800 more employees in the next three years. Presently, 68 percent of Utah's information technology companies are located in Salt Lake County. They employ 66 percent of the industry's workers and generate 55 percent of the revenue.

Utah's population growth is more than double that of the nation

The construction sector, both residential and nonresidential, reached record levels during 1994. Population growth, enhanced by net in-migration, strong economic and job growth, and low mortgage rates, were all contributors to the robust construction economy. Projected to be about 2.4 percent for 1995, Utah's population growth is more than double that of the nation.

Residential construction should slow in 1995 because of higher interest rates, less migration and more moderate job growth. Vacancy rates will remain low and, as a result, demand for multifamily housing will remain relatively strong. Nonresidential construction should experience another strong year in 1995. Continued work on the Kennecott expansion and low vacancy rates for industrial, office, and retail buildings will keep nonresidential values high [1].

The Utah workforce is known for its low unionization (fewer than 5 percent of manufacturing employees are affiliated with unions), earning wages lower than the U.S. average. Like its neighboring states, Utah has relatively low average annual pay compared to the nation. For example, in 1993, per capita personal income of $16,140 ranked only 48th among the 50 states. Nonetheless, for the sixth straight year, Utah has been gaining ground with respect to the nation in this economic measure. Utah's low wage levels are largely the result of demographic and social factors, including: (1) a much higher proportion of young and part-time workers, (2) a higher female labor force participation rate, and (3) the lower union affiliation.

Looking at another measure— median household income— Utah appears in a somewhat more favorable light where it ranks 21st among the 50 states [1]. For "employers", these figures make for more economic operations. However, for "sellers" of retail and other services locally, the impact may be negative and needs to be considered along with other demographic information in your new venture plans.

Education

Utah claims the nation's highest literacy rate at 94 percent. Also, Utah ranks second in the nation in percent of persons 25 years and older who have completed high school—85.1 percent. It has a young workforce and will continue to have a work force younger than the national average.

Utah claims the nation's highest literacy rate at 94 percent

Technology Opportunities

The Provo/Orem area has the nation's third largest cluster of high-tech companies after Silicon Valley and North Carolina's Research Triangle Park. Also, most of the population and information systems jobs reside in the 35-mile stretch between Salt Lake City and Provo. Nearly half of the high-tech companies in the Salt Lake City/Provo area are PC software developers. It is possible that this "clean industry" was a major factor in the U.S. Conference of Mayors naming Provo "1991 America's Most Livable City". Provo was also named "1991 America's Most Livable Community" by *Money* magazine.

The Provo/Orem area has the nation's third largest cluster of high-tech companies

Salt Lake City has an excellent economy which is based mostly on high-tech and biomedical companies. The Corporation for Enterprise Development has named Utah as the fourth best state in the nation in which to start a small business. Utah's highest score came in development capacity, and was ranked second in the nation in that category.

Quality of Life

Salt Lake City boasts a wealth of fine local and national entertainment as well as many dance clubs. Utah arts enthusiasts enjoy a unique mix of performing arts groups including the Utah Symphony, Ballet West, the Utah Opera Company and the Mormon Tabernacle Choir. Utah's culture emphasizes a family and community lifestyle enhanced by a low violent crime rate. Utah is well known around the country for its national parks and outdoor opportunities and is also home to the U.S. Ski Team. The Wasatch mountain range contains a great number of ski resorts with international reputations.

Weather in winter is mild, and winter facilities are easily and quickly accessed. Salt Lake City is within 20-35 minutes of most ski resorts. This makes the city an ideal site for major winter sports events; Salt Lake City has been selected by the U.S. Olympic Committee as America's bid city for the 2002 Winter Olympic Games. But Utah sport life is not exclusively focused on winter sports. Utah's professional sports teams include NBA's Utah Jazz and the Buzz of the Pioneer Baseball League.

General Business Climate

Utah was recognized in 1991 by *Financial World* magazine as being the best fiscally managed state. Utah is considered pro-business. Financial incentives include an exemption of sales and use taxes on the purchase or lease of new equipment or machinery and a number of other financial incentives and services are available to companies relocating or expanding operations in the area. Utah businesses pay no inventory or worldwide unitary taxes. The corporate franchise tax in Utah is 5 percent of net taxable income. The Economic Development Office offers a number of programs beneficial to businesses. Among others, the Foreign Trade Zone service in Salt Lake City (a customs port city) allows duties to be deferred or reduced. Additionally, Utah's Freeport Law excludes ad valorem taxes on inventories of any kind. "Custom Fit Training" helps subsidize company training expenses by using state and federal funds. Redevelopment area tax increment financing is used in areas in need of economic revitalization.

Utah is considered by most people to be pro-business

Salt Lake City has excellent infrastructure. It serves as the major western hub for Delta Air Lines, and eight commercial airlines provide daily flights to and from Salt Lake City. Having a major airport five miles from downtown, with extensive service by Delta and Southwest, is a major selling point when promoting the state pro-business policy by encouraging companies to relocate or expand their operations in Utah. Additionally, the area has a well developed railway system, including the Rio Grande Western, Southern Pacific and Union Pacific, and Amtrak serves the area.

Some major companies in Utah are responding to bold future economic forecasts for the Utah economy, and many are planning expansion of their operations. For example Kennecott is continuing a $880 million modernization and expansion of their copper smelter and refinery. The existing smelter will be replaced with the most environmentally clean and efficient smelter in the world. This investment will complete the modernization of the integrated Utah copper operation from mining through refining. The modernized facilities will produce copper at a lower cost than any other major operation in the world. The project will require more than 1,100 construction workers and an additional 2200 jobs in support of the construction for three years. In addition, this investment is expected to generate $80 million in state and local government taxes. This will be one of the largest construction jobs in the country. The contracts, plus materials and equipment purchases, will stimulate substantial economic activity in the State. Kennecott's investment represents by far, the largest private investment ever undertaken in Utah. This decision reflects a confidence in Utah and its economy.

Many companies are planning to expand their operations

Salt Lake City offers attractive growth opportunities not only for existing businesses but also for business buyers. Utah has been emerging from the recession sooner than many areas of the country, and investors recognized that by making a stake in the city to capitalize on its strength and growth potential as a trade and services center. Cooperation between education, government, and business has earned the Salt Lake Metropolitan Area an "A+" from *Fortune* magazine in a recent "Best Cities for Business" article, as well as recognition by *Time*, *Newsweek*, *Inc.* , and *Entrepreneur* magazines as one of the nation's economic bright spots.

Salt Lake City offers attractive growth opportunities not only for existing businesses, but also for buyers

Economists expect Utah's economy to slow down and gradually return to still strong, but more sustainable levels of growth in 1995. The 1994 rate of job growth of 6.2 percent is over one-and-a-half times the historical average of 3.5 percent. Like all booms, Utah's current one will subside. The monthly construction and employment data suggest that Utah's economy peaked in mid-1994 and growth rates are either slowing down or flattening as the year ends.

The construction boom is the major driver in the current expansion. As housing prices rise in response to demand and the impact of higher mortgage rates take effect, the number of new permits issued should fall. The values of both residential and nonresidential construction are expected to decrease in 1996. The scenario of over-building that caused such dramatic decreases in construction in the late 1980's has not repeated itself in the current market. The supply of housing is much more in balance with the demand and bodes well for a smooth, moderate adjustment ahead. Nonresidential construction is not burdened with an oversupply of space, but instead experiences very competitive and strong market forces. This lack of over-building means the expected cooling down in construction should be less severe and more gradual and this will benefit the stability of the overall economy.

The percentage changes in employment, personal income, total wages, retail sales, population, and consumer sentiment, to name just a few, are all expected to decline from 1994 to 1995. These declines are expected to be gradual and moderate and will place Utah's economy in 1995 again as one of the top performers in the country.

Utah's future economy will be significantly impacted by the military base closure process which involves the critical review of two Utah military bases: the Air Logistics Center at Hill Air Force Base and the Defense Depot at Ogden. The Base Closure and Realignment Commission must present its recommendations to the President by mid-1995. Hill Air Force Base is the largest basic employer in the Utah economy and realignment or closure of the base would have serious impacts on the state's economy [1].

References

1. *1995 Economic Report to the Governor*, Utah State Economic Coordinating Committee.

2. Edmondson, Brad. *Children in America.* American Demographics - Desk Reference Series, No.1. February 1994, Page 14.

16

Utah Business Resource Database

On the following pages are descriptions of federal, state, and local public programs which provide assistance to Utah businesses. Programs which offer capital to Utah businesses are also discussed in Chapter 7— Raising Capital.

Contents

State and Local Resources

Business Incubators

Small business incubators are designed to support companies in their pre-startup and startup stages before the companies are able to apply for loans. Small business incubators may also support established firms that wish to begin a new division or subsidiary in manufacturing, mail order, wholesale distribution, etc. Business incubators provide facilities in which small companies may share overhead expenses such as office equipment, support staff, technical and financial advisors, business planning services and assistance in obtaining outside financing.

Contact:

Marie Yoder, Director
Uintah County Economic
Development Incubator Center
134 West Main Street
Vernal, UT 84078
(801) 789-1354

DeLance Squire, Director
Commission for Economic Development in Orem
777 South State Street
Orem, UT 84058
(801) 226-1521

Contact local government offices for information about business incubators operating in other areas.

Centers of Excellence Program

In 1986 Utah began the **Centers of Excellence Program,** which focuses on high-technology research that is being conducted in colleges and universities throughout the state. The primary goals are (1) to accelerate the growth of targeted technologies by assisting research activities within Utah's colleges and universities; (2) to expedite the translation of research products from university laboratories to Utah's economy; and (3) to enhance the image of Utah as a center for technological growth and economic development.

To receive state funding, a center must identify the type of research it will be doing, show that its research has industrial sponsorship, and show that the product will have an impact on Utah's economy. Another requirement is that the research must attract at least $2 of private or federal funds for each dollar of state funds used. At the present time, there are 26 centers conducting research in the following four targeted areas: (1) aerospace technology; (2) biomedical and biotechnology; (3) information technology; and (4) natural resources, including agriculture.

Theratech, a once-fledging company that has developed advanced transdermal drug-delivery systems, known as patches, is the best known high-tech start-up that can trace part of its success to the Centers of Excellence program. The company received $200,000 in financing from Utah eight years ago, and today it employs almost 100 people.

Since starting its Centers of Excellence program in 1986, Utah has invested in a number of businesses, from molecular design to interactive videos. So far, the program has led to the creation of almost 70 new high-tech companies and 2,220 jobs with an average salary of about $28,500; about one third higher than the State's average.

Contact: Mr. G. Michael Alder, Director
Mr. Jerold L. Foote, Deputy Director
Center for Excellence Program
324 South State Street
Salt Lake City, UT 84111
(801)538-8771

SBA 504 Certified Development Companies

Three Utah development companies, located in Salt Lake City and Ogden, lend to small and medium-sized businesses at fixed rates for terms of 10 to 20 years. Companies must create one job for every $35,000 received in financing. A 504 loan is funded through the sale of a debenture that is guaranteed by the U.S. Small Business Administration for up to $750,000 or 40 percent of the total cost of land, buildings, and equipment.

Contacts: Mr. Scott Davis, President
Deseret Certified Development Company
7050 Union Park Center, Suite 570
Midvale, UT 84047
(801) 566-1163
Fax: (801) 566-1632

Mr. Robert Richards, Director
Weber Capital Development Company
2404 Washington Boulevard, Suite 1100
Ogden, UT 84401-2316

(801) 627-1333
Fax: (801) 392-7609

Chambers of Commerce

Chambers of Commerce are an excellent source of business information. Phone numbers of Chambers of Commerce in Utah are:

American Fork	756-5110	Monticello	587-2884
Bear River	257-7585	Mount Pleasant	462-2456
Beaver Valley	438-2975	Nephi Area	623-2411
Blanding	678-2539	Ogden Area	621-8300
Bountiful Area	295-6944	Panguitch	676-2311
Brigham City	723-3931	Park City	649-6100
Cache	752-2161	Payson Area	465-0355
Carbon County	637-2788	Pleasant Grove	785-3400
Cedar City	586-4484	Provo/Orem	224-3636
Central Valley	263-2632	Richfield	896-4241
Clearfield	825-5893	Roosevelt Area	722-4598
Delta Area	864-4316	Salt Lake Area	364-3631
Emery County	381-2453	Sandy	566-0344
Flaming Gorge	784-3392	South Salt Lake	466-3377
Hurricane Valley	635-2811	Spanish Fork	789-8352
Kaysville	544-4178	Springville	489-4681
Layton	546-1293	St. George Area	628-1658
Magna	250-5685	Sugarhouse	467-0844
Manti	835-9691	Vernal Area	789-1352
Midvale	561-3880	Wasatch	654-3666
Moab	259-7531	West Jordan Area	566-3600
		West Valley City	969-8755

Committee of Consumer Services

The Committee of Consumer Services represents Utah small business and agricultural consumers of gas, electric, or telephone services in utility matters before the Utah Public Service Commission. The committee studies the impact of utility rates and regulatory actions onbusinesses and advocates those actions that will be most beneficial to consumers. Contact:

Dr. Joseph L. Ingles, Administrative Secretary
Committee of Consumer Services
408 Heber M. Wells Building
160 East 300 South
Salt Lake City, UT 84145
(801) 530-6645

Department of Commerce

The Department of Commerce enhances commerce in the state by setting and enforcing fair standards of conduct for business and professionals, assisting in regulation of public utilities, and providing consumer education and assistance. The Department is comprised of seven divisions: Consumer Protection, Corporations and Commercial Code, Occupational and Professional Licensing, Public Utilities, Real Estate and Securities. The Committee of Consumer Services, an independent advocacy for utility matters, is also housed administratively in the Department.

Contact: Department of Commerce
160 East 300 South
P.O. Box 45802
Salt Lake City, UT 84145-0802
(801) 530-6955

Department of Community and Economic Development

The Department of Community and Economic Development has a number of excellent programs that provide assistance to small businesses throughout the state:

The *International Business Development Office* assists businesses by developing marketing efforts, providing technical assistance in exporting, and matching foreign market opportunities with Utah sources.

Contact: Mr. Dan Mabey, Director
International Business Development Office
324 South State Street, Suite 200
Salt Lake City, UT 84111
(801) 538-8737

The *Utah Procurement Outreach Program* helps Utah small businesses bid on federal contracts. The office maintains a bid board for all major federal agencies operating within the state. In addition, this program assists companies in obtaining commercial contracts.

Contact: Mr. James Odle, Director
Federal Procurement Office
324 South State, Suite 235
Salt Lake City, UT 84111
(801) 538-8790

The *Utah Rural Development Program* provides employment alternatives that are not dependent solely on agriculture markets or energy-related industries. The primary goal of this program is to identify and market the economic strengths of rural Utah in a way that will encourage the creation and expansion of Utah businesses.

Contact: Mr. L. Edward Meyer, Director
Utah Rural Development Program
324 South State Street, Suite 230
Salt Lake City, UT 84111
(801) 538-8781

The *Office of Hispanic Affairs*, the *Office of Asian Affairs*, the *Office of Black Affairs*, and the *Office of Indian Affairs*
These programs work to improve the educational, employment, and economic status of minorities in the state. The Office of Hispanic Affairs is charged with overseeing economic development and business-related issues for all minority enterprises in the state. The office works with Utah's Federal Procurement Assistance Office to match federal contracts with Utah minority-owned businesses. The office also sponsors workshops to help minorities do business with the federal government, and publishes the Minority Business Directory, a list of more than 400 minority businesses that is mailed to federal procurement agencies.

Contacts: Mr. Ruben J. Jiminez, Director
Office of Hispanic Affairs
324 South State Street, Suite 250
Salt Lake City, UT 84111
(801) 538-8815

Mr. Will Numkena, Director
Office of Indian Affairs
324 South State Street, Suite 250
Salt Lake City, UT 84111
(801) 538-8808

Ms. Betty Sawyer, Director
Office of Black Affairs
324 South State Street, Suite 250
Salt Lake City, UT 84111
(801)538-8815

Mr. Louie Tong, Director
Office of Asian Affairs
324 South State Street, Suite 250
Salt Lake City, UT 84111
(801)538-8815

Department of Employment Security

The Department of Employment Security provides comprehensive labor market information, including labor supply and demand, hours and earnings, and unemployment rates by county and state. It also provides employers placement assistance through a statewide network of local offices. There is no fee for this service.

Contact: Department of Employment Security
140 East 300 South, 4th Floor
Salt Lake City, UT 84111
(801) 536-7400

Bureau of Economic and Business Research

This office maintains a comprehensive and timely information base on the Utah and Rocky Mountain regional economies and uses computer models for data analysis. Periodicals include (1) *Utah Economic and Business Review*, featuring articles on economic development with monthly selected business statistics; (2) *Utah Construction Report* reporting statistics on construction permits in Utah; (3) *Utah Statistical Abstract*; (4) *Utah Facts* summarizing data supporting economic development; and (5) *County Economic Profiles* containing statistics on Utah's 29 Counties. The Bureau is headquarters for the Travel and Tourism Research Association.

Contact: Bureau of Economic and Business Research
401 Kendall D. Garff Building
University of Utah
Salt Lake City, UT 84112
(801) 581-6333

Economic Development Corp. of Utah

This program works to attract companies to Utah, develops targeted industry strategies for attraction, provides research on the local economy, and assists local businesses in expansion and retention.

Contact: Economic Development Corp. of Utah
215 South State Street, Suite 850
Salt Lake City, UT 84111
(801) 328-8824

Impact, U.S. Department of Commerce

This program provides assistance to minority businesses through programs that provide information, referrals, planning, and loan packaging expertise.

Contact: Impact, U.S. Dept. of Commerce
350 East 500 South, Suite 101
Salt Lake City, UT 84111
(801) 328-8181

Bureau of Indian Affairs, U.S. Department of the Interior

The BIA loan is a direct loan guarantee and non-reimbursable grant designed to assist Indian tribes to expand their businesses and move towards self-sufficiency. The BIA Area Offices serving Utah area are as follows:

Beaver, Sevier, Piute, Iron and Washington Counties:
Contact: Dee Wilcox
BIA Area Office, Box 720
St. George, UT 84771
(801) 674-9720

Duchesne, Uintah, and Tooele Counties:
Contact: Perry Baker, Superintendant
Uintah-Ouray Indian Agency
P.O. Box 130
Fort Duchesne, UT 84026
(801) 722-2406

San Juan County:
Contact: Tom Martin, Credit/Finance Officer
Navaho Area Office
P.O. Box 1060
Gallup, NM 87301
(602) 871-5151, Ext. 5112 (Windowrock, AZ)

Shiprock Agency:
Contact: Wilbert Pioche, Credit/Finance Officer
P.O. Box 966
Shiprock, NM 87420
(505) 368-4427

Western Navaho Agency:

Contact: Leander Kansaswood, Credit/Finance Officer
P.O. Box 127
Tuba City, AZ 86045
(602) 283-4531

Metro Utah

This program aids in the recruitment and expansion of businesses in the metropolitan areas of Utah. Responds to requests for information and distributes a quarterly newsletter, the *Metro Utah News.*

Contact: Metro Utah Inc.
324 South State Street, #500
Salt Lake City, UT 84114-7320
(801) 538-8746

Mountain West Venture Group is a venture capital club which provides a public, non-aligned forum for business development. Investors, entrepreneurs, venture capitalists, and others can readily mingle. The group has no funds of its own to lend. Regular monthly meetings are well attended and a monthly newsletter is published.

Contact: Mountain West Venture Group
50 South Main
P.O. Box 210
Salt Lake City, UT 84144
(801) 521-3200

Office of Women's Business Ownership (OWBO)

OWBO has been established by Small Business Administration in order to assist women business owners. OWBO offers pre-business workshops, conferences, technical and financial information, export and procurement conferences and other forms of business assistance.

Contact: Jean Fox, Business Development Specialist
SBA, 125 South State Street
Salt Lake City, UT 84138
(801) 524-3204

Another related association is:

National Association of Women Business Owners
600 South Federal Street, Suite 400
Chicago, IL 60605

SCORE (Service Corps of Retired Executives)
SCORE is a volunteer program sponsored by the U.S. Small Business Administration. There are chapters throughout the state. They provide the management expertise of volunteer business owners and executives to prospective entrepreneurs and to small businesses.

Contact: SCORE
125 South State
Room 2237 Federal Bldg.
Salt Lake City, UT 84138
(801) 524-3212

Small Business Development Centers
The Utah Small Business Development Center's (USBDC) lead office is hosted by the David Eccles School of Business through its Programs in Emerging Business office at the University of Utah. It is conveniently located in downtown Salt Lake City. The USBDC provides assistance to existing and new businesses, primarily through one-on-one consulting and through specific training programs and seminars. Currently the USBDC has subcenters located at Snow College in Ephraim, Utah State University in Logan, Weber State University in Ogden, College of Eastern Utah in Price, Utah Valley State College in Orem, Southern Utah University in Cedar City, and Dixie College in St. George.

Contact:

Utah Small Business Development Center
Mr. David A. Nimkin, State Director
University of Utah
102 West 500 South, Suite 315
Salt Lake City, UT 84101
(801) 581-7905
Fax: (801) 581-7814

Southern Utah University SBDC
Mr. Greg Powell, Director
351 West Center
Cedar City, UT 84720
(801)586-5401

Weber State University SBDC
Mr. Bruce Davis, Director
School of Business and Economics
3750 South Harrison
Ogden, UT 84408-3806
(801) 626-7232

College of Eastern Utah SBDC
Mr. Gary Ward, Director
Applied Sciences
451 East 400 North
Price, UT 84501
(801) 637-1995

Snow College SBDC
Mr. Lynn Schiffman, Director
345 West First North
Ephraim, UT 84627
(801)283-4021

Utah State University SBDC
Mr. Frank Prante, Director
E. Campus Bldg, Coll of Business
Logan, UT 84322-8330
(801) 750-2277

Utah Valley State College SBDC
Michael Finnerty, Director
800 West 1200 South
Orem, UT 84058
(801)222-8000, ext. 8230

Dixie College SBDC
Mr. Keldon Bauer
225 South 700 East
St. George, UT 84770
(801) 673-4811, ext. 455

Small Business Institutes
A Small Business Institute (SBI) provides free, customized management assistance to small businesses. Senior and graduate students from business colleges act as consultants under the guidance of business faculty advisors. Students consultant groups (usually 4-5 students) work with the small firms for one full quarter. They then provide the business with a written as well as an oral report (e.g., marketing plan, feasibility analysis, new accounting system, etc.). SBIs are located within several Utah colleges:[1] Any small business person may call their local college or university and request assistance:

University of Utah
Dr. Roger H. Nelson, Director
Programs in Emerging Business
David Eccles School of Business
Salt Lake City, UT 84112
(801) 581-7415

Brigham Young Univ
Dr. Keith Hunt, Director
Grad School of Business
660 Tanner Building
Provo, UT 84602
(801) 378-2080

Steven P. Grizzell
Utah Technology Finance Corporation
185 South State Street #208
Salt Lake City, UT 84111
(801) 364-4346

Joe Ollivier
SBI Instructor
P.O. Box 633
Provo, UT 84602

Southern Utah University
Ed Harris, Director
Southern Utah University
351 West Center
Cedar City, UT 84720
(801) 586-5403

Weber State University
Bruce Davis, Director
Center for Business &
Economic Training
Ogden, UT 84408-3815
(801) 626-7232

Utah State University
David Baucus
College of Business UMC 3555
Utah State University
Logan, UT 84322-3555
(801) 797-1658

Small Business Investment Companies (SBICs)
SBIC is a term used to refer to both Small Business Investment Companies and Minority Enterprise Small Business Investment Companies (MESBICs). Both companies are private venture capital firms which are licensed, regulated and partially funded by the Small Business Administration and are primarily focused on first stage financing. SBICs provide funds in smaller amounts than do most venture groups: typical SBIC loans are around $150,000, and may provide loans for less than $100,000. Most SBIC lending is provided through exchange of partial ownership in a company using convertible loans, loans with warrants or convertible bonds. SBICs may also purchase common or preferred stock in companies directly.

There are two SBIC's or MESBIC's currently operating in Utah, they are:

Contact: Wasatch Ventures
(a venture partnership of Zions First Natnl Bank and UTFC)
Managed by Draper & Associates
102 West 500 South
Salt Lake City, UT 84101
(801) 596-0071

First Security Business Investment Corporation
79 South Main Street #800
Salt Lake City, UT 84111

There are about 500 SBICs nationwide, and most of them are members of the National Association of SBICs. Inquiries about Utah and national SBICs can be obtained from the NASBIC offices.

Contact: National Association of Small Business Investment Companies
1199 North Fairfax Street, Suite 200
Alexandria, VA 22314
(703) 683-1601

Utah Association of Women Business Owners

The Salt Lake Chapter of the National Association of Women Business Owners is an organization for current and prospective women business owners. It provides networking, support, and information.

Contact: Veda Barrie, President
Utah Association of Women Business Owners
941 East 3300 South
Salt Lake City, UT 84106
(801) 486-2181

Utah Microenterprise Loan Fund (UMLF)

UMLF is a non-profit corporation organized by local banks and other private and public enterprises in order to provide support and financing to entrepreneurs. At present, UMLF operates in Salt Lake County only. The UMLF offers small moderately-secured loans up to $10,000 along with substantial business development assistance. To register for an informational meeting, call the Utah Small Development Center at (801) 581-7905.

Utah Small Cities Inc.

This program aids in the recruitment and expansion of businesses in the rural areas of Utah and responds to requests for information.

Contact: Utah Small Cities Inc.
324 South State Street, Suite 500
Salt Lake City, UT 84114
(801) 538-8780

Utah Supplier Development Council

This program is a purchasing council made up of major Utah firms that specifically look for small businesses owned by minorities and women to be suppliers for the Council. The Council also prints a directory of these businesses.

Contact: Utah Supplier Development Council
University of Utah Purchasing Department
151 Annex Building
Salt Lake City, UT 84112
(801) 581-8169

Utah Technology Finance Corporation

The purpose of the Utah Technology Finance Corporation is to encourage the growth of new and emerging high technology businesses throughout Utah and assist with product commercialization. A complete description of their services is included in Chapter 7.

Contact: Don Welty, Executive Director
Utah Technology Finance Corporation
185 South State, Suite 208
Salt Lake City, UT 84111
(801)364-4346
Fax (801)364-4361

Utah Ventures

This is a private venture capital firm which accepts unsolicited, written proposals for venture funding for high-growth-potential business ideas.

Contact: Utah Ventures
419 Wakara Way Suite 206
Salt Lake City, Utah 84108
(801) 583-5922

The Wayne Brown Institute

This program's primary purpose is to accelerate economic growth by developing and implementing programs and processes that will assist entrepreneurs in developing their ideas into viable, high-growth companies that can attract funding and management. Annually, the Institute sponsors a "Utah Venture Capital Conference." This is usually held in February. Small firm participants are screened and selected for participation. Those chosen, are coached and given professional assistance in making a brief, compacted presentation at the venture conference. Venture capitalists from all over the country are invited to participate and to listen to the presenters. The object of the conference is to bring the entrepreneur in contact with the venture capital firms in hope that mutually profitable funding deals can be struck.

Contact: Wayne Brown Institute
P.O. Box 2135
Salt Lake City, UT 84110-2135
(801) 595-1141

Utah Information Technologies Association (UITA)

UITA is a state-wide, industry trade association representing and providing services to Utah's information technologies (IT) enterprises, and to the suppliers that provide products and services to the industry. IT enterprises are defined as, "developers, producers, and sellers of computer, software and/or communications-related products or services, that are headquartered or have operations in Utah." UITA is committed to developing and sustaining the business success of Utah's IT industry by enhancing awareness of the industry's characteristics and prominence—inside and outside of Utah—offering and referring services which increase the industry's competitiveness and commerce, and provide and refer products and services which enhance the competitiveness of industry and supplier enterprises. UITA offers three types of memberships and various membership benefits. If your new venture involves information technology, it would be useful to join UITA.

Contact: Randy G. Hurst, Executive Assistant
Utah Information Technologies Association (UITA)
6995 Union Park Center, Suite 490
Midvale, UT 84047
(801) 568-3500
Fax: (801) 568-1072

[1]Wambhiem, Bruce A. with the Small Business Department of Zions First National Bank. *How to Finance a Utah Business.* Zions Capital and Business Resource Guide. Publishers Press, June 1993, Page 163.

Federal Programs

AGRICULTURAL RESEARCH - BASIC AND APPLIED RESEARCH

Assistance: project grants (100 percent)

Purposes: for discovery research: development of scientific technical information on agriculture. Recent projects have emphasized animal and plant productivity, soil and water conservation, commodity conversion and delivery, human nutrition, and integration of agricultural systems.

Eligible applicants/beneficiaries: nonprofit higher education institutions, nonprofit organizations.

Range: $1,000 to $25,000. Average $3,000.

Activity: most projects conducted with in-house staff, there are limited discretionary research funds.

HQ: Administrator, Agricultural Research Service -USDA, 6303 Ivy Lane, Greenbelt, MY 20770-1433. Phone: (301)344-2854.

COMMODITY LOANS AND PURCHASES

Assistance: direct payments/unrestricted use; direct loans

Purposes: to help growers stabilize their income from commodities they produce. Producers receive non-recourse loans against the support price established for their crops which serve as loan collateral. If market prices rise above the support price, farmers can market the commodity and repay the loan; if not, the loan is repaid through forfeiture of collateral to the ASCS which makes a deficiency payment to the grower for the difference between the support and the market price. Commodities eligible for purchases include feed grains, wheat, rice, rye, peanuts, tobacco, and dairy products. Loans are available only for honey, upland cotton, extra-long staple cotton, sugar, soybeans, canola, flaxseed, mustard seed, rapeseed, safflower, and sunflower seed, with special per-year limitations for certain crops. USDA may permit loan repayments in amounts less than the original loan principal under a "marketing loan" provision. In return for deficiency payments participants must forego loans on the eligible quantity; they usually must also agree to reduce their future planting of the crop and to use acreage removed from production in approved conservation uses, for which cost-share assistance may be available from ASCS.

Eligible applicants/beneficiaries: owner, landlord, tenant, or sharecropper on farms producing eligible commodities; for sugar, processors or refiners that agree to pay sugar beet or sugar cane producers the established minimum support prices.

Range: loans, $50 to $76,000,000. Average: $24,288 NOTE: for the 1991 through 1995 crop years the following maximum payments to any one person apply: $50,000 in total for cotton, feed grain, wheat, and rice deficiency and diversion payments; $75,000 in total for gains realized by repaying a loan at a lower level than the original loan, deficiency payments for wheat or feed grains attributable to a reduction in the statutory loan level, and loan deficiency payments. A total payment limitation of $250,000 exists for each crop, combined with payments previously mentioned, covering inventory reduction payments and payments for the compensation of resource adjustment (other than the diversion payments and cost-share assistance), or public access for recreation.

Activity: FY 91,252,000 new loans.

HQ: Cotton, Grain and Rice Support Division, ASCS-USDA, P.O. Box 2415, Washington, DC 20013. Phone: (202)720-7641
Farmers Home Administration (FmHA)

Farmers Home Administration

Purpose: FmHA provides credit and management advice to farm and rural individuals.

Program Eligibility: This program is open to anyone.

Program Details: FmHA provides supervised credit and management advice to farm and other rural people unable to get credit from other sources at reasonable rates and terms. The basic programs are designed to strengthen businesses, family farms, and rural communities, and alleviate rural poverty. Some types of loans include:

Business and industrial loans: FmHA guarantees up to 90% of principal and interest on loans made by commercial lenders to establish or improve businesses and industries, if they primarily are used to help preserve or create new employment opportunity for rural people. Loans may assist enterprises located

in rural areas and towns having populations less than 50,000.
Farm ownership loans: Loans are made to eligible farmers to enlarge, develop, and buy family farms, refinance debts, and install farm-based recreation or other nonagricultural income-earning facilities. Many other non-business related loans also are available.

Application Procedure: To receive more information on the Farmers Home Administration program, call or write to:

U.S. Department of Agriculture
Culpeper Building, Suite 238
1606 Santa Rosa Road
Richmond, VA 23229
(804) 287-1550

DEPARTMENT OF COMMERCE

Economic Development Administration
Business Loan Guarantee Program

For businesses who are located in a designated redevelopment area. Many Virginia counties have this designation. EDA will guarantee up to 80 percent of the bank loss on a loan. The loans guaranteed range from $500,000 to more than $10 million. Interest rates are 1.5 to 2.5 above the lenders prime rate. Terms are limited to 25 years for fixed assets and five years for working capital.

700 Centre, Suite 550
704 East Franklin Street
Richmond, VA 23291
(804) 771-2246

MARKET NEWS

Assistance: technical information.

Purposes: provide reports on prices, demand, movement, volume, and quality of agricultural commodities. Information is spread through news media, printed reports, bulletin boards, phone, facsimile machines, data networks, and telegraph.

Eligible applicants/beneficiaries: anyone.

Activity: FY 93 estimate, 1,755 markets covered.

HQ: Deputy Administrator/marketing Program Operations, AMS-USDA, P.O. Box 96456, Washing
ton, DC 20090. Phone: (202)720-4276.

Information Division
Economic Research Service

Purpose: Offers production and marketing reports detailing agricultural activities.

Program Eligibility: This program is open to anyone.

Program Details: This division carries out research on the production and marketing of major agricultural commodities, foreign agriculture and trade, economic use, conservation, and development of natural resources; trends in rural population, employment, and housing; rural economic adjustment problems; and performance of the U.S. agricultural industry. It provides objective and timely information to farmers, farm organization members, farm suppliers, marketers, processors, consumers, and others who make production, marketing, and purchasing decisions.

Application Procedure: For a listing of the reports which are available and to get on the mailing list for the quarterly catalog of reports, contact this office at:

Information Division
Economic Research Service
U.S. Department of Agriculture
1301 New York Ave. N.W., Room 237
Washington, DC 20005
(202) 219-0515

MARKETING AGREEMENTS AND ORDERS

Assistance: specialized services; advisory services/counseling.

Purposes: to help maintain adequate prices to producers of agricultural products. This is done by issuing federal marketing orders or agreements relating to marketing and economic problems of the commodity or area covered by the federal actions. Marketing orders are issued by USDA, only after a public hearing where milk, fruit and vegetable producers, marketers, and consumers testify, and after farmers vote approval through a referendum.

Eligible applicants/beneficiaries: generally, growers of certain fruits, vegetables, and specialty crops (like nuts, raisins, olives, and hops); also dairy farmers.

Activity: FY 93 estimate, $19.3 billion in marketing.

HQ: Deputy Administrator/Marketing Program Operations, AMS-USDA, P.O. Box 96456, Washington, DC 20090. Phone: (202)720-4276.

FEDERAL-STATE MARKETING IMPROVEMENT PROGRAM

Assistance: Project grants (50 percent)

Purposes: for pilot marketing service projects to improve the marketability of agricultural products, expand export markets, and improve economic and physical marketing efficiency as well as competitive trading. Activities involve direct marketing, international trade, alternative crop production, and aquaculture.

Eligible applicants: appropriate state agencies

Eligible beneficiaries: producers, processors, marketing agencies, and consumers.

Range: $5,000 to $150,000. Average: $59,000

Activity: FY 92, 32 states funded to conduct 31 projects.

HQ: Staff Officer, Federal-State Marketing Improvement Programs, AMS-USDA, P.O. Box 96456, Rm 4006 South, Washington, DC 20090-6456. Phone: (202)720-2704.

MARKET PROTECTION AND PROMOTION

Assistance: specialized services; advisory services/counseling; training.

Purposes: to assure a fair and open marketing distribution system through the elimination of deceptive, unfair, or fraudulent trade practices in the processing and marketing of food and agricultural products. Various activities fall under the national dairy promotion research and nutrition education program, the Federal Seed Program, the Plant Variety Protection Program, the Research and Promotion Program, and the Pesticide Data Program.

Eligible applicants/beneficiaries: any state government, public or private organization, business, or individual.

Activity: FY 93 estimates, 4,300 seed samples tested; 350 plant variety certificates of protection issued.

HQ: Deputy Administrator/marketing Program Operations, AMS-USDA, P.O. Box 96456, Washington, DC 20090. Phone: (202)720-4276.

WHOLESALE MARKET DEVELOPMENT

Assistance: advisory services/counseling; project grants.

Purposes: to provide marketing assistance to food producers through studies on food wholesaling, conducted in cooperation with other government agencies and private industry.

Eligible applicants: government agencies and private industry.

Eligible beneficiaries: producers, processors, marketing agencies, and consumers.

Range/Average: N.A.

Activity: FY 93 estimate, 16 active projects.

HQ: Director, Transportation and Marketing Division, AMS-USDA, P.O. Box 96456, Rm 4006 South, Washington, DC 20090-6456. Phone: (202)690-1300.

TRANSPORTATION SERVICES

Assistance: advisory services/counseling; project grants.

Purposes: to develop and promote agricultural transportation policies and systems, toward improved farm income and larger exports. Assistance is provided where it is determined that a significant regional impact is at stake or that a significant policy is at issue.

Eligible applicants/beneficiaries: any state government, public or private organization, business or industry, or individuals.

Range/Average: N.A.

Activity: new program in FY 90; annually, 5 reports published, program personnel participating in 6 regulatory proceedings.

HQ: Director, Transportation and Marketing Division, AMS-USDA, P.O. Box 96456, Rm 4006 South, Washington, DC 20090-6456. Phone: (202)690-1300.

GRANTS FOR AGRICULTURAL RESEARCH, SPECIAL RESEARCH GRANTS

Assistance: project grants (50 percent/ 1-5 years).

Purposes: for research in the food and agricultural sciences, and for ongoing state-federal research. Emphasis presently is on research related to aquaculture, water quality, integrated pest management, and rangelands.

Eligible applicants/beneficiaries: research organizations, corporations, state agricultural experiment stations, colleges and universities, and federal laboratories with rangeland research capacity.

Range: $6,000 to $352,000. Average: $100,000.

Activity: FY 91, 124 grants.

HQ: Administrator, Cooperative State Research Service, CSRS-USDA, 901 D Street SW, Washington, DC 20250. Phone: (202)720-4423.

GRANTS FOR AGRICULTURAL RESEARCH-COMPETITIVE RESEARCH GRANTS

Assistance: project grants (100 percent/to 3 years).

Purposes: for basic research in food, agriculture, and related fields. Emphasis is in such areas as: plant and animal systems, natural resources and environment, nutrition and health, markets, and trade policy and processes.

Eligible applicants/beneficiaries: state agricultural experiment stations, U.S. colleges and universities, other research institutions and organizations, federal agencies, private organizations or corporations, and individuals.

Range: $4,000 to $540,000. Average: $118,000.

Activity: 1991, 590 grants.

HQ: Chief Scientist, National Research Initiatives Competitive Research Grants Program, USDA, 901 D. Street, Rm 323, Washington, DC 20250-2200. Phone: (202)401-5022.

SMALL BUSINESS INNOVATION RESEARCH

Assistance: project grants (100 percent).

Purposes: for research by small business concerns to stimulate technological innovation, mainly in the areas of: forests and related resources; plant, animal production and protection; air, water, and soils; food science and nutrition; rural and community development; aquaculture; and industrial applications. Phase I grants range up to $50,000 for six months of activity; phase II, up to $250,000 for up to two years; phase III covers pursuit of commercialization of research products, and receives no federal funding. A principal objective of SBIR programs is to foster and encourage participation by minority and disadvantaged firms.
Eligible applicants/beneficiaries: small, U.S. for-profit businesses.

Range: $42,000 to $240,000. Average: $91,000.

Activity: FY 91, 52 grant awards including 36 for phase I and 16 for phase II.

HQ: SBIR Coordinator, Office of Grants and Program Systems, USDA CSRS-AMD, 901 D. Street SW, Ag Box 2245, Washington, DC 20250-2245. Phone: (202)401-6852.

AGRICULTURAL AND RURAL ECONOMIC RESEARCH

Assistance: technical information

Purposes: to provide reports on economic conditions, social science information and analysis on international, national, or regional problems related to agriculture and rural policies and programs. Reports are authored annually by USDA staff, and are available in printed or electronic form.

Eligible applicants/beneficiaries: any individual or organization in the U.S. and U.S. territories.

Activity: FY 93 estimate, 120 active projects.

HQ: Economic Research Service, USDA, 1301 New York Ave. NW, Room 1212, Washington, DC 20005. Phone: (202)219-0310.

EMERGENCY LOANS

Assistance: direct loans (4.5 percent interest).

Purposes: to repair, restore, or replace damaged or destroyed farm property, as a result of declared natural disasters; loans may also cover farm operating expenses and other costs necessary to return disaster victims and their operations to a financially sound condition. Loans may cover: 100 percent of the cost of physical loss, with terms up to 40 years; 80 percent of actual production loss, with terms up to 20 years. Prospective applicants should contact FmHA county offices immediately after sustaining the loss.

Eligible applicants/beneficiaries: established farmers, ranchers, or aquaculture operators (tenant-or owner-operator) conducting a farming operation at the time of the disaster, as proprietors, partnerships, cooperatives, corporations, or joint operations. They must also be U.S. citizens or legal resident aliens, or entities operated by citizens owning over a 50 percent interest. Recipients are unable to obtain necessary credit from other sources to qualify for subsidized loss loans and have county committee eligibility certification. They must provide suitable security to support the loan request and have crop insurance if available for affected crops (except for the 1988-1990 crops). Available also in Puerto Rico, Virgin Islands, Guam, American Samoa, Pacific Trust Territories, and the Northern Marianas, when those areas are designated.

Range: $500 to $500,000. Average: $42,300 in FY 92.

Activity: Fy 92, 600 loans expected.

HQ: Administrator, FmHA-USDA, 5410 S.Building, ELF Room, 14th and Independence Ave. SW, Washington, DC 20250. Phone: (202)720-1632.

FARM OPERATING LOANS

Assistance: direct loans; guaranteed/insured loans (7-22 years).

Purposes: to enable beginning, existing, and expanding family farm operators to purchase livestock, farm, forestry recreation, or nonfarm enterprise equipment, and to provide funds for operating expenses for such enterprises. The loans are used to meet family subsistence needs, purchase essential home equipment, make minor real estate improvements, refinance secured and unsecured debts, pay property taxes and property insurance premiums, plant softwood timber on marginal land, finance youth projects, and to make annual operating loss loans to delinquent borrowers for production purposes. Guaranteed loans may be subsidized up to four percent and direct loans are awarded at an interest rate of one percent above the cost of government borrowing.

Eligible applicants/beneficiaries: U.S. citizens with experience or training to operate a farm, legal capacity to incur a loan obligation. They are unable to obtain a reasonable loan elsewhere and they will become owners or tenants operating family farms through the program. Certain corporations, cooperatives, partnerships, and joint operations conducting family farms may also apply. Available in the states, Puerto Rico, Virgin Islands, Guam, American Samoa, Northern Marianas, Pacific Trust Territories.

Range: insured, to $200,000; guaranteed, to $400,000. Average: insured, $46,000; guaranteed, $101,000.

Activity: FY 91 10,679 insured and 10,745 guaranteed loans.

HQ: Director, Farmer Programs Loan Making Division, FmHA-USDA, 14th and Independence Ave., Washington, D.C. 20250. Phone: (202)720-1632.

FARM OWNERSHIP LOANS

Assistance: direct loans; guaranteed/insured loans (30-40 years)

Purposes: to purchase, enlarge, and improve family farms, to refinance debts, provide necessary water and water facilities, take necessary basic soil treatment and land conservation measures. The loans may also be used to construct, repair, or improve buildings needed in family farm operations; improve, establish, or buy a farm forest enterprise; provide facilities to produce fish under controlled conditions; finance nonfarm enterprises on part of the farm, including recreation; buy and develop land for forestry purposes; and to develop energy conserving measures. Guaranteed loans may be subsidized up to four percent and direct loans are awarded at below-market interest rate.

Eligible applicants/beneficiaries: U.S. citizens with experience or training to operate a farm, with legal capacity to incur a loan obligation, inability to obtain a reasonable loan elsewhere, and who will become owners or tenants operating family farms through the program. Certain corporations, cooperatives, partnerships, and joint operations conducting family farms are also eligible. Loans are available in the states, Puerto Rico, Virgin Islands, Guam, American Samoa, Northern Marianas, and Pacific Trust Territories. If an individual, not have a combined farm ownership loan, soil and water loan, and recreation loan indebtedness to FmHA of more than $200,000 for insured loans, and $300,000 for guaranteed loans, or a total indebtedness against the property securing the loan of more than the market value of the security, whichever is the lesser amount.

Range: insured, to $200,000; guaranteed, to $300,000. Average: insured, $89,000; guaranteed, $150,000.

Activity: FY 91, 641 insured and 2,509 guaranteed loans.

HQ: Director, Farmer Programs Loan making Division, FmHA-USDA, 14th and Independence Ave., Washington, DC 20250. Phone: (202)720-1632.

COOPERATIVE EXTENSION SERVICE

Assistance: formula grants (matching, 56 percent).

Purpose: for land grant institutions to operate state and county agricultural extension service programs providing educational and technical assistance to farmers, producers, and marketing firms in applying technical developments ensuing from research, community organizations to develop natural, economic and human resources. They provide programs to homemakers and youth regarding food and nutrition, home economics, child development, and parent education. USDA's current national priority initiatives are: Competitiveness of American Agriculture, Water Quality, Revitalizing Rural America, Improving Nutrition, Diet and Health.

Eligible applicants: designated state land grant institutions, Puerto Rico, Guam, Virgin Islands, American Samoa, Micronesia, Northern Marianas, and District of Columbia. State and local governments, other organizations, and individuals are not eligible for these payments.

Eligible beneficiaries: general public.

Range: $853,000 to $19,929,000. Average: $7,106,000.

Activity: FY 91, 232,000 Expanded Food and Nutrition Program participants; 5.4 million 4-H youth.

HQ: Extension Service, USDA, Management Office, 14th and Independence Ave, Washington, DC 20250. Phone: (202)720-3377.

OTHER FEDERAL RESOURCES FOR RURAL SMALL BUSINESS ASSISTANCE

The following programs may be beneficial to rural small businesses under particular circumstances:

The Rural Electrification Administration (REA) has a Rural Economic Development Loan and Grant Program that provides zero interest loans and grants to REA borrowers for the purpose of promoting rural economic development and job creation projects. Feasibility studies, start-up costs, and incubator projects can be included. Preference is to zero interest loans rather than grants. A few loans have been made in Washington through REA cooperatives. Contact: State Manager, U.S. Dept. of Agriculture, 14th and Independence Avenue, Washington, DC 20250-1500. Ph: (202) 690-3594.

The Bureau of Indian Affairs promotes business development on or near Native American reservations through several financial assistance programs. The financial assistance programs are available to Native Americans, Native American owned corporations, and partnership or cooperative arrangements with Native Americans. The Indian Revolving Loan Fund, The Indian Loan Guarantee Fund, and the Business Development Grant Program are the major financial assistance programs. These programs typically require at least a 20% equity investment by the business. There are few limits on loan size, but loans to individuals are typically limited to $350,000 for the Revolving Loan Fund and $500,000 for the Loan Guarantee Fund. Grants are limited to $100,000 for individuals and $250,000 for tribes. Contact: Bureau of Indian Affairs Regional Office, Bureau of Indian Affairs, Regional Office, Washington, DC. Ph: (202) 208-3710

National Rural Development and Finance Corporation (NRD&FC) is a private, nonprofit rural that provides technical assistance and loans for rural business expansion and creation. Since 1979, NRD&FC has lent over $6.5 million to 64 businesses throughout the United States - retaining over 400 jobs and creating more than 300 in the process. NRD&FC typically makes loans to manufacturing or service industries that are either expanding or starting up. Average loan size is $125,000 with terms of 5 to 7 years and an interest rate of prime rate plus 1.5 points. NRD&FC is currently developing a Rural Lending Partnership Program that will extend NRD&FC's loan making, fund management, and training to local development organizations. Contact:NRD&FC, 1818 N Street NW, Suite 410, Washington, DC 20036, (202) 429-9017; FAX (202) 331-0349.

Community Reinvestment Fund (CRF) is a nonprofit organization that purchases development loans from community based development organizations and government agencies. This secondary market function makes it possible for local communities and nonprofit organizations to raise money for new projects by selling their existing loans. CRF purchases a variety of loan types, including economic development loans, affordable housing loans, and loans originally funded under a variety of programs including the community Development Block Grant Program, the Urban Development Action Grant Program, or certain state-funded programs. In addition, CRF also offers contract portfolio management, portfolio review, training, and capacity building. Contact:CRF, 2400 Foshay Tower, 821 Marquette Avenue, Minneapolis, MN 55402, (612) 338-3050; FAX (612) 338-3236.

RURAL ECONOMIC DEVELOPMENT LOANS AND GRANTS

Assistance: direct loans (no interest/10 years); project grants (100 Percent).

Purposes: for rural economic and job development projects, including the costs of feasibility studies, project start-up, and other reasonable expenses. Project examples: business incubators, establishment or expansion of factories or businesses, and industrial development parks.

Eligible applicants/beneficiaries: electric and telephone utilities with current REA loans.

Range: $10,000 to $100,000. Average: $83,000.

Activity: cumulatively 1989 - January 1992, 200 loans approved.

HQ: REA-USDA, 14th and Independence Ave. SW, Rm 2245 South, Washington, DC 20250. Phone: (202)720-9552.

AGRICULTURAL STATISTICS REPORTS ("Agricultural Estimates")

Assistance: technical information.

Purposes: collection and publication of statistics related to agriculture, resources, and rural communities. Reports cover crops, livestock and poultry estimates, prices received by farmers, process for commodities and services, data on farm employment and wage rates.

Eligible applicants/beneficiaries: farmers and agricultural producers, marketing and processing groups, transportation and handler groups, consumers, state governments, educational institutions, and the general public, including the U.S. territories.

Activity: estimates on some 120 crops and 45 livestock item, published in 400 reports.

HQ: National Agricultural Statistics Service, USDA, Rm 4117 South, Washington, DC 20250. Phone: (202)720-2707.

TECHNICAL AGRICULTURAL ASSISTANCE

Assistance: project grants (100 percent/1-2 years).

Purposes: for technical research and assistance projects dealing with international agricultural problems. Current projects include expansion of developing-country agricultural management concepts and technologies, guidance on the development of private enterprise, livestock production and health. This program is conducted in cooperation with the state Department's Agency for International Development.

Eligible applicants/beneficiaries: U.S. institutions of higher learning; public and private nonprofit scientific research organizations, including those in U.S. territories.

Range: $20,000 to $200,000. Average: $80,000.

Activity: no specific numbers provided.

HQ: Development Resources Division, Office of International Cooperation and Development, USDA OICD/DRD, Rm 3219 South, Washington, DC 20250-4300. Phone: (202)690-1924.

INTERNATIONAL AGRICULTURAL RESEARCH PROGRAM ("International Research")

Assistance: project grants (cost sharing).

Purposes: for research abroad on international agricultural problems in collaboration with foreign scientists, in furtherance of research priorities of USDA, of state agricultural experiment stations, and of U.S. agricultural education and research institutions. Current program emphasis includes pest disease prevention and control germ plasm and genetic improvement, soil and water resources, forestry and wood products, dry land agriculture, and aquaculture. Only U.S. researchers are funded under this program.

Eligible applicants/beneficiaries: U.S. institutions of higher learning; public and private nonprofit scientific research organizations, including those in U.S. territories.

Range: $15,000 to $300,000. Average $60,000.

Activity: no specific numbers provided.

HQ: Research and Scientific Exchange Division, Office of International Cooperation and Development, USDA, Rm 3222 USDA-OICD-RSED, Washington, DC 20250-4300. Phone: (202)690-4872.

INTERNATIONAL TRAINING-FOREIGN PARTICIPANT

Assistance: project grants (100 percent).

Purpose: for international research in food, agricultural, and related subjects. Mainly in the areas of course development and evaluation. Funding currently supports projects involving short-term agricultural and trade-related training and orientation for senior and mid-level officials, including marketing and production of forestry and wood products, soybean utilization, rice processing, food safety, and dairy production and livestock management.

Eligible applicants/beneficiaries: U.S. institutions of higher education, nonprofit organizations.

Range: $10,000 to $40,000. Average: $19,000.

Activity: no specific numbers provided.

HQ: Food Industries Division, Office of International Cooperation and Development, USDA, 14th and Independence Ave., Washington, DC 20250. Phone: (202)690-1339.

SCIENTIFIC AND TECHNICAL COOPERATION

Assistance: project grants (cost sharing); direct payments/specified use.

Purposes: for international cooperation in agriculture and forestry through short-term exchange visits of U.S. and foreign scientists. Also for international meetings, conferences, or workshops on high priority topics of mutual concern to participating countries.

Eligible applicants/beneficiaries: U.S. institutions of higher learning, public or private nonprofit scientific research organizations-including those in U.S. territories.

Range: $500 to $4,000 per individual for travel costs, representing one-half of total costs. Average: $1,500

Activity: new program in FY 90; no specific numbers provided.

HQ: Research and Scientific Exchange Division, Office of International Cooperation and Development, USDA-OICD-RSED, Rm 3222, Washington, DC 20250. Phone: (202)690-4872.

CENSUS BUREAU DATA PRODUCTS ("CENSUS BUREAU PUBLICATIONS, COMPUTER TAPES, AND MICROFICHE")

Assistance: technical information.

Purposes: dissemination of statistical results of censuses, surveys, and other programs. Data cover population, housing, agriculture, retail and wholesale trade, selected service industries, governments, foreign trade statistics, and other subjects. Certain estimates and projections are also available. Various types of geographic areas are covered. Distribution is through printed reports, computer tapes, microfiche, directories, CD-ROMs, catalogs, statistical compendia, indexes, and guides, all usually sold by the GPO.

Eligible applicants/beneficiaries: anyone.

Activity: FY 91, 2,000 reports published; 10,000 computer tapes, CD-ROMs, and related products were ordered.

HQ: Chief Data user Serviced Division, Bureau of the Census-USDC, Washington, DC 20233. Phone: (301)763-5820. Customer Services, Bureau of the Census-USDC, Washington, DC 20233. Phone: (301)763-4100.

CENSUS DATA USER SERVICES

Assistance: advisory services and counseling, technical information and training.

Purposes: assistance to census data users in the access to and the use of census data. Assistance is provided through newsletters, technical guides, conferences, training courses and related activities including development of user oriented computer programs for processing census files. Staff members are available to participate as speakers and resource persons in training activities and conferences on the censuses and other programs of the Census Bureau.

Eligible applicants/beneficiaries: officials of federal, state, and local governments, universities, community organizations, and the private sector are eligible for data user training, at a nominal fee. Materials and consultation are available to all.

Activity: monthly newsletter, 4 seminars for librarians and information specialists, 16 specialized workshops and training courses.

HQ: Bureau of the census, 306 Washington Plaza, Suitland Fed. Center WP 306, Washington, DC 20233. Phone: (301)763-4100.

MEASURES AND ANALYSES OF THE U.S. ECONOMY

Assistance: technical information.

Purposes: provides measures and analyses of the national income and product accounts as summarized by the gross national product, as well as a series of related economic data analyses-used to formulate and execute fiscal, financial, international and other policies. Analyses include the wealth accounts of the U.S., the input-output accounts, personal income and related economic series by geographic area, the U.S. balance of payments accounts and associated foreign investment accounts, measures relating to environmental change within the framework of the national economic accounts. Additional analyses include measures of business activity such as a system of leading coincident, and lagging economic indicators.

Eligible applicants/beneficiaries: general public.

Activity: monthly "Survey of Current Business" and periodic supplements.

HQ: Public Information Office, Bureau of Economic Analysis - USDC, 1441 Elf Street NW, Washington, DC 20230. Phone: (202)606-9900.

EXPORT PROMOTION SERVICES

Assistance: advisory services and counseling.

Purposes: to stimulate exporting by providing information on overseas trade markets and opportunities. Information is provided through non-financial assistance, in export promotion with displays, trade and industrial exhibits, trade missions, catalogs, video catalogs, and foreign buyer shows. Information is provided on trade statistics, foreign tariffs, customs regulations and procedures.

Eligible applicants/beneficiaries: anyone.

Activity: Agent/Distributor Reports, World Trader Data Reports, Export Contact Lists, and Trade Lists.

HQ: Office of the Director General, U.S. and Foreign Commercial Service-USDC- Rm 3804, 14th and Constitution Ave. NW, Washington, DC 20230. Phone: (202)482-5777.

TRADE DEVELOPMENT

Assistance: advisory services and counseling.

Purposes: the central source of industry-specific expertise, policy development, industry competitiveness analysis, and international trade promotion assistance. Services include regular statistical reports, economic studies on current policy issues such as international trade and industry competitiveness, forecasts of industry/sector outputs and cost trends. Information is provided on technological developments, export promotion events, and foreign market information.

Eligible applicants/beneficiaries: general public.

Activity: "United States Trade Performance and Outlook",competitive assessment studies of selected U.S. industries.

HQ: International Trade Administration-USDC, 14th and Constitution Ave. NW, Rm 2800A, Washington, DC 20230. Phones: Technology and Aerospace Industries; (202)482-1872; Basic Industries, (202)482-0614; Service Industries and Finance, (202)482-5261; Export Trading Company Affairs, (202)482-5131; Textiles Apparel, and Consumer Goods Industries, (202)482-3737; Trade and Economic Analysis, (202)482-5145.

U.S. & Foreign Commercial Service
International Trade Administration

Purpose: To assist businesses in importation and exportation. This service provides a myriad of different types of assistance and is important for any business wishing to export or import.

Program Eligibility: This program is open to anyone. A fee schedule is available from the U.S. Department of Commerce.

Program Details: The service is made available for businesses with four distinctive areas of assistance: (1) To find and assess your markets; services include comparison shopping service, foreign market research, and World Traders' Data Reports. (2) To make contacts; services include Agent/Distributor service, export contact list service, and trade opportunities program. (3) To promote your products; services include catalog & video exhibitions, Commercial News USA, foreign buyer program, matchmakers, trade missions and trade shows, and (4) Individual counseling; services include U.S. & Foreign Commercial Service and Caribbean Basin Program.

The service also assists in obtaining proper exporting licensing and status of trade relationships with target countries.

The service offers an Export Mailing List which attempts to bring buyers and sellers together for a $25 setup fee and a $.25 per name charge.

The service also offers the Commercial Information Management Service (CIMS) which offers many data bases on CD-ROM. These data bases include National Trade Data Bank and other trade information and industry sector analysis.

A World Traders' Data Report for $100 answers 13 important credit questions about specific exporters.

Application Procedure: For more information, call or write:

U.S. & Foreign Commercial Service
U.S. Department of Commerce
International Trade Administration
700 W. State St., 2nd Floor
State House Mail
Boise, ID 83720-2700
(208) 334-3857

Economic Bulletin Board (EBB)
International Trade Administration
United States and Foreign Commercial Service

Purpose: This program helps companies obtain sales leads from overseas firms seeking to buy or represent American products.

Program Eligibility: This program is open to anyone.

Program Details: This subscription service provides timely sales leads, joint ventures, and licensing opportunities from overseas firms and foreign governments seeking to buy or represent U.S. products and services. U.S. Commercial Officers worldwide gather leads through local channels. Lead details, such as specifications, quantities, end-use, delivery, and bid deadlines, are delivered daily to Washington, and then made available electronically within 24 hours directly to the U.S. business community in both printed and electronic form through private sector nationwide distributors. Electronic distribution is through the Economic Bulletin Board. There is an annual $35 charge which comes with a $12 connect-time credit thereafter it costs 50 cents a minute with an estimated down load time of 10-15 minutes a day. The printed form is offered through a daily subscription to The *Journal of Commerce* at a cost of $68 for 3 months, $225 for one year. Both new and established exporters can use EBB as a fundamental sales tool.

Application Procedure: For more information on this program, call or write:

Economic Bulletin Board
U.S. Department of Commerce
Office of Business Analysis
14th and Constitution Ave. N.W., Room 4885
Washington, DC 20230
(202) 482-1986

FOREIGN-TRADE ZONES IN THE UNITED STATES

Assistance: specialized services.

Purposes: assistance in the establishment and operation of foreign trade zones which may be authorized in localities to encourage and streamline import and export activities and to stimulate domestic production of export goods. Foreign-Trade zones function like public utilities, subject to U.S. Customs and other requirements providing access to businesses and manufacturers on a nondiscriminatory basis.

Eligible applicants/beneficiaries: public and private corporations in states with appropriate enabling legislation.

Activity: annually, 60-80 FTZ orders issued, covering zones, sub-zones, and expansion applications.

HQ: Executive Secretary, Office of the Executive Secretary, Foreign-Trade Zones Board, U.S. Department of Commerce, 14th and Constitution Ave. NW, Room 3716, Washington, DC 20230. Phone: (202)482-2862.

EXPORT LICENSING SERVICE AND INFORMATION

Assistance: advisory services and counseling.

Purposes: information, training, seminars, and other assistance on export licensing requirements, regulations, and policies.

Eligible applicants/beneficiaries: general public.

Activity: FY 92 estimate, counseling 309,000 exporters; processing 100,000 phone inquiries through the automated STELA; 308 export licensing seminars with 8,100 participants.

HQ: Exporter Counseling Staff, Office of Export Licensing, USDC-Rm. 1099, P.O. Box 273, Washington, DC 20044. Phones: status & trade fair (202)482-2753; regulatory and policy questions, (202)482-4811; STELA, (202)482-2752.

Exporting Licensing and Controls Seminars
Bureau of Export Administration

Purpose: Assist businesses in understanding the U.S. export licenses and regulations regarding high technology products.

Program Eligibility: This program is open to anyone.

Program Details: The seminar staff teaches exporters about the national security requirements for international sales. U.S. exporters and foreign importers of American products around the world increase their knowledge and understanding of U.S. Export Regulations by attending classroom instruction offered by export administration specialists. The Export Administration Regulations Course is a professional seminar featuring a full day of classroom training on export controls and licensing procedures. There are two 2-day update conferences each year.

Seminars are held once a month in major cities throughout the United States as well as in foreign countries several times a year. Both introductory, intermediate and specialized courses on the Export Administration Regulations are offered. Completing the introductory course is a prerequisite for receiving advanced instruction. The seminars assist a business to understand the requirements for compliance with U.S. export laws and procedures, to improve its ability to use and understand federal export regulations, to prepare better license applications and other documentation, to find out how a company can avoid the costly fines and time-consuming seizures that result from violation of export laws, and to discover ways to increase productivity, ease license application efforts and lower costs of doing business abroad.

These seminars have proven valuable to manufacturers, carriers, shipping agents, freight forwarders, international sales and marketing specialists, contracts administrators, materials and traffic managers, customer service representatives, buyers, accountants, attorneys, technical supervisors, order processors and export licensing coordinators.

Application Procedure: To find out more about this program call or write to:

Export Seminar Staff
Bureau of Export Administration
U.S. Department of Commerce
14th and Pennsylvania Ave. N.W., HCHB Room 1099D
Washington, DC 20230
(202) 482-6031

ECONOMIC DEVELOPMENT-BUSINESS DEVELOPMENT ASSISTANCE

Assistance: guaranteed loans (to 80 percent)

Purposes: for the acquisition of fixed assets or for working capital used to create or retain permanent jobs, through the establishment or expansion of EDA-approved redevelopment area plants. Loan pricing is up to prime interest rate plus 1.25% with a guarantee of 80%; prime plus 2.5% with a 65% guarantee. Working capital loans have terms of up to seven years, whereas the terms of fixed assets are the average life of the assets. Business development guarantees won't be extended to projects in which the prospective borrower meets the following: (1) contemplates relocation any or all of its facilities, resulting in a loss of jobs at existing facilities; (2) produces a product or service for which there is a sustained and prolonged excess of supply over demand; (3) will use the funds in connection with research or development or for retail merchandising. EDA expects one job to be created or saved for every $20,000 of loan assistance.

Eligible applicants: private lending institutions making loans to private borrowers whose projects have been approved by the appropriate state or political subdivision.

Eligible beneficiaries: privately owned firms including partnerships, sole proprietorship, public or private corporations, and employee stock ownership trusts.

Range: $500,000 to $111,100,000. Average: $2,000,000.

Activity: FY 91, no guarantees approved.

HQ: Director, Credit and Debt Management Division, EDA-USDC, Rm. H7830b Herbert C. Hoover Bldg., 14th and Constitution Ave NW, Washington, DC 20230. Phone: (202)482-4731.

National Trade Data Bank (NTDB)

Purpose: This program is a convenient electronic source for international trade and export information to start or boost your export sales.

Program Eligibility: This program is open to anyone. Requirements include any IBM-compatible PC with at least 512k memory, an ISO 9660 CD-ROM reader, and Microsoft CD-ROM extensions (version 2.0 or higher)

Program Details: This subscription service provides the best international trade and export data from 15 U.S. Federal Government agencies. A special "BROWSE" feature is user friendly for those not familiar with CD-ROM technology. "BROWSE" and "ROMWARE" perform databank searches based on country and product information, or searches for specific words in the titles of documents. Subscription rates for 12 months is $360 or $35 per two disk package. The program contains over 100,000 documents and is released monthly.

Application Procedure: For more information, call or write:

National Trade Data Bank (NTDB)
U.S. Department of Commerce
Office of Business Analysis
HCHB Room 4885
Washington, DC 20230
(202) 482-1986

TRADE ADJUSTMENT ASSISTANCE

Assistance: project grants (50-100 percent).

Purposes: trade adjustment assistance to firms and industries adversely affected by increased imports, in the form of technical assistance in which the participants must share expenses. Assistance may consist of detailed aid as industrial engineering, marketing, product diversification, computer systems, export promotion, management improvements. To receive the Trade Act certification, the firms must demonstrate that increased imports of articles like or directly competitive with those that they produce contributed significantly to declines in sales or in production, and to separation or threat of separation of their workers. Firms must also submit an acceptable adjustment proposal to be eligible to apply for technical assistance. Industry associations or other organizations must submit evidence demonstrating import competition, and that the industry includes a substantial number of Trade Act-certified firms or workers.

Eligible applicants/beneficiaries: intermediary organizations including Trade Adjustment Assistance Centers or industry groups that can demonstrate injury from imports.

Range: N.A.

Activity: FY 91, 155 firms certified; 122 adjustment proposals accepted; technical assistance to 792 firms; 4 trade-injured industry projects assisted.

HQ: Trade Adjustment Assistance Division, EDA-USDC, 14th and Constitution Ave. NW, Rm 7023, Washington, DC 20230. Phone: (202)482-3373.

NATIONAL TECHNICAL INFORMATION SERVICE ("NTIS")

Assistance: technical information.

Purposes: main source for the maintenance and sale of federally-sponsored technological and technical information, products, services, research and engineering reports, register of research in progress, machine-processable data files, and computer programs. NTIS also licenses federally-owned patents and assists in filing foreign patent applications. Fees are charged and trust funds help support the program also.

Eligible applicants/beneficiaries: any U.S. and most foreign organizations or individuals.

Activity: FY 91, 421,000 printed reports, 1,501,000 microfiche reports, 78 patent licenses granted, 138 foreign-filed, 23,000 foreign technical reports acquired.

HQ: Director, NTIS-USDC, 5285 Port Royal Rd., Springfield, VA 22161. Phone: (703)487-4636.

MINORITY BUSINESS DEVELOPMENT CENTERS

Assistance: project grants (85-100 percent/1-5 years).

Purposes: for MBDCs organizations offering management and technical assistance in all phases of business development and management by minority firms. No loans are offered to businesses.

Eligible applicants: states, Indian tribes, local governments, educational institutions, nonprofit organizations, individuals, businesses.

Eligible beneficiaries: existing or proposed minority-owned businesses.

Range: $165,000 to $622,000. Average: $212,000.

Activity: FY 91, MBDCs in 100 locations received grants; assistance provided to 17,000 clients which, in turn, obtained $358 million in financial packages and over $867 million in procurement contracts.

HQ: Assistant Director/Program Development, MBDA-USDC, 14th and Constitution Ave. NW-Rm 5096, Washington, DC 20230. Phone: (202)482-5770.

AMERICAN INDIAN PROGRAM

Assistance: project grants (85-100 percent/1-5 years).

Purposes: to six Indian Business Development Centers and one American Indian Business Consultant, to provide management and technical assistance of all types to new or existing American Indian businesses. No loans or grants are awarded to businesses under this program, however help is provided in obtaining financial assistance.

Eligible applicants: states, Indian tribes, local governments, educational institutions, nonprofit organizations, individuals and businesses.

Eligible beneficiaries: new or existing American Indian businesses.

Range: $158,000 to $303,000.

Activity: FY 91 clients obtained over $16 million in financial packages and $30 million in procurement contracts.

HQ: Assistant Director, Office of Operations, 441 4th St. NW, Suite 1120 Washington, DC 20230 Phone: (202)727-6053.

MINORITY BUSINESS RESOURCE DEVELOPMENT (PUBLIC AND PRIVATE)

Assistance: project grants (85%/1-3 years)

Purposes: for activities advocation the expansion of opportunities for minority businesses by identifying and developing private markets and capital sources, decreasing minority dependence on government programs, expanding business information and services through trade associations, and promoting and supporting the mobilization of resources of federal, state and local governments at the local level.

Eligible applicants/beneficiaries: established business, industry, professional, trade associations, and chambers of commerce.

Range: $25,000 to $320,000.

Activity: FY 90, 10 projects funded.

HQ: Assistant Dircetor/Program Development, MBDA-USDC, 14th and Constitution Ave. NW - Rm. 5096, Washington, DC 20230. Phone: (202)482-5770.

PATENT AND TRADEMARK TECHNICAL INFORMATION DISSEMINATION

Assistance: technical information.

Purposes: to provide support for the growth of American commerce and technology through the utilization and dissemination of technical information available through patents, and for the maintenance of public search centers containing patents and trademarks. The office examines patent and trademark applications, grants patents, and approves trademarks when legal requirements are met. There is a fee charged for services.

Eligible applicants/beneficiaries: general public.

Activity: annually, approximately 130,000 searches and 8,600 patents sold.

HQ: Patent and Trademark Office-USDC, Commissioner of Patents and Trademarks, Washington, DC 20231. Phone: (703)305-8341.

FEDERAL PATENT LICENSING OFFICE
National Technical Information Service (NITS)
Center of the Utilization of Federal Technology (CUFT)
U.S. Department of Commerce

Purpose: Offers patent licensing opportunities, often exclusive, for U.S. businesses.

Program Eligibility: This program is open to anyone.

Program Details: This office licenses (often exclusively) U.S. Government-owned inventions. If a business wishes to license a particular U.S. Government-owned invention, it should contact this office. The business either will negotiate directly with CUFT or will be referred immediately to the appropriate licensing office at another agency.

Each year Federal laboratories disclose hundreds of new technologies, many of which have significant commercial potential and are thus patented. These patents create property rights which the Government can license to industry as an incentive to develop these into commercial products and processes. Resulting industrial and commercial activities benefit the national economy, create jobs, and improve international competitiveness.

The office administers a routine program of publicly announcing all U.S. Government inventions being made available for licensing. It evaluates many of these inventions and promotes those identified as having commercial potential. In addition, the office obtains foreign patent protection on selected inventions to protect valuable foreign commercial markets for domestic licensees. Current licensees have pledged tens of millions of dollars to bring U.S. Government inventions to market.

Application Procedure: For more information on this program, call or write to:

Federal Patent Licensing Office
National Technical Information Service (NTIS)
Center of the Utilization of Federal Technology (CUFT)
U.S. Department of Commerce
Room 304F
5285 Port Royal Road
Springfield, VA 22161
(703) 487-4732

PRODUCTIVITY AND ECONOMIC GROWTH

Assistance: technical information.

Purposes: to encourage the formation of Industrial Technology Partnerships to achieve advances in technology and innovation. Also to identify and remove governmental barriers to and incentives for productivity growth and international competitiveness, to disseminate productivity and manufacturing systems know-how, in addition to coordinating the formulation and implementation of policies for technology transfer, federal patent policy, and metric conversion.

Eligible applicants/beneficiaries: any U.S. firms or business organizations.

Activity: no specific numbers provided.

HQ: Technology Administration, USDC, 14th and Constitution Ave. NW Rm 4230, Washington, DC 20230. Phone: (202)482-0940.

U.S. DEPARTMENT OF HOUSING AND URBAN DEVELOPMENT (HUD)

Community Development Block Grants
Provides direct grants of federal funds to selected small cities and counties to undertake a wide range of housing, public facilities and economic development activities. Communities may use the economic development funds to make attractive loans to businesses in their areas. The program is described in greater detail in the State Finance section of the Resource Database.

Urban Development Action Grant
Designed to encourage private development projects in eligible cities. Funds are available for a variety of commercial and industrial projects which help revitalize a city's economic base and provide new permanent employment

opportunities. HUD awards a UDAG to an eligible city for a specific project and the city lends the money to a private developer as part of the project's financing package. The borrower repays the city based on the loan agreement. The proceeds become an endowment to the city for future economic development projects.

COMMUNITY DEVELOPMENT BLOCK GRANTS/ENTITLEMENT GRANTS ("CDBG")

Assistance: formula grants (100%)

Purposes: CDBG funds to localities with more than 50,000 population for a broad range of activities intended to result in decent housing in suitable living environments, and/or community economic development, and/or improved community facilities and services. Program policy requires the "principal benefit" be to low-moderate income persons (at least 70 percent of the grant allocation). Projects may be operated by the locality or through sub-grantees, including public or nonprofit agencies, neighborhood-based organizations, local development corporations, small business investment companies, and other groups. Permitted uses of funds include virtually any aspect of residential or nonresidential rehabilitation, including historic preservation and energy conservation, energy development, grants or loans to businesses. Revolving loan funds for rehabilitation or for economic development purposes, real property acquisition, relocation of households or businesses, demolition, redevelopment site clearance and preparation for reuse, improvement or installation of public works, certain social service program funding, housing code enforcement, city planning and related studies. Ineligible uses include, facilities for the general conduct of government, community-wide facilities, new housing construction, housing subsidies paid directly to occupants, income maintenance payments. Cities must have approved Housing Assistance Plans to be eligible for funds. For "entitlement" communities CDBG grants require no matching funds, and the amounts are based on a statutory formula.

Eligible applicants: cities in Metropolitan Statistical Areas with populations over 500,000, qualified urban counties of at least 200,000 (excluding the population in entitlement cities), and cities with populations of under 50,000 that are central cities in Metropolitan Statistical Areas.

Eligible beneficiaries: low and moderate-income residents, including those benefiting from projects sponsored by CDBG sub-grantees or others who obtain CDBG funds. The grantee must certify that at least 70% of the grant received during a one to three year period will principally benefit low and moderate income persons.

Range: N.A.

Activity: FY 92, 888 eligible local government units (FY 91, 843 grants approved).

HQ: Entitlement Communities Division, Office of Block Grant Assistance, Community Planning and Development, 451 7th St. SW, Washington, DC 20410. Phone: (202)708-1577.

COMMUNITY DEVELOPMENT BLOCK GRANTS/SMALL CITIES PROGRAM

Assistance: project grants (formula-based, 100%)

Purposes: funding for "Small cities" which are those with populations under 50,000 and that are not central cities within metropolitan areas; there is no minimum population.

Eligible applicants: under the CDBG Program/State Program, each state elects whether to administer the Small Cities Program for the non-entitlement communities within its jurisdiction, those with population under 50,000. HUD now administers the Small Cities Program only in the states of Hawaii and New York where eligible applicants are general local government units, except metropolitan cities, urban counties or units participating in an urban county's CDBG Program, and Indian tribes eligible for assistance under section 106(a) of the Act.

Eligible beneficiaries: low and moderate income residents, including those benefiting from projects sponsored by CDBG sub-grantees or others who obtain CDBG funds.

Range/Average: to $327,000 for "Single Purpose" grants; "Comprehensive," to $547,000.

Activity: FY 91, 96 grants.

HQ: State and Small Cities Division, Office of Block Grant Assistance, Community Planning and Development, HUD, Rm 7184, 451 7th St. SW, Washington, DC 20410. Phone: (202)708-1322.

INDIAN COMMUNITY DEVELOPMENT BLOCK GRANT PROGRAM

Assistance: project grants (100%)

Purposes: funds are provided for activities resulting in decent housing in suitable living environments, community economic development, and improved community facilities and services.

Eligible applicants/beneficiaries: any Indian tribe, band, group, or nation, including Alaskan Indians, and Eskimos, and any Alaskan native village eligible for assistance under the Indian Self-Determination and Education Assistance Act.

Range/Average: $276,000.

Activity: FY 91, 95 awards.

HQ: Office of Block Grant Assistance, Community Planning and Development, HUD, 451 7th St. SW, Rm 7286, Washington, DC 20410. Phone: (202)708-1322.

LABOR FORCE STATISTICS

Assistance: project grants(100%) technical information.
Purposes: to develop statistical data and analyses of labor force activities such as, employment and unemployment, wages, occupations, layoffs, and plant closings. Quarterly and monthly reports are produced, covering national, state, and local statistics. The data and analyses appear in publications such as "Monthly Labor Review" and "Unemployment in States and Local Areas" published by BLS.

Range: $13,000 to $4,638,000. Average: $1,079,000.

Activity: FY 90, cooperative agreements in effect with all states, Puerto Rico, District of Columbia, Guam, Virgin Islands, and American Samoa.

HQ: Office of Employment and Unemployment Statistics, BLS-DOL, 2 Mass. Ave. NE, Postal Square Bldg., Rm 4675, Washington, D.C. 20212. Phone: (202)606-6400.

EMPLOYMENT PROJECTIONS DATA

Assistance: technical information.

Purposes: development of data for interpretation; analysis of current and long-run economic developments affecting employment and related studies. Provided are such data as projections of labor force size, rate and patterns of growth in the economy, interindustry sales and purchases, demand for labor in various industries.

Eligible applicants/beneficiaries: general public.

Activity: FY 92, new edition of Occupation Outlook Handbook, projections for the year 2005.

HQ: Office of Employment Projections, BLS-DOL, Rm 2135, 2 Massachusetts Ave. NE, Washington, DC 20212. Phone: (202)606-5700.

JOB TRAINING PARTNERSHIP ACT ("JTPA")

Assistance: formula grants.

Purposes: to provide job training and related services to the economically disadvantaged, including adults, youth, and others facing significant employment barriers to permanent, self-sustaining employment. Partnerships between the private sector and state and local governments are authorized. Matching funds (20%) must be provided for sub-state projects. A summer youth employment and training component is funded through this program.

Range: N.A.

Activity: FY 92, over 1,400,000 total participants.

HQ: Employment and Training Administration-DOL, Rm N4703, 200 Constitution Ave. NW, Washington, DC 20210. Phone: (202)219-5580.

BUSINESS SERVICES ("COUNSELING ON DOING BUSINESS WITH THE FEDERAL GOVERNMENT")

Assistance: advisory services/counseling.

Purposes: promotion of participation by businesses in government procurement contracts for products and services, in surplus property sales contracts, in concession contracts, and in repair and renovation contracts. Special services are available to small and disadvantaged businesses.

Eligible applicants/beneficiaries: any business concern.

Activity: FY 93 estimate, 185,000 business counseling actions, 442 business opportunity meetings.

HQ: Director, Office of Small and Disadvantaged Business Utilization (AU), GSA, Rm. 6029, 18th and F. NW, Washington, DC 20405. Phone: (202)501-1021.

ECONOMIC INJURY DISASTER LOANS

Assistance: direct loans; guaranteed/insured loans (to 30 years)

Purposes: to assist small businesses in recovering from disasters. Uses include debt payments and working capital, but not realty or equipment acquisition or repair. Direct loans are from SBA at no more than 4% interest.

Eligible applicants/beneficiaries: small businesses, small agricultural cooperatives, or nursery victims in declared disaster areas, unable to obtain credit elsewhere, with evidence of the cause and extent of economic injury.

Range: to $500,000. Average: $54,000.

Activity: FY 92, 1,622 Loans.

HQ: Office of Disaster Assistance, SBA, 409 Third St. SW, Suite 8100, Washington, DC 20416. Phone: (202)205-6734.

LOANS FOR SMALL BUSINESSES

Assistance: direct loans; advisory services/counseling.

Purposes: to establish, preserve, or strengthen small businesses owned by low-income persons, or those located in high unemployment areas.

Eligible applicants/beneficiaries: persons with income below basic needs, or businesses in areas of high unemployment that have been denied the opportunity to acquire adequate business financing through normal lending channels on reasonable terms.

Range: to $150,000. Average: n $68,000.

Activity: FY 91, 255 loans.

HQ: Director, Loan Policy and Procedures Branch, SBA, 409 Third St. S.W., Washington, DC 20416. Phone: (202)205-7511.

BUSINESS DEVELOPMENT ASSISTANCE TO SMALL BUSINESS

Assistance: advisory services/counseling; technical information; training.

Purposes: counseling on management and operation of small businesses through workshops, expertise from the Service Corps of Retired Executives, courses, publications, Small Business Institute Program and other volunteer programs, and training.

Eligible applicants/beneficiaries: existing and potential small business persons, veterans, and, in some cases, members of community groups.

Activity: FY 91, 450,000 persons counseled.

HQ: Associate Administrator for Business Initiatives, SBA, 409 Third St. S.W., Washington, DC 20416. Phone: (202)205-6665.

MINORITY BUSINESS DEVELOPMENT

Assistance: specialized services, up to 9 years.

Purposes; procurement contracts by SBA with other federal agencies for subcontracts, in turn, with disadvantaged businesses. The program incorporates contract, financial, technical, and managerial assistance to participants.

Eligible applicants/beneficiaries; small businesses controlled by U.S. citizens with social and economic disadvantages, or by disadvantaged Indian tribes, Alaska native corporations, or native Hawaiian organizations.

Activity: FY 91, 3,863 contracts valued at $4 billion.

HQ: Office of AA/MSB&COD, SBA, 409 Third St. SW, Washington, DC 20416. Phone: (202)205-6410.

MANAGEMENT AND TECHNICAL ASSISTANCE FOR SOCIALLY AND ECONOMICALLY DISADVANTAGED BUSINESSES

Assistance: project grants, 100%

Purposes: for management, technical assistance, and training services through qualified individuals or public or private organizations, to businesses that are socially or economically disadvantaged or located in areas of high unemployment.

Eligible applicants; state and local governments, education institutions, public or private organizations, Indian tribes, and individuals with the capability to provide the necessary assistance.

Eligible beneficiaries: business or potential businesses that are economically or socially disadvantaged, or participants in the Minority Business Development program.

Range: $1,800 to $388,000. Average: $79,000.

HQ: Associate Administrator/Minority Small Business and Capital Ownership Development, SBA, 409 hird St. SW, Washington, DC 20416. Phone: (202)205-6423.

PHYSICAL DISASTER LOANS

Assistance: direct loans (4-8 percent interest/3-30 years); guaranteed/insured loans.

Eligible Applicants: Indian tribe, band, group, pueblo, or community located on a state reservation; nonprofit, tax-exempt organizations such as schools, colleges, universities, public libraries, schools for the mentally retarded or physically handicapped, educational radio or TV stations, child care centers, museums, medical institutions, hospitals, health centers, clinics and programs for older individuals or for the homeless; public airports; private service and educational organizations.

Ineligible applicants: animal hospitals, summer camps, or playgrounds that are not part of a public agency; or schools, Sunday schools, church and nonprofit tax-exempt public health and education organizations that provide grants, scholarships, and funds to support approved or accredited public health and educational institutions, but do not themselves operate such programs. Questions concerning eligibility of others should be addressed to the state agency responsible for disposal of surplus property.

Activity: FY 93 estimate, $570,000,000 in original acquisition cost of property donated.

HQ: Director, Property Management Division, Office of Transportation and Property Management, Federal Supply Service, GSA, Washington, DC 20406. Phone: (703)305-5234.

DEPOSITORY LIBRARIES FOR GOVERNMENT PUBLICATIONS

Assistance: technical information.

Purposes: availability of government publications for public reference in 1,400 depository libraries, in the U.S. and its possessions.

Eligible applicants: depository libraries are designated by members of Congress, with two Representative designations provided for in each congressional district and four Senatorial designations provided for in each state at large. By law, all state libraries, highest state appellate court libraries, land grant college libraries, and law school libraries are eligible for designation.

Eligible beneficiaries: general public.

Activity: FY 93 estimate, 27,900,000 publications distributed.

HQ: Chief, Library Division, Library Programs Service-Stop SLL, U.S. GPO, 701 Capital St. NW, Washington, DC 20401. Phone: (202)512-0571. Or Director, Library Programs Service-Stop SL, U.S. GPO, Washington, DC 20401. Phone (202)512-1114

GOVERNMENT PUBLICATIONS SALES AND DISTRIBUTION

Assistance: sale, exchange, or donation of property and goods; technical information.

Purposes: availability of government publications for sale to the general public. Discounts are available to dealers. A revolving fund supports this program.

Eligible applicants/beneficiaries: general public.

Activity: FY 93 estimate, 1,233,000 mail orders processed.

HQ: Superintendent of Documents, U.S. GPO, Washington, DC 20402. Phone: (202)512-2332.

SMALL BUSINESS ADMINISTRATION (SBA)

Provides various services to small businesses, including financial assistance, business development, small business advocacy, special assistance for minority-owned businesses, federal procurement assistance and innovative research contracts. A small business is generally defined by the SBA as one which is independently owned and operated and is not dominant in its field. Unless otherwise noted, all programs are available through each SBA district office.

Financial Assistance Programs

Provides financial assistance through loans, surety bonds, community development companies and small business investment companies.

Guaranteed Loans - Provide financial assistance to qualified small businesses that are unable to obtain credit without government aid. SBA guarantees up to $750,000 of loans granted by lending institutions. Most state and national banks and some savings and loans associations in Virginia participate in the SBA Guaranty Loan Program.

Direct Loans - If a private lender will not provide financial assistance either on their own or with SBA's guaranty, then SBA may consider direct government financing. However, funds are extremely limited.

Small General Contractor Loans - Designed to provide financing for the construction and rehabilitation of property to be sold. Available under SBA Guaranty Program only.

Contract Loan Program - To assist small firms with short term financing of labor and material costs on contracts in which the contract proceeds are assignable. Available under SBA Guaranty Program only.

Export Revolving Line of Credit Program - To provide short term revolving financing for specific export transactions or to finance labor and materials for pre-export production. In some cases, funds may be used to penetrate or develop foreign markets. Available under SBA Guaranty Programs only. SBA's Guaranty may be up to $1,000,000 with a co-guaranty from an Export-Import Bank.

7(a)(11) Program - Loans may be made to businesses located in areas with proportions of unemployment or low income individuals. See your SBA district office for more details.

Handicapped Assistance Loans - To assist persons who have a physical, mental or emotional disability of a permanent nature which, in any way, limits the selection of any type of employment for which the person would otherwise be qualified.

Physical Disaster Loans - To assist businesses located in an area that suffered damage as a result of a physical disaster. Must be declared a disaster area by the President of the United States.

Surety Bond Guaranty Program - To make the bonding system more available to small contractors who may be denied access to the system. SBA can guarantee up to 80 percent of surety's loss on a bond that has a maximum in total contract value of up to $1,250,000.

Community Development Companies - There are three types of development companies: state(501), local(502), and certified development companies(504). State and local development companies (501 and 502) provide long-term financing to small business concerns with funds provided by SBA guaranteed direct loans to the development companies. Both types are corporations chartered for the purpose of promoting economic growth within specific areas. SBA's guaranteed loans to these development companies supplement private equity capital and long-term loan funds. Funds are limited for 501 and 502 funding. Certified Development Companies (504) use SBA guaranteed debenture bonds for long term, fixed asset financing. Projects generally range in size from $200,000 to $1,000,000. A bank or other private lender typically provide 50 percent of project financing. SBA's share of the project is generally 40 percent, not to exceed $500,000. The Business would then contribute the final 10 percent of the costs. Significant job creation / economic impact is a prerequisite to qualify. A Certified Development Company can be organized as a private nonprofit corporation or for-profit stock corporation.

Small Business Investment Companies (SBIC) - Provide equity investment and long-term loans to small firms for growth, expansion and modernization. SBIC's primarily assist small firms with significant growth potential or new small firms in new industries. There are also Minority Enterprise SBIC's licensed solely to help small businesses owned and managed by socially or economically disadvantaged persons.

Veterans loans may be made to Vietnam-Era veterans 30% or more disabled, or veterans discharged due to disability.

PROCUREMENT ASSISTANCE TO SMALL BUSINESSES

Assistance: specialized services.

Purposes: assistance to small businesses in all phases of obtaining and administering government procurement contracts; small business "set-asides" in federal contracts, restricting awards to small businesses only, consultation by SBA with other federal procuring agencies, toward encouraging small business participation.

Eligible applicants/beneficiaries: existing and potential small businesses.

Activity: FY 91 representative activity, $13.4 billion in set-asides, 561 contract awards valued at $635,000,000 resulting from issuance of SBA Certificates of Competency.

HQ: Associate Administrator/Procurement Assistance, US-SBA, 409 Third St. SW, Washington, DC 20416. Phone: (202)205-6460.

SMALL BUSINESS INVESTMENT COMPANIES

Assistance: direct loans, guaranteed and insured loans (75-80 percent); advisory services and counseling.

Purposes: for SBA-licensed small business investment companies, including minority enterprise SBICs, to provide venture capital, in turn, to small businesses-through long-term loans, equity purchases, or loan guarantees. The investment companies provide management and other assistance to firms that obtain the loans.

Eligible applicants: any chartered SBIC with a combined paid-in capital and surplus of at least $2,500,000 ($1,500,000 for minority enterprise SBICs), with qualified management and evidence of sound operation, and that an establish the need for SBIC financing in the geographic area in which the applicant proposes to operate.

Eligible beneficiaries: individual businesses (single proprietorship, partnership, or corporation) also small businesses owned by disadvantaged persons.

Range: guarantee loans, $50,000 to $35,000,000. Average: $1,000,000.

Activity: FY 91, $90,500,000 in disbursements.

HQ: Director, Office of Investments - Investment Division, SBA, 409 Third St. S.W., Washington, DC 20416. Phone: (202)205-6510.

SMALL BUSINESS LOANS

Assistance: guaranteed and insured loans.

Purposes: for small businesses to construct, expand, or convert facilities, to purchase equipment or materials; for working capital. Eligible projects include the design, manufacture, marketing, installation, or servicing of specific energy measures.

Eligible applicants/beneficiaries: small businesses, including those owned by low-income and handicapped individuals or located in high unemployment areas, also nonprofit sheltered workshops.

Range: guaranty, to $750,000. Average: $192,000.

Activity: FY 91, 17,323 loans.

HQ: Director, Loan Policy and Procedures Branch, SBA, 409 3rd St. SW, Washington, DC 20416. Phone: (202)205-7510.

LOCAL DEVELOPMENT COMPANY LOANS

Assistance: guaranteed and insured loans (40%/25 years).

Purposes: for local development companies to make loans, in turn, to small businesses for the purchase of land, buildings, machinery, equipment, construction, or modernization- but not for working capital or to refinance existing debt.

Eligible applicants: local development companies incorporated under general state corporation statues, either on a profit or nonprofit basis, to promote economic growth in a particular community within the state.

Eligible beneficiaries: small businesses.

Range: guarantee loans, $62,000 to $1,000,000. Average: $359,000.

Activity: FY 91, 38 loans.

HQ: Office of Rural Affairs and Economic Development, SBA, 409 3rd St. SW, Mail Code 6123, Rm 8300, Washington, DC 20416. Phone: (202)205-6485.

BOND GUARANTEES FOR SURETY COMPANIES

Assistance: insurance, 90% guaranteed surety bonds.

Purposes: for surety companies for bid, payment, and performance or other bonds provided to small businesses on contracts up to $1,250,000.

Eligible applicants: surety companies holding certificates of authority from the Secretary of the Treasury as an acceptable surety for bonds on federal contracts, or other companies that can meet the requirements of the SBA.

Eligible beneficiaries: small contractors with gross annual receipts of no more than $3,500,000 as averaged for the last three fiscal years.

Range: $475 to $1,250,000. Average: $110,000.

Activity: FY 91, 7,500 guarantees issued.

HQ: Assistant Administrator, Office of Surety Guarantees, SBA, 409 3rd St. SW, Washington, DC 20416. Phone: (202)205-6540.

HANDICAPPED ASSISTANCE LOANS

Assistance: direct loans

Purposes: for nonprofit sheltered workshops (HAL-1) and for small businesses owned by handicapped persons (HAL-2) producing goods and services. Loan proceeds may be used for working capital, equipment, materials, or construction, but not for training, education, housing or other supportive services.

Eligible applicants/beneficiaries: HAL-1 is incorporated nonprofit organizations operating for and employing handicapped individuals for at least 75% of the man-hours required for the direct production of commodities or in the provision of services which it renders. HAL-2 are small businesses concerns that are 100% owned by handicapped individuals, whose handicap is of a nature that it would limit the individual in engaging in normal competitive business practices without SBA assistance.

Range: $500 to $350,000. Average: $95,300.

Activity: FY 90, 105 loans.

HQ: Director, Loan Policy and Procedures Branch, SBA, 409 3rd St. SW, Washington, DC 20416. Phone: (202)205-7511.

SERVICE CORPS OF RETIRED EXECUTIVES ("SCORE")

Assistance: project grants; advisory services/counseling.

Purposes: to pay the out-of-pocket expenses of retired or active business executives who volunteer their services to counsel and train new and existing small businesses.

Eligible applicants/beneficiaries: existing and potential small businesses.

Activity: currently, 12,500 volunteers, serving in all 50 states and in U.S. possessions.

HQ: SBA, 409 3rd St. SW, Washington, DC 20416. Phone: (202)205-7414.

PROCUREMENT AUTOMATED SOURCE SYSTEM ("PASS")

Assistance: specialized services.

Purposes: computerized national data system providing information to federal agencies and certain private sector firms on capabilities of small businesses, including minority- and women-owned firms, interested in obtaining government procurement contracts. Registration is free.

Eligible applicants/beneficiaries: small business concerns.

Activity: currently, 230,000 small businesses registered, 800 access locations.

HQ: Procurement Assistance, 409 3rd St. SW, Washington, DC 20416. Phone: (202)205-6469.

SMALL BUSINESS DEVELOPMENT CENTER ("SBDC")

Assistance: specialized services.

Purposes: for Small Business Development Centers to provide management counseling, training, and technical assistance to small businesses.

Eligible applicants: any public or private higher education institutions, including community or junior colleges.

Eligible beneficiaries: small businesses.

Range: $200,000 to $3,404,000. Average: $972,000.

Activity: currently, funding to 57 centers in 50 states, DC, Puerto Rico, and the Virgin Islands.

HQ: Office of Small Business Development Center, SBA, 409 3rd St. SW 5th floor, Washington, DC 20416. Phone: (202)205-6766.

VETERANS LOAN PROGRAM

Assistance: direct loans.

Purposes: for Vietnam-era or disabled veterans to construct, expand, or convert business facilities; to purchase building equipment or materials; or for working capital.

Eligible applicants/beneficiaries: small business concerns owned, a minimum of 5%, owned by eligible veterans. Management and daily operation of the business must be directed by one or more of the veteran owners, whose status is used to qualify for the loan. Vietnam-era veterans are those who served for a period of more than 180 days, any part of which was between August 5, 1964 and May 7, 1975, and were discharged other than dishonorably. Disabled veterans are those of any era with a minimum compensable disability of 30% or a veteran of any era who was discharged for disability.

Range: $1,000 to $150,000. Average: $76,000.

Activity: FY 91, 204 loans.

HQ: Director, Loan Policy and Procedures Branch, SBA, 409 3rd St. SW, Washington, DC 20416. Phone: (202)205-7511.

CERTIFIED DEVELOPMENT COMPANY LOANS

Assistance: guaranteed/insured loans (10-20 years)

Purposes: to assist small businesses, through the sale of debentures to private investors, in acquiring fixed assets-e.g., land, buildings, equipment; loans may also cover construction, expansion, renovation, or modernization. Ten percent of project costs must be provided by the certified development company, and 50% by a private lender.

Eligible applicants: nonprofit certified development companies recognized by SBA.

Eligible beneficiaries: small businesses.

Range: to $1,000,000. Average: $292,000.

Activity: FY 91, 1,517 loans.

HQ: Office of Rural Affairs and Economic Development, SBA, 409 3rd St. SW, Rm 8300, Washington, DC 20416. Phone: (202)205-6485.

BUSINESS LOANS FOR 8(A) PROGRAM PARTICIPANTS

Assistance: direct loans; guaranteed and insured loans for up to 25 years.

Purposes: for socially or economically disadvantaged businesses to construct, expand, or convert facilities, also to acquire machinery, buildings, equipment, supplies, or materials. Working capital loans are limited to manufacturers.

Eligible applicants/beneficiaries: socially and economically disadvantaged owners of small businesses, who cannot obtain funds on reasonable terms in the private credit marketplace.

Range: direct loans, to $150,000; guaranteed, to $750,000. Average: direct, $114,000.

Activity: FY 90, 22 loans.

HQ: Director, Loan Policy and Procedures Branch, SBA, 409 3rd St. SW, Washington, DC 20416. Phone: (202)205-7511.

WOMEN'S BUSINESS OWNERSHIP ASSISTANCE

Assistance: project grants 33-50%

Purposes: to conduct demonstration projections for the benefit small businesses owned and controlled by women, including financial, management, and marketing training and counseling.

Eligible applicants: profit or nonprofit organizations. Educational institutions, state and local governments, and SBA-funded SBDCs are ineligible.

Eligible beneficiaries: women entrepreneurs.

Range: \$35,000 to \$1,033,000. Average: \$408,000.

Activity: currently, 26 sites with programs.

HQ: Office of Women's Business Ownership, SBA, 409 3rd St. SW, Washington, DC 20416. Phone: (202)205-6673.

VETERANS ENTREPRENEURIAL TRAINING AND COUNSELING

Assistance: project grants (50%).

Purposes: for projects to provide training, counseling, and technical and managerial assistance to veterans and their dependents in starting or operating small businesses.

Eligible applicants: nonprofit volunteer organizations, which may subcontract with other entities to provide the services, also public or private organizations, and Small Business Development Centers.

Eligible beneficiaries: veterans and their dependents.

Range: \$45,000 to \$100,000. Average: \$71,000.

Activity: FY 93, 5 grants.

HQ: Assistant Director, Office of Veterans Affairs, SBA, 409 3rd ST. SW Sixth Floor, Washington, DC 20416. Phone: (202)205-6773.

NATURAL RESOURCE DEVELOPMENT

Assistance: project grants (formula based 75%).

Purposes: for states to contract with small businesses to plant trees on land owned by state or local governments.

Eligible applicants: states and U.S. territories and possessions.

Eligible beneficiaries: small tree planting businesses.

Range/Average: N.A.

Activity: new program in FY 91.

HQ: Office of Procurement Assistance, SBA, 409 3rd St. SW, Washington, DC 20416. Phone: (202)205-6470.

MICROLOAN DEMONSTRATION PROGRAM

Assistance: formula grants, project grants, and direct loans.

Purposes: to make loans to eligible intermediary lenders that will, in turn, provide small-scale loans of up to $25,000 to newly established or growing small businesses for working capital or for the acquisition of supplies or equipment. Also used to make matching grants with intermediaries to provided intensive grants to nonprofit nonparticipating entities to provide business assistance to low-income entrepreneurs and other low-income individuals, to assist them in obtaining private sector financing for their businesses- with or without loan guarantees, to report to Congressional committees on program effectiveness. Loans to intermediaries may be up to $750,000 in the first year, to $1,250,000 subsequently, and require a non-federal match of 15%; loans must also be secured by SBA and have a maturity of 10 years.

Eligible applicants: intermediary lenders that are private nonprofit entities, private nonprofit community development corporations- with one year of in-house experience in making and servicing micro-loans, as well as in providing intensive marketing management, and technical assistance to borrowers.

Eligible beneficiaries: small businesses, minority entrepreneurs and women, low-income and other persons.

Range/Average: N.A.

Activity: new program in 92, FY 93, 35 intermediary lenders from 30 states approved.

HQ: Office of Financing, Loan Policy and Procedures Branch, SBA, 409 3rd St. SW, Rm 8033, Washington, DC 20416. Phone: (202)205-6570.

FOREIGN INVESTMENT GUARANTIES

Assistance: guaranteed and insured loans.

Purposes: loan and other investment guarantees against loss, to U.S. investors doing business in developing countries. Examples of funded projects include power plant, food processing, credit union, hotel, mining, agri-business and paper.
Eligible applicants/beneficiaries: U.S. citizens, corporations, partnerships, other associations- and their foreign subsidiaries that are 95% owned by U.S. citizens.

Range: $4,000,000 to $50,000,000. Average: $16,000,000.

Activity: FY 91, 16 guarantees.

HQ: Information Officere, Overseas Private Investment Corporation, 1100 New York Ave. NW, Washington, DC 20527. Phone: (202) 336-8400.

FOREIGN INVESTMENT INSURANCE

Assistance: provides insurance up to 20 years.

Purposes: protection of U.S. investment in developing countries, against certain economic and political risks, including inconvertibility, expropriation, war, revolution, and civil strife. The investments must contribute to the economic and social development of host countries, and not adversely affect U.S. employment. Special programs insure contractors and exporters against arbitrary drawings of letters of credit posted as bid, performance, or advance payment guarantees. The maximum insurance term is 20 years.

Eligible applicants/beneficiaries: U.S. citizens, corporations, partnerships, other associations-and their foreign subsidiaries that are 95% owned by U.S. citizens.

Range: $18,000 to $100,000,000. Average: $23,680,000.

Activity: FY 91, 127 projects insured.

HQ: Information Officer, Overseas Private Investment Corporation, 1100 New York Ave. NW, Washington, DC 20527. Phone: (202) 336-8400.

DIRECT INVESTMENT LOANS

Assistance: direct loans.

Purposes: for private sector projects in developing countries, in which there is substantial involvement by U.S. small businesses or cooperatives.

Eligible applicants/beneficiaries: privately owned firms or firms of mixed private and public ownership sponsored by or significantly involving U.S. small businesses or cooperatives.

Range: $250,000 to $6,000,000. Average: $2,700,000.

Activity: FY 91, 12 loans.

HQ: Information Officer, Overseas Private Investment Corporation, 1100 New York Ave. Washington, DC 20527. Phone: (202)336-8400.

SUPERFUND INNOVATIVE TECHNOLOGY EVALUATION PROGRAM ("SITE")

Assistance: project grants (50% for up to 2 years)

Purposes: for programs involving the research, development, and demonstration of alternative and innovative treatment technologies that can be used in response actions under the Comprehensive Environmental Response, Compensation and Liability Act of 1980(CERCLA). Technologies may involve treatment, recycling, separation, detoxification, destruction, or stabilization of hazardous chemical wastes- including chemical, biological, thermal, physical, and stabilization or solidification treatment processes. Assistance is available through various programs to developers of emerging technologies at bench, pilot, or full scale to reach commercialization through actual field demonstrations at uncontrolled hazardous waste sites.

Eligible applicants/beneficiaries: private developers and individuals.

Range: to $3,000,000; emerging technologies, $121,000 to $300,000.

Activity: FY 93 estimate, 10 new programs.

HQ: Chief, Office of Environmental Engineering Technology Demonstration, EPA, 401 M St. SW (RD 681), Washington, DC 20460. Phone: (202)260-2583.

Appendix A

The Patent Process

You may decide that you want to do some, or all, of the patent application work yourself. Described below are the general steps involved in applying for a patent.

The Patent Search

Inventions should be "searched" for patentability. A patent search will help you determine if your invention is novel. If you don't do the search, you run the risk of investing significant time and money into a patent application which will be rejected. The search may even unearth a better product, in which case you may decide to forget the whole endeavor. Or, you may decide to license the already patented item and make or market it instead.

An advantage of doing a patent search yourself is that you can review the latest patents in your area of interest. You may get some ideas and you will certainly gain an understanding of what has previously been patented. You will also learn the style used in filing patent applications.

You can hire someone to do the search for you or you can do it yourself. Most people hire an attorney to do it. He doesn't do the search himself; rather, he hires an agent who specializes in patent searches and then he bills you for the searcher's fee (plus a commission, which averages about 40 percent.) You can save some money if you work directly with the agent. They are usually listed in "yellow pages" under "patent searchers." The greatest concentration of them is in the Washington, D.C. area. Find out about the searcher's charges, technical background, on-the-job experience, and typical amount of time spent on a search. You should also ask for the names of some clients, preferably local, that you can call to verify the searcher's honesty, competency, and diligence.

The best place to conduct a patent search is at the Patent and Trademark Office (PTO) in Arlington, Virginia. The PTO has every patent ever issued arranged into subclasses, and it also has foreign patents and literature classified in the subclasses. The PTO also maintains Patent Depository Libraries (PDL's) in each state.Check with your local libraries to determine which library(ies) are PDL's in Utah.

The PDL Librariesoffer a variety of media, as well as trained personnel, to assist you in your search. In order to conduct your search in the most efficient manner, it will be beneficial to you to adhere to the following steps.

1. Write down all the features of your invention in a brief, concise format. This is done to simplify your invention so that you will know exactly what to look for when searching. Take this description, as well as any drawings you may have of your invention, to the PDL with you.

2. Since patents are classified by subject matter into over 300 main classifications, each of which has an average of about 220 subclasses, you need to find the relevant subclasses in which to search. To find subclasses into which prior art on your invention may be classified, use the *Index to the U.S. Patent Classification*. This is the starting place that gives you an alphabetical list of classes and subclasses.

   Look over the index, observe the cross-references, and familiarize yourself with the system. You should then obtain what you believe to be the correct subclasses. After you find one or more subclasses which you believe may be relevant, check these in the *U.S. Patent Classification Definitions* (which you will find on microfiche at the PDL's) to be sure that you have obtained the correct subclasses. The *U.S. Patent Classification Definitions* will also give you valuable searching hints and cross-references. You should also refer to the *Manual of Classification* (which is arranged by classes and subclasses) to see if there are any other relevant subclasses near your selected subclasses.

3. After you have decided on the class and subclass numbers that your patent idea may fall under, ask a librarian to search on the computer for a list of the patents that have been granted under your given subclass. The librarian will use the "Classification and Search Support Information System" (CASSIS), which links directly to the U.S. Patent Depository computer base. Once you have obtained this list, you need to review the applicable patents.

4. After you have obtained all applicable patents and other references, study them to see if the concepts of your invention are shown and described in any of the references you have selected. This will probably be the most difficult and time-consuming part of your search.

5. After you have made your search, obtained all your references, and looked them over, you should have a pretty good idea of the patentability of your invention.

The Disclosure Document

One of the services provided for inventors is the acceptance and preservation for a two-year period of papers disclosing an invention. This disclosure is accepted as evidence of the dates of conception of the invention. It will be retained for two years at which time it will be destroyed unless it is referred to in a separate letter in a related patent application.

This disclosure must be accompanied by a stamped, self-addressed envelope and a separate paper in duplicate also signed by the inventor. The papers will be stamped with an identifying number and returned with the reminder that the Disclosure Document may be relied upon only as evidence and that an application must be filed in order to provide patent protection.

It should be noted, and cannot be emphasized too strongly, that the Patent and Trademark Office's Disclosure Document Program exists and operates for one purpose: to provide inventors with a very creditable witness to their disclosures. The program is not a substitute for filing a patent application or for building and testing the invention. Also, filing a disclosure under the program will not provide the inventor with any "grace period" or any other justification for delaying the filing of a patent application.

The Patent Application

U.S. Patent law states: "Application for patent shall be made, or authorized to be made, by the inventor, except as otherwise provided in this title, in writing to the Commissioner. Such application shall include (1) a specification; (2) a drawing; and (3) an oath by the applicant. This application must be accompanied by the fee required by law. The fee and oath may be submitted after the specification and any required drawing are submitted, within such period and under such conditions, including the payment of a surcharge, as may be prescribed by the Commissioner. Upon failure to submit the fee and the oath within such prescribed period, the application shall be regarded as abandoned, unless it is shown to the satisfaction of the Commissioner that the delay in submitting the fee and oath was unavoidable. The filing date of an application shall be the date on which the specification and any required drawing are received in the Patent and Trademark Office." [7]

A *specification* should contain a written description of the invention, and of the manner and process of making and using it, in such a manner as to enable any person skilled in the art to which it pertains, to make and use the item. A specification should conclude with one or more claims pointing out and distinctly claiming the subject matter which the applicant regards as his invention.

A drawing should be furnished where it is necessary for the understanding of the subject matter to be patented. The drawings you send to the PTO must be drawn clearly and carefully on strong, white, smooth paper, preferably in India ink on the stiff, thick, calendared paper called bristol board. The drawing sheet must be 8 1/2 inches wide and 14 inches long. The top margin must be 2 inches and the side and bottom margins must be 1/4 inch each. This leaves a drawing area of 8 inches by 11 3/4 inches. All work must be confined to this drawing area. You may not use margin border lines. If your drawings do not comply strictly to the rules, you may ask a Patent Office draftsman to correct them. You will be charged a nominal fee for this work.

The oath that an applicant makes states that he/she believes himself/herself to be the original and first inventor of the process, machine, manufacture, or composition of matter, for which he/she is seeking a patent. The applicant must make various other allegations required by law and various allegations required by Patent and Trademark rules. The applicant will also state the country in which he/she is a citizen. The oath must be sworn to by the inventor before a notary public or other officer authorized to administer oaths.

You must also include a filing fee with your application. This fee is based on the number of claims you submit. The basic fee is $340.00 and entitles an applicant to present twenty (20) claims, including not more than three (3) in independent form.

Filing the Patent Application

Once the Patent Office has received your application, you will be notified and you may mark your product with "Pat. Pend.," "Patent Pending," or "Patent Applied For." It is against the law to use these terms unless you actually do have an application pending or on file in the Patent Office.

It usually takes about a year for the Patent Office to respond to your application. During this time however, do not let a potential buyer see the claims, declaration, serial number, or filing date. An unscrupulous manufacturer with this knowledge may try to file an application and concoct evidence of prior inventorship to win an interference against you.

References

1. Jones, Stacy V. *The Inventor's Patent Handbook.* New York: The Dial Press, 1969.

2. Levy, Richard C. *Inventing and Patenting Sourcebook.* Detroit: Gale Research, 1990.

3. Pressman, David. *Patent It Yourself.* New York: McGraw-Hill Book Company, 1979.

4. Richardson, Robert O. *How to Get Your Own Patent.* New York: Sterling Publishing Co., 1981.

5. Russell, J. Thomas et. al. *Kleppner's Advertising Procedure,* 10th Ed. Englewood Cliffs, New Jersey: Prentice Hall, Inc., 1986.

6. Samuels, Jeffery M. *Patent, Trademark, and Copyright Laws.* Washington, D.C.: The Bureau of National Affairs, Inc., 1987.

7. *General Information Concerning Patents*. Washington, D.C.: U.S. Department of Commerce, Patent and Trademark Office, 1989.

Appendix B

Computer Financial Templates

Computer spreadsheet programs are wonderful tools that help you generate financial projections. They allow you to quickly and easily change assumptions and do "what-if" analyses that otherwise are extremely time-consuming if done with pencil and paper.

Financial spreadsheet templates have been provided for you to generate the typical financial projections in a business plan--breakeven, cash flow, income statement, and balance sheet. A loan amortization template has been included to assist in generating the other statements. Printouts of each of these templates are included at the end of Chapter 13, The Business Plan. Any version of Lotus 1-2-3, or spreadsheet that reads 1-2-3 files, can use these templates. However, the macross embedded in the program will probably not work in any program except 1-2-3. The templates are still usable; however, you will have to do some operations manually, such as printing, instead of relying on the macros to do them for you automatically. You must already have a spreadsheet to run these programs—they are not stand-alone programs. Make a backup copy of the template diskette either onto your hard drive or a floppy diskette.

You must have at least a beginner's knowledge of your spreadsheet program for these templates to be of value. This appendix does not teach you how to use Lotus 1-2-3 or any other spreadsheet program. Take a spreadsheet class, go through the self-learning tutorial supplied with your spreadsheet, or else buy a book that teaches you the program. If you are really brave, you can even wade through your user's manual. You *can* learn the basics of a spreadsheet program from a book. For the steps outlined in this section, commands are given in 1-2-3. If you have a spreadsheet that has commands different than 1-2-3, you will have to translate them.

Breakeven Analysis

The first projection that you want to generate is a breakeven analysis. Review Chapter 11, Cash Flow Management, to refresh your memory on breakeven. Follow these steps:

1. Load your spreadsheet.
2. Retrieve the file named BKEVEN. /FRBKEVEN~
3. Change the account titles so they are the expenses in your business.
4. Decide whether you want this to be a monthly or yearly breakeven. The first tells you how much you have to sell in a month to break even, the second tells you how much you have to sell in a year. If sales are highly seasonal, do it on an annual basis. If most months are fairly consistent, do it on a monthly basis.
5. Classify every expense item as either fixed, variable, or combination (see Chapter 11). Type fixed dollar amounts in the B column. Variable decimal percentages go in column C. For example, if utilities are fixed and run about $500, enter 500 in the B column. If merchandise expense is typically 50 percent of sales, type in .50 in column C.
6. Save often! /FSFILENAME~
   If you don't save your spreadsheet often, a power surge or a child who turns your computer off can lose a lot of work for you. Save your worksheet every ten minutes-- it is a quick insurance policy against data loss. When you save a worksheet, give it a name different than the original template (in this case BKEVEN). If you try to save it under the same name, you will get an error message since the original files are "locked" and cannot be overwritten.
7. Move the cursor down to the total line and see what your total fixed and variables expenses are. If your variable column adds to more than one, you probably mistyped a figure. Go back and review your numbers.
8. Your breakeven amount in dollars is shown on line 32.
9. If you have a single-product company, type in your selling price in cell B34. B35 will show you how many units that represents. This figure is valid *only* if you sell only one product.
10. To print this worksheet, type Alt-P. This means hold down the Alt Key and type P once. It will automatically print the whole worksheet.

11. View the breakeven graph. /GV
12. Add any options you want to the breakeven graph. This includes adding titles, grids, and other features in your spreadsheet program. You will have to learn the graphing section of your program to do this.
13. When the graph is what you want, save the graphic image. /GSNAME~
14. If you are using 1-2-3, exit the program, enter Printgraph, select the images that you want to graph, then print them.

Cash Flow Projections

Your cash flow projection is critical. You want to demonstrate that with your forecasted cash inflows and outflows you are able to pay your bills and finance the growth that you anticipate. For the cash flow statement to be of value, you need to accurately forecast the *timing* of cash inflows and outflows. If you pay insurance once a year, show it as such. Don't average it across all months. The same principle applies to purchases of inventory. When and how much are you going to spend on purchases?

Two templates are provided for cash flow projections. One is for the first year of operations and is broken down by months. The title of the template is CASHYR1. The second is for years two and three and is broken down by quarters. It is entitled CASHYR2. Review Chapter 11, Cash Management, before going through the following steps:

1. Load your spreadsheet.
2. Retrieve the file named CASHYR1. /FRCASHYR1~
3. Don't be dismayed by the zeroes all over the screen-- formulas are in those cells. Also, when you type in numbers, you will see numbers "appearing everywhere." The formulas recalculate every time you type in a new figure.
4. Change the account titles if you need to. To do so, turn off the titles command-- /WTC . Go to the cells that need to be changed. When you are finished, move the cursor to C5 and reinvoke the titles command-- /WTB . You are thus able to see account titles no matter where you are on the worksheet.
5. Enter the beginning cash on hand in row 5.
6. Enter cash inflows in rows 8, 9, and 10.
7. Enter cash outflows starting on line 17. The accounts down to line 37 are mostly "expense" cash outflows. Lines 41 to 45 are "non-expense" cash outflows.

8. Look at line 49 for your end-of-month cash balance. If you want to do "what-if" analysis, you need to divide your screen into two "windows." In 1-2-3, the command is /WWH. The F6 key flips you back and forth between windows. If you do this, you are able to change assumptions in the top window and see the effect on cash position in the bottom window.
9. Save often! Save under a name other than CASHYR1.
10. To print your work, type Alt-P.
11. To save time in doing your income statement projection, type Alt-U before you leave the program. This saves information that will be used in your income statement and thus does not have to be retyped.
12. Before exiting the worksheet, write down the ending cash balance in December. This will be used as the starting cash balance in next cash flow projection.
13. When you have completed this statement, you are ready to work on years two and three. Retrieve the cash flow statement for years two and three, /FRCASHYR23.
14. Type in the beginning cash balance as your previous ending cash balance from CASHYR1.
15. Repeat steps 4-12 for years two and three.

Income Statement Projections

The income statement shows revenues, expenses, and the difference between them, which is net profit. Most of the expenses can come directly from your cash flow sheet, and the template is automated so that it brings those expenses in without your having to retype them.

While the cash flow statement shows the exact timing of cash inflows and outflows, the income statement should show when revenues and expenses *occurred*, even though cash was paid at another time. Consider employer payroll taxes, which are due quarterly. They are shown on the cash flow statement in the months when checks are written. In the income statement, it would be misleading to allocate all of that expense in one month. You would have two months with low expenses and one month with high expenses. Therefore, you distribute that expense over each of the three months. Sales are shown in the month in which an invoice is written, rather than when cash is collected. When expenses are loaded in from your cash flow statement, review each one and decide if the timing of the expense is different than when cash is paid out. Consult an accountant if you need help in making these adjustments.

Two income statement templates are provided. ISYR1 is for year one and is broken down by months. ISYR2 is for years two and three and is broken down by quarters. Follow these steps in completing your income statement projections:

1. Load your spreadsheet.
2. Retrieve the income statement template for year one. /FRISYR1
3. If you want to change account titles, turn off the Titles Command. /WTC
4. Change account titles (if desired) to fit your business. Remember that you will be pulling expenses in from your cashflow worksheet and thus those expenses must be the same as on your cashflow projections.
5. Move the cursor to C5, and reinvoke the Titles Command. /WTB
6. If you want to use the expenses that you typed in your cashflow projection, type Alt-U. Otherwise, you will need to type in all expense items.
7. Type in revenues and costs of goods sold. The space provided allows you to type in profit centers or product names in these sections. For example, if there are two divisions in your company, you should type in names for both divisions in the space provided under revenues and costs of goods sold. Then for each division you can keep track of these items separately.
8. Notice that depreciation is an expense that does not appear on your cash flow statement. Consult someone with good accounting skills to calculate your depreciation.
9. As described above, consider each expense item and decide if the timing needs to be changed to properly allocate when the expense will be incurred.
10. As with the cash flow statement, you may want to create two "windows" to see what effect changes in the worksheet have on net profit. /WWH
11. Save often!
12. To print the income statement projection, type Alt-P.
13. When you have completed the income statement projection for the first year, save it a final time. Retrieve the worksheet for years two and three. /FRISYR23
14. Repeat steps 3-12 for years two and three.

Balance Sheet Projections

A balance sheet shows what your company owns, what it owes, and the difference between the two, which is called net worth or equity. For the business plan, you want to show the projected balance sheet at startup and at the end of years one, two, and three. The balance sheet is more difficult to project than the statements described above and an accountant's advice would be valuable when putting it together. Project the balance sheets only after your other statements are completed. Follow these steps:

1. Load your spreadsheet.
2. Retrieve the balance sheet template. /FRBS
3. Change the titles (optional) if you need to adapt it to your specific business.
4. Fill in balance sheet amounts at startup.
5. Cash balance at startup comes from your cash flow statement. Look at the same statement to arrive at a year-end cash position.
6. Accounts receivable balance depends upon your credit policy. To generate your cash flow statement, you had to estimate how quickly customers would pay you. Based on those estimates, calculate how much would be owed to you at the end of each year. For example, if 80 percent of your accounts are collected in thirty days, and the remaining 20 percent are collected in thirty days, use your sales projections for the last two months of each year to determine the amount of receivables at year end.
7. Inventory usually fluctuates with the level of sales. If you foresee your company following a different inventory pattern, type in your estimates. If you show inventory increasing, be sure to reflect that in your cash flow statement. Purchases will be higher than what you actually sell (an accountant can calculate this for you).
8. Land is shown at purchase price and is neither appreciated nor depreciated.
9. Building, furniture, and equipment are shown consistently at original purchase price, but depreciation on them increases.
10. Enter depreciation as a negative number beneath the corresponding asset.
11. Accounts payable depend upon the terms that vendors give you. Most give you thirty days to pay, therefore accounts payable at year end would be the amount of purchases during December.
12. Notes payable are short-term notes that are to be paid off in under one year.
13. The amount of long-term debt can be calculated by the template AMORT. This amortization program calculates loan balances, monthly payments, and shows how much of each payment is principle and interest.
14. Total equity is the difference between assets and debt. If your firm is incorporated, the value for common stock remains at the

original issuance price. The balancing figure appears in retained earnings. If you are not incorporated, the balancing figure appears as owners equity. Write a formula which balances the two sides of the balance sheet. If you are incorporated, the formula at startup is +C24 - (C43+C46+C47). If you are not incorporated, the formula at startup is C24 - C43.

15. If you wrote the formula correctly, total debt plus equity should equal total assets. If they don't, you need to check the formula that you wrote.
16. Save often!
17. To print the worksheet, type Alt-P.

Loan Amortization

A loan amortization template is included to assist you in calculating all of the above financial statements. This program calculates loan balances, monthly payments, and shows how much of each payment is principle and interest. To use it, follow these steps:

1. Load your spreadsheet.
2. Retrieve the amortization template. /FRAMORT
3. The initial screen gives instructions on using the template.
4. Type Alt-B to begin plugging in numbers.
5. The program prompts you for loan value. Type it in without commas or dollar signs and hit Return.
6. It prompts you for interest rate. Type it in decimal form (12%= .12)
7. Type in number of payments/year.
8. If you made a mistake in typing, you can go back now and change it.
9. Type Alt-C to calculate the amortization schedule.
10. To print it, type Alt-P.
11. There is little reason to save your work, since it can be regenerated by typing in only three numbers.
12. To restart the program, retype Alt-B.

Appendix C

Sample Business Plan

The business plan on the following pages is presented as example of what one looks like. The plan was written in 1989; hence, some of the information may be outdated. The plan is not without flaws, and it does not conform exactly with the outline in this book. No business plan is perfect, however, and so hopefully this plan will give you a sense of what a fairly technical plan looks like.

Table of Contents

EXECUTIVE SUMMARY

The Opportunity

Every computer system requires a disk operating system (DOS) to function. The microcomputer DOS world is dominated by Microsoft's MS-DOS. Sales for MS-DOS are projected to be approximately 10 million copies in each of the next several years. Microsoft has remained nearly unchallenged in the DOS market for IBM compatible computers.

Microsoft, located near Seattle, Washington, is the world's largest software company. The company has been accused by many of being slow to respond to demands for improvement because of the lack of competition. Only one company, Digital Research, has marketed an alternative single-user, single-tasking operating system that will run MS-DOS application programs. Its product, DR DOS, is basically an MS-DOS clone which sells for less than MS-DOS. Total sales of DR DOS to date are reportedly over 4 million copies. Digital Research has demonstrated that Microsoft can be challenged in the microcomputer DOS world.

ITS is completing development of a disk operating system called HI-dos. It is completely compatible with, but possesses far greater capabilities than, MS-DOS. HI-dos runs faster, contains more powerful commands, is easier to use, and "looks nicer" than MS-DOS. Since HI-dos sells for less than either MS-DOS or DR DOS, and is a superior product, ITS faces significant opportunities in the microcomputer DOS industry.

Management Team

Three people have been centrally involved in managing ITS. Leonard O , an experienced businessman with a proven entrepreneurial track record, has been the driving force behind the company. He has owned and run his own businesses for over thirty years, primarily in the construction industry. A search is currently underway for a President who has considerable experience and contacts in the microcomputer industry. Thierry G , the head software engineer, has an M.B.A. and an M.S. in computer science and has considerable experience in software development. Michael A , another engineer, started and managed an international computer marketing firm. Several engineers and other employees will be added to staff in the next several months.

Financial Returns

The breakeven point in dollars for 1991 is approximately $2.1 million. Sales are projected to be $3.5 million, which will result in a profit after taxes of approximately $1 million. Sales are projected to increase to $14 million by 1993, with a resulting profit after taxes of $5.6 million. Returns (after taxes) on equity for the first three years of operations are projected to be:

1991	63%
1992	87%
1993	110%

Proposed Company Offering

ITS is offering 1,000,000 shares of common stock at $1.00 per share. 3,500,000 shares are currently outstanding. The new shares issued thus represent 22% ownership of the company. The earnings per share in 1993 are projected to be $1.24. At an estimated P/E ratio of 15, the stock would be evaluated at $18.6. The increase in net worth for any investor will obviously be considerable.

THE COMPANY AND ITS OVERALL STRATEGY

1. THE OPPORTUNITY

Every computer system requires a disk operating system (DOS) to function. DOS controls the basic functioning of computers before any application software, such as a word processor, spreadsheet, or a database program, can be run. Applications programmers must write their software to be compatible with specific disk operating systems.

The microcomputer world is dominated by MS-DOS, a disk operating system that was developed by Microsoft for IBM and compatible computers. Sales for MS-DOS are projected to be approximately 10 million copies in each of next several years. Microsoft has remained nearly totally unchallenged in the disk operating system market for IBM compatible computers. Microsoft, located in Redmond, Washington, is the world's largest software company. The company, in the opinion of many, has been slow to respond to demands for an improved DOS because of its lack of competition. Only one company, Digital Research, has marketed an alternative single-user, single-tasking operating system that will run MS-DOS applications programs. It is called DR DOS. Digital Research has reportedly sold over 4 million total copies of DR DOS since June 1988, thus demonstrating that Microsoft can be challenged in systems software.

ITS is completing development of a disk operating system called HI-dos. It is completely compatible with, but possesses far greater capabilities than, MS-DOS. HI-dos runs faster, contains more powerful commands, is easier to use, and "looks nicer" than MS-DOS. Digital Research has demonstrated that MS-DOS can be challenged, and ITS's operating system is superior to either of these companies'.

A pre-release version of HI-dos has been reviewed in the French computer magazine, DECISION. Regarded by the columnist as a technical revolution in the MS-DOS world, HI-dos was designated the "Clone of the Year." A translation of the original article entitled "HI-DOS: LE CLONE DE L'ANNEE," which appeared in the July 1989 issue of the magazine, is included in Appendix A. HI-dos also received high marks in functionality and compatibility from Van Wolverton, industry expert and author of the popular DOS handbooks "RUNNING MS-DOS" and "SUPERCHARGING MS-DOS." In his opinion, DOS will continue to be the dominant operating system for IBM compatible computers for at least another 4 years, and HI-dos has the potential to be the most serious rival to MS-DOS. A copy of Wolverton's letter is included in Appendix B.

ITS anticipates capturing 14% of the original equipment manufacturers (OEMs) MS-DOS compatible market, which results in tremendous financial returns. The OEMs will first be approached to license the operating system and provide it with every computer that they sell. License agreements with only a few OEMs can result in sales in the hundreds of thousands of units. Initial reactions on the OEMs parts to HI-dos have been very favorable. According to a survey of more than ten OEMs, conducted recently by ITS representatives in Taiwan, most of the OEMs indicated an interest in evaluating HI-dos on their systems when the program becomes available.

2. THE COMPANY

ITS was organized in 1988 in Taiwan and was moved to the United States in 1989. Three people have been centrally involved in the company -- Leonard O , an experienced businessman with a proven entrepreneurial track record; Thierry G , a software engineer with an M.B.A.; and Michael A , a computer specialist who previously started and managed a computer marketing firm.

ITS is in the final stages of product development and testing of HI-dos and will begin marketing it in the fall of 1990. The company is preparing for tremendous growth in the next year. A new office is being opened in Seattle. The search for a President with a successful track record in the microcomputer industry is underway, and three new software engineers will be added to the staff by summer.

INDUSTRY ANALYSIS

DOS was the operating system selected by IBM in 1981 for its first personal computer, the IBM PC. Since then, it has been the predominant operating system for IBM and IBM-compatible personal computers.

1. THE STAYING POWER OF DOS

DOS, known originally as QDOS and 86-DOS, was developed by (Tim Paterson of the now defunct) Seattle Computer Products for computers that use the Intel 8088 or 8086 microprocessors. Microsoft bought the right to DOS and licensed it to IBM as PC-DOS and later to clone makers and other customers as MS-DOS. Eventually, IBM became the co-developer of DOS with Microsoft.

It is estimated that there are more than 40 million copies of DOS in use. Despite its popularity, DOS is hardly any PC user's most favorite operating system. The often cited drawbacks include the lack of functions and the enigmatic command-line user interface. The slew of third-party and public domain DOS add-in utilities that have been developed attest to the deficiencies of DOS. These programs provide DOS users essential features such as intuitive file and disk management and customized menu system.

The most critical limitation of DOS, perhaps, is its failure to catch up with the advances in computer hardware. Even though DOS has undergone a number of upgrades (see Table 1), it remains a single-tasking operating system that allows programs to run only in the 640K-byte memory space defined by the 8088/8086 microprocessors and IBM's original PC design.

There was speculation about the imminent demise of DOS when IBM rolled out the IBM PC/AT in 1984. At the heart of this new personal computer is the Intel 80286 microprocessor which provides programs access to 16M-bytes of memory as well as multitasking capability. Unlike the launch of the IBM PC, however, IBM did not introduce the ATs with an operating system that could immediately utilize the full potential of the more advanced microprocessor. Indeed, it took IBM and Microsoft three years to announce a new operating system; the first '286-specific operating system, known as the OS/2, was released in 1987. Meanwhile, market acceptance of the '286-based systems was exceptional, and as more and more DOS applications that could use the speed of an AT became available, DOS gained an opportune moment to establish itself as the preeminent operating system.

It turns out that most '286 machines would require costly hardware enhancements to run OS/2 adequately. The lack of applications also contributes to the sluggish start of OS/2.

Understandably, most software publishers would hesitate to invest on an untried operating system.

The gap in hardware and software technologies continued as the personal computer industry entered the '386-era. More than three years after Compaq delivered the first 80386-based machine, the '386 version of OS/2 is still on the drawing board. Like the '286s, a majority of the installed '386s are used to run DOS applications. A recent survey of 500 U.S. corporations and institutions confirms the dominance of DOS -- as of November 1989, over 92 percent of all commercial software packages in use were running under DOS (PC Week, February 5, 1990, p.142).

While OS/2 is touted as the operating system of the future, it will not be selling in large numbers any time soon. It is becoming obvious that the transition from DOS to OS/2, if and when it happens, will be slow. The large installed base of DOS-systems means DOS will continue to be a vital force in personal computing.

Table 1
Upgrade Path of DOS

Version	Year	Functionality
1.0	1981	Original disk operating system
1.25	1982	Support for double-sided disks
2.0	1983	Support for subdirectories
2.01	1983	Support for international symbols
2.11	1983	Bug fixes
2.25	1983	Extended character set support
3.0	1984	Support for 1.2 MB floppy disks
3.1	1984	Support for PC networks
3.2	1986	Support for micro floppies
3.3	1987	Allows partitioning of larger than 32 MB hard disks
4.0	1988	Easy to use shell interface and installation programs Support for larger than 32 MB non-partitioned disks
4.01	1988	Bug fixes

Source: Datapro Report on Microcomputers, Datapro Research Corp., September 1989.

2. GROWTH POTENTIAL

Three generations of the Intel 80-series microprocessors have gone by and DOS is still the standard operating system for the Intel-based systems. DOS is an outdated technology. However, a great number of operational and functional enhancements from third-party software developers are available for DOS users. These independent efforts together contribute to extend the useful life of DOS and the possibilities of DOS programs. It is likely that DOS will continue its dominance of the operating system market in the foreseeable future.

2.1. DOS Helpers

The durability of DOS is by no means accidental. Thanks to the ingenuity of software engineers, frustrated DOS users have had help from a large variety of utility programs which overcome the many shortcomings of DOS.

The negligence of IBM and Microsoft, in spite of DOS's ineptness, opens a window of opportunity for third-party software developers. Many of them thrive in the DOS add-in market with programs which make DOS easier and more intuitive to use. These programs fill the voids in DOS by adding features such as file management, full screen text editor, data recovery, disk diagnostic and maintenance, sector editor, etc. Most of these features can be found in commercial packages such as PC Tools, the Norton Utilities, and the Mace Utilities (see Table 2 for a summary of features).

In addition to extending the functionality of DOS, the other notable contribution of the DOS utilities is the improvement in user interface. Most utility packages implement a menu system with on-line help to guide the users through all the built-in functions. A similar concept is applied in the design of the DOS shell or front end programs, which feature point and shoot operation for both DOS and DOS add-in commands. Popular DOS shells such as The Norton Commander and 1dir+ also provide a menu generator for managing DOS applications. Starting version 4.0, a shell developed by IBM has been added to DOS.

Many DOS utility programs regularly make PC Magazine's Top Ten Sellers list. Based on the number of units sold in the week ending January 27, 1990, three of the ten best sellers were utility software (see Table 3). Capitalizing on DOS users' interests, most computer magazines have a regular segment on DOS utilities. Some even include diskettes with a collection of utility programs as a bonus for magazine subscriptions.

Table 2
Popular DOS Utilities
Summary of Features

	PC Tools Deluxe	The Norton Utilites, Advanced Edition	The Mace Utilities
File and Editing:			
Text Editor	yes	no	no
Sector Editor	yes	yes	yes
File attribute editor	yes	yes	yes
File finder	yes	yes	yes
Text finder	yes	no	yes
Edit within text finder	yes	no	no
Unerase	yes	yes	yes
Quick unerase	no	yes	yes
File compress/decompress	yes	no	no
Extended filename creation	no	no	yes
Directory Features:			
Directory sorting	yes	yes	yes
Visual tree	yes	yes	yes
Move files between directories	yes	yes	no
Disk Features:			
Defect analysis	yes	yes	yes
Reformat recovery	yes	yes	yes
Defragmentation	yes	yes	yes
Disk mapping	yes	yes	yes
Backup	yes	no	no
Benchmark tests	no	yes	yes
Format conversion	yes	no	no
Caching	yes	yes	no
Restore damaged boot sector and partition table	yes	yes	yes
Application Management:			
Application execution	yes	no	no
Security Features:			
File encryption/decryption	yes	no	no
Password protection	yes	no	no
Antivirus features	no	yes	no
Wipeout file permanently	no	yes	yes
Printer Management:			
Printer setup	no	no	yes

Note: PC Tools Deluxe also features four desktop managers, including calendar, calculator, clock, and alarm clock.

Source: PC Magazine, v.9, n.6, March 27, 1990, p.106

The popularity of the utility programs reflects, on the one hand, users' dissatisfaction with DOS, and on the other, their commitment to the DOS-based system. Each and every DOS utility in the marketplace is in essence a negative vote on IBM and Microsoft for their insensitiveness to the users' demand. As a group, these programs shed lights on how and what features should be incorporated in DOS. DOS users cherish their favorite DOS applications and they need a better DOS. The vast interest among DOS users for a more competent operating system represents great market potential for a revamped DOS.

2.2. Unconventional Memory Management

While both IBM and Microsoft fail to take the lead in bringing DOS up-to-date with the advances in microprocessor technology, the DOS world does not stand still. One of the significant technical achievements is in the area of memory management, which provides DOS applications a mechanism to preserve and/or push beyond the 640K-byte work space accessible by DOS.

Table 3
DOS Application and Utility Programs
Top Ten Sellers

	Title	Publisher
1.	WordPerfect 5.1	WordPerfect Corp.
2.	Fastback Plus 2.0	Fifth Generation Systems
3.	Quicken 3.0	Intuit
4.	Microsoft Works 2.0	Microsoft Corp.
5.	Lotus 1-2-3 2.2	Lotus Development Corp.
6.	The Norton Utilities, Advanced Edition 4.5	Peter Norton Computing
7.	PC Tools Deluxe 5.5	Central Point software
8.	Carbon Copy Plus	Microcom
9.	Microsoft Word 5.0	Microsoft Corp.
10.	ProComm Plus	Datastorm

Note: Ranking based on net sales by unit in the week ending January 27, 1990

Source: PC Magazine, v.5, n.6, March 27, p.63.

2.2.1. Expanded Horizon

An important break-through is the expanded memory specification (EMS), which was jointly developed by Lotus and Intel and later endorsed by Microsoft in 1985. Known as the Lotus/Intel/Microsoft expanded memory specification, or LIM spec, it uses a "bank-switching" scheme to break the 640K barrier imposed by DOS. Most significantly, expanded memory can be installed on all Intel-based systems, including the low end 8088/8086s, and software support for EMS is easy to implement.

Not surprisingly, Lotus was the first to release software products with EMS upgrades. The use of expanded memory in its 1-2-3 spreadsheet program and Symphony multi-purpose package allows for larger and more sophisticated worksheets.

EMS is instrumental in pumping new life into the DOS-based machines. In addition to directly enhancing the capability and size of DOS applications, EMS has also been applied in many other ways useful to DOS users:

- On 8088/8086s and '286s with expanded memory, memory management tools such as Move'em by Qualitas Inc. and QRAM by Quarterdeck Office Systems, Inc. can move device drivers and terminate-and-stay-resident (TSR) programs out of the 640K-byte memory addressed by DOS, thus freeing memory space for DOS applications.

- '386-specific memory management tools such as Qualitas' 386Max and Quarterdeck's QEMM-386 can transform the extended memory on the '386-based systems into expanded memory, which can then be used by DOS applications that support EMS. They can also preserve the DOS work space by relocating device drivers and TSR programs.

- Operating environments such as Quarterdeck's DESQview and Microsoft Windows, which bring task-switching and multitasking into the DOS world and are themselves the contributing factor of DOS's endurability, can utilize expanded memory for running and swapping different programs. The availability of expanded memory also increases the number of DOS applications that can be installed for multitasking.

- Simple task-switching programs, like Software Carousel from SoftLogic Solutions, are capable of opening and switching up to ten DOS programs. They also use expanded memory.

- EMS emulation software programs such as Above Disc from Above Software and TurboEMS from Lantana Technology Inc. use hard disk space to emulate expanded memory.

2.2.2. DOS Extenders

In the DOS environment, the massive capabilities of the '386s and '486s, or even the '286s, are wasted. The '286 microprocessor, for instance, can address up to 16M-bytes of memory. The '386 and '486, moreover, are 32-bit microprocessors which have an even larger addressable memory. Known as extended memory, this is not available for regular DOS applications. The demand for more powerful and sophisticated software, on the other hand, has put increased pressure on the 640K barrier.

For software developers who are bumping their heads on the limited memory space of DOS, the availability of a special type of memory management tool, called the DOS extender, is a welcome relief. By incorporating this technique, application programs will be able to prod the DOS memory wasteland, while at the same time maintain compatibility with DOS. Unlike the implementation of EMS, only the programs which directly support DOS extenders can benefit from the increased memory, and these programs cannot be run on the 8088/8086s.

The concept of DOS extender was separately developed in 1986 by three different companies -- Eclipse, PharLap Software, and Rational Systems. Since then, it has been endorsed by major corporations such as IBM, Hewlett-Packard, Lotus, and Borland. Lotus 1-2-3 Release 3.0 and Paradox/386 are among the prominent DOS applications that incorporate the extender technology.

2.3. The Virtue of 80386s

As prices plummet, the '386-based machines are fast becoming the desktop computing standard. A recent PC Week survey shows that the '386s and '386SXs together account for almost 60 percent of the year-ahead planned purchase of the Intel-based personal computers at U.S. corporations and institutions (see Table 4).

The emergence of the '386 class computers is perceived by industry experts as the dawn of true multitasking and multi-user computing. With the '486s already in the horizon, DOS is undoubtedly outdated. As noted earlier, however, a clear-cut replacement for DOS has been very slow in the making. And without a capable operating system, the potential of these mighty new personal computers remains largely untapped.

Contrary to the conventional wisdom, however, the increased popularity of the '386s does not necessarily spell the end for DOS. A vast majority of the '386s are still installed as DOS-based systems. They have the speed advantage unmatched by the '286s, and can enhance the performance of many heavy-duty DOS applications, particularly the CPU- and data-intensive programs such as database management, statistical analysis, and CAD.

By virtue of the Virtual-86 mode of the '386 microprocessor, multitasking of DOS applications on a '386 is more efficient than on a '286. DESQview 386, Microsoft Windows/386, and VM/386 from Intelligent Graphics Corp. are examples of '386-specific operating environments that are DOS compatible and are able to make use of the features of the '386s. These programs provide multitasking capabilities without having to switch to OS/2 or other operating systems.

With the support of the existing base of popular DOS applications, and the availability of technical enhancements which enable current and future programs to take advantage of the advanced microprocessors, there is no compelling reason to abandon DOS.

2.4. Opportunity "Windows"

Microsoft Windows is a very unique program in the DOS world. It is Microsoft's attempt to implement the Macintosh look and feel on the DOS-based systems. It features a graphical user interface that consists of drop-down menus, dialog boxes, pop-up messages, icons, and mouse support.

Table 4
Intel-Based Personal Computers
Share of Year-Ahead Planned Purchases
As of September 1989

	IBM	Compaq	Others	Total
80386s	17%	5%	12%	34%
80386SXs	10%	3%	12%	25%
80286s	13%	5%	16%	34%
8088/8086	4%	0%	3%	7%
Total	**44%**	**13%**	**43%**	**100%**

Note: Results based on survey of 500 U.S corp. and institutions.

Source: PC Week, January 8, 1990, p.122.

On appearances, Windows is essentially a command shell that loads after DOS and then takes control of the machine. It allows the users to select and perform DOS functions without having to enter the DOS commands. Unlike other DOS shells, however, it also provides an integrated environment in which the users can put different applications in windows on the same display, and quickly switch applications or transport data among them. Windows can run both Windows applications and regular DOS programs in full screen display, in windows, or as icons. For applications which are specially written to run under Windows, they have the additional advantage of a uniform user interface.

Due to the lack of Windows applications, market acceptance of Windows has been slow after its release in 1985. In recent years, however, there is a growing list of excellent Window-based programs such as Aldus' PageMaker, Microsoft Excel, Microsoft Word for Windows, Micrografx's Designer, Samna' Ami, etc., and it appears that the market is finally ready for Windows.

The forthcoming release of Windows 3.0, the latest upgrade, is scheduled for May 1990. Among other changes, this version of Windows will have significant improvement in speed and memory management. It can run on a 8088/8086-based machine with 640K-bytes of memory, albeit slowly. On a '286 or '386, it allows Windows programs to address the extended memory on the system, thus breaking the 640K limit without requiring the users to switch to a whole new operating system.

These and other technologies incorporated in Windows 3.0 will prolong the useful life of the DOS-based systems, and its success will certainly have a positive impact in securing DOS as a viable operating system. Bill Gates, the Chairman of Microsoft Corp., recently predicted that half of all DOS users will adopt Windows this year. By his own admission now, OS/2 is not an immediate successor to DOS. As he said, "With the improvements we're making to Windows and the incredible wealth of applications there, there's no reason why a user shouldn't start out in this environment" (PC Week, March 26, 1990, p.5).

3. SALES OUTLOOK

The market for DOS will continue to grow, topping 11.5 million units this year, according to one study. The outlook for 1991 is less certain, and may depend on the outcome of two important product releases -- Windows 3.0 in May, and the '386-specific version of OS/2 later this year. The technology incorporated in Windows 3.0 is expected to breathe new life into the DOS-based systems. The new OS/2, on the other hand, is intended to replace DOS as the operating system for the high end '386- and '486-based computers.

3.1. Against All Odds

If one takes count of the adversities that DOS is facing, it is hard to be optimistic about the future of this operating system. DOS is a mismatch for the '386s, or even the '286s. Both IBM and Microsoft, the key players in the operating system market, are grooming OS/2 as a replacement for DOS. As software developers attempt to satisfy the users' demand for power and features, the 640K limit imposed by DOS is fast becoming a serious impediment to software development.

On the other hand, the pessimistic view about this venerable operating system is also unfounded. Evidenced by the number of installed base, DOS is perhaps the best known and most widely used software package ever written. It has the support of a very large number of popular application software. And the functional and technical enhancements to DOS, made possible by the unyielding efforts of many software and hardware engineers, are most crucial in maintaining the viability of DOS.

A lesson for OS/2 and other competing operating systems vying to replace DOS is that DOS does not achieve its status overnight by itself; the popularity of DOS is the result of lots of application software and third-party support. Not surprisingly, the installed base of OS/2 totals only about 300,000 almost three years after its debut. The relatively high price tag of OS/2, its excessive hardware requirements, and the fact that it was introduced during the period of skyrocketing RAM prices are other reasons for its sluggish start.

The original version of OS/2 was targeted at the '286-based systems. In order to make OS/2 compatible with DOS applications, IBM and Microsoft have gone to great lengths to overcome an inherited flaw in the design of the '286 microprocessor. The performance of OS/2 running on the '286s, even with the necessary hardware upgrade, is lethargic. In retrospect, industry experts agree that OS/2 should have been developed directly for the '386s. With the advent of the '386s, it is obvious that OS/2 will not be used much on the '286s after all. Until the '386-specific version becomes a reality and application programs are available, OS/2 will not be a serious threat to DOS in the foreseeable future.

Ironically, Microsoft's effort in developing the Windows operating environment may further delay market acceptance of OS/2. Running under DOS on the '286s or '386s, the latest version, Windows 3.0, provides DOS users much of the functionalities and capabilities promised by OS/2. Owners of the low end 8088/8086 machines can also benefit from Windows 3.0's user-friendly graphical interface and utility programs. Windows 3.0 is perceived by industry experts as a watershed type of product -- its success should truly fortify DOS as a viable operating system for all Intel-based machines.

3.2. 1990 And Beyond

According to a recent report from Montgomery Securities, Inc. in San Francisco, the combined shipments of PC- and MS-DOS are expected to peak at 11.5 million units in 1990, then drop 7 percent, to 10.8 million units in 1991 (see Table 5). OS/2, on the other hand, is expected to grow from 0.5 million units in 1990 to 1.5 million units in 1991. The optimistic projection for OS/2 is based on the assumption that the release of the '386-specific version would provide the much needed impetus for market acceptance. Nonetheless, DOS will still dominate the operating system market, outnumbering OS/2 in unit sales by a margin of 7 to 1 in 1991.

Montgomery analysts also predict a surge in Windows sales, rising from 1.0 million units in 1990 to 1.6 million units in 1991. This outlook is modest in light of the immediate success of Windows 3.0 anticipated by Bill Gates. Windows 3.0 has indeed generated substantial interest among users and software developers. AT&T, Zenith Data Systems, Northgate Computer Systems, Inc., CompuAdd Corp., and many other companies have already signed on to bundle Windows, together with DOS, with their computers. And Microsoft will have an aggressive marketing strategy, offering a $50 upgrade to anyone with an old run-time version, with no proof of purchase required.

Since Windows is an operating environment that runs on top of DOS, it is not, as the Montgomery report portraits, an operating system that competes with DOS. Quite the contrary, Windows complements DOS, and its success would have a positive impact on the market potential of DOS.

With Windows 3.0's ability to make use of the features of the advanced microprocessors, DOS can be a viable operating system for the high end computers. The combined force of DOS and Windows would put OS/2 on the defensive end. Even if OS/2 is able to pick up immediate support from software developers, a full suit of OS/2 applications will not be ready for at least a couple years. Meanwhile, the advantage of switching to OS/2 is not obvious to the users, and it is unlikely that OS/2 will make significant inroads into the operating system market.

In contradiction to the projection by Montgomery and other industry experts, there is no reason to believe that DOS will lose sales to OS/2 in 1991, or even 1992. At the very least, DOS should be able to maintain its current market share in the next two years.

Realizing the rapid progress in microprocessor technology, and the fact that DOS must rely on patches and other interim techniques to maintain its viability, it is naive to believe that DOS can continue its unchallenged dominance. A downturn in sales is likely in 1993, particularly if OS/2 applications could finally catch up with the users' demand. The long-run outlook beyond 1993 calls for a gradual decline in DOS's market share.

3.3. The OEM Market

The original equipment manufacturers (OEMs) have been the major outlet for MS-DOS. Most OEMs sell their computers with DOS installed. The anticipated success of Windows 3.0 will reinforce the continued popularity of the DOS-based systems. Some OEMs may be inclined to bundle Windows with their hardware; they too will have to include a copy of DOS in the package.

Excluding PC-DOS, which is sold exclusively by IBM and IBM authorized dealers, and end-users purchases of MS-DOS through retail channels, it is estimated that the OEMs as a group account for about half of the total shipments of DOS, or an equivalent of 5.6 million units in 1989.

Table 5
Sales of Operating Systems
Actual and Projected As of January 1990
(in million units)

	1989	1990	1991
DOS	11.3	11.5	10.8
Windows	0.7	1.0	1.6
OS/2	0.1	0.5	1.5
Unix	0.4	0.5	0.7
Macintosh	1.1	1.2	1.4

Source: Montgomery Securities, Inc., San Francisco, CA, 1990.

PRODUCT ANALYSIS

HI-dos, developed by ITS Corp., is a single-user, single-tasking operating system designed to run on computers that use the Intel 80-series microprocessors. It is a technologically superior product in comparison to PC- or MS-DOS, and yet it maintains full compatibility with the industry standard. HI-dos also provides the users the functions and features that are lacking in DOS.

1. WHY A DOS-CLONE?

Indeed, as the '386s are replacing the '286s as the desktop computing standard, and DOS is a mismatch for the power and capabilities of these machines, why develop a DOS-clone? The answer, surprising as it may sound, is because the market for DOS remains strong and there is a demand for a better DOS.

In the previous section, DOS's staying power and the operational and functional enhancements that are available to make DOS a viable operating system were described. The general conclusion is that it is premature to write off DOS. With the support of a large installed base and popular DOS applications, DOS and DOS-based systems will continue to dominate the personal computer market in the foreseeable future.

The advent of the '386s and '486s has led many industry observers to believe that personal computing will move in the direction of multitasking and multi-user systems. The reality is that a vast majority of the installed '386s are running in single-user mode, while OS/2 is facing a long and tough fight for adoption. It is true that market acceptance of OS/2 has been hampered by the lack of application programs. It is also possible that there is just a lack of genuine interest in OS/2. Capable and sophisticated as it is, OS/2 represents overkill for most PC users, who are satisfied with their DOS-based systems. With the help of third-party software developers, there are many ways to exploit the '286s and '386s without leaving DOS.

How does a DOS-clone fit in this scenario? Well, DOS is outdated. Sure, many of DOS's shortcomings can be overcome by the utility programs that are available, but DOS users should not have to turn to third-party software developers for these productivity enhancement tools, most of them are indispensable and should be a part of DOS to begin with. With a product like HI-dos, the users will have the convenience of a DOS-compatible operating system and the functionalities of DOS add-ins in one complete package. They no longer have to waste time searching or pay for the extra features.

Riding on the popularity of DOS, there has never been much pressure on IBM and Microsoft to improve their revered "cash cow." With the two market leaders preoccupied with OS/2, the DOS market presents a real opportunity. Thanks to the foresight of its founders and software engineers, ITS Corp. is ready to take advantage of this exceptional opportunity. By incorporating the much needed improvements in HI-dos, ITS has developed a product which is at least a year ahead of its competitors. HI-dos represents the first legitimate contender to replace PC- and MS-DOS.

2. HI-dos HIGHLIGHTS

HI-dos has been under development for about 2 years. Another 3 months of development remain before Beta testing. Product release is scheduled for November 1990. Many design ideas have been adapted from successful third-party utility packages such as PC Tools, Norton Utilities, and Sidekick.

Present users of PC- or MS-DOS can install HI-dos on their computers in a few minutes and immediately begin using their old programs and data files just as they always have. In fact, they will find it easier and more productive to use their old programs due to the greatly enhanced capabilities of HI-dos.

HI-dos is written in Assembly language. This means it takes up less memory than other DOS programs, which is important with today's memory-hungry graphics based applications. HI-dos also provides considerably more power than PC- and MS-DOS.

The laptop computer market is one of the fastest growing computer markets. There is, therefore, a sizable market for an operating system that is truly ROMable. Before its final release, HI-dos is expected to be ROMable so that the kernel of the operating system can fit into the ROM BIOS on laptop computers. This is a market niche that may prove quite valuable for market entry. Microsoft has not been able to produce a ROMable version of the last two releases of DOS, so their customers have to be content with the outdated, but ROMable, 3.2 release (see Appendix C).

HI-dos is more user-friendly than PC- and MS-DOS. With the latter, routine operations require the users to have thorough knowledge of the system command language. HI-dos overcomes this situation by offering the users easily accessible on-line help and full-screen menus to help speed command execution. HI-dos also supports CGA, EGA, and VGA color displays for further convenience for the users.

For the first time, the users will view their DOS as a productive tool that is easy to use. There are over 110 useful commands and special features, far more than PC- or MS-DOS provides. Most of these additional features are carefully selected to conform with most users wish lists, in one way or another. The following is an outline of some of HI-dos's innovations and improvements:

Look and Feel

- Works in color at the command line.
- Several HI-dos commands are menu-based and feature color support.
- Support for 43 and 50 line text modes without loading ANSI.SYS.
- On-line help on all commands.
- Full-screen HELP command with extensive help on all HI-dos commands.
- All menu-based HI-dos commands feature support for a mouse.
- Powerful command line editor with support for function key and alias definitions. Works with a mouse.
- Many possibilities for the user to customize the command line colors.
- Permits execution of several commands at the same time from the command line. Also allows multiple commands to use the same parameter(s) and multiple parameter sets to be used with a command. Any poweruser will appreciate these timesaving additions.

Installation

- HI-dos comes with a full-screen, menu-based installation program that will install both the user's CONFIG.SYS and AUTOEXEC.BAT files. It is able to detect the user's current configuration if he has already installed a different operating system on his computer.
- The design of HI-dos enables it to be installed onto any hard disk or diskette with its SYS command, regardless of whether or not the target disk already contains another disk operating system and/or data. The HI-dos system file can reside anywhere in the root directory of the boot drive.
- The SYS command in HI-dos allows the user to keep his previous DOS on a disk when installing HI-dos. This should make the user feel comfortable trying out HI-dos since he can always reinstall his previous DOS without having to reformat his disk.
- HI-dos can prepare a hard disk without the need of other disk management programs. It provides full-screen commands to set the user's CMOS configuration, low-level format the hard disk, partition the hard disk, and format the hard disk. HI-dos supports partitions up to 512M-bytes each.

- The partition manager in HI-dos supports MS-DOS extended partitions, Disk Manager partitions, Speedstor partitions, as well as its own HI-dos partitions. Even though the user can still use the partition managers supplied with both Disk Manager and Speedstor if he should wish so, he can save precious memory by using the internal HI-dos partition manager.

General Commands

- HI-dos comes with a full-screen, user-friendly command SHELL which enables the user to take advantage of all the HI-dos features without having to rely on the notorious DOS prompt. The user has access to an application menu with one-key application execution and password protection. The file management section gives a graphic depiction of the directory structure of up to two directories at a time and allows for easy and fast file management.
- Full-screen editor with powerful editing capabilities including wordwrap, margins, block editing, undelete, text justification, search and replace, etc. Can edit files in "Wordstar" format.
- Full-screen TYPE command which can scroll up, down, and sideways in the displayed file. Can display binary files and files in "Wordstar" format. Supports 43 line and 50 line text modes.
- Full-screen MODE command that takes the guessing out of setting up peripheral devices. Can also set the keyboard speed and supports laptop displays.
- Full-screen COPY command with 11 different switches for a multitude of copying options. COPY can display the files on the screen and the user can pick the files he wants to copy.
- Full-screen DISKCOPY command with on-screen depiction of the diskcopying process.
- Full-screen DISKCOMP command with on-screen depiction of the diskcomparing process.
- Full-screen CHKDSK command with several enhanced features. These include depiction of disk usage map, checking for bad sectors including data recovery, display of low-level disk information, and display of repeated files on a drive.
- Full-screen DEBUG command with several new and powerful features.
- WHEREIS command that can search through a drive for a file or range of files.
- WD command which repeats the execution of a command throughout a range of directories or the whole drive.

- Full-screen FIND command which can find any occurrence(s) of a range of characters in a file or range of files. Support for multiple directories.

- Full-screen COMP command which compares two files and displays any discrepancies on the screen. No limit for the number of differences in the two files. Also performs a file comparison on files with different lengths.

- CD command that does not need a path to find a directory. It even works with wildcards. A real timesaver.

Security and Recovery Features

- Password protection of partitions at system level. Very secure. The LOCK and UNLOCK commands are provided to manage password protection from the command line.

- HI-dos can install Read-Only partitions.

- HI-dos can encrypt files with a password, making files unreadable for anyone without the correct password.

- The virus checking utility can monitor the user's files for a possible virus attack.

- Safe formatting option of hard disks and diskettes so the user can recover an accidentally formatted hard disk or diskette.

- CHKDSK command that can check the user's hard disk or diskette for bad sectors, mark any bad sectors unusable, and recover any valid data in the cluster containing the bad sector.

- Menu-based backup and restore utility for backup of hard disks. Includes file compression and "intelligent" data transfer for both disk and speed efficiency.

- Total deletion of files so that they are unrecoverable.

- Undelete command to recover accidentally deleted files.

Memory Resident Utilities

- ASCII table which can insert up to 16 characters into an application program.

- Floating point calculator with support for decimal, hexadecimal, and binary calculations. Features readout tape and can insert a result at the cursor position in an application program.

- Screen capturing utility which can capture all or part of a screen and write the captured text to a file, insert it at the cursor position, or send it to a printer.

- ❑ Phone book with search capabilities. Can automatically dial phone numbers if a modem is connected to the computer.
- ❑ Foreign keyboard manager with graphics keyboard support. Supports 16 different foreign keyboard layouts. Can pop-up a display of the current keyboard configuration.
- ❑ WHEREAMI command that displays the default directories on all drives.
- ❑ Other desktop management utilities including timehandler, notepad, and calendar.
- ❑ MARK, RELEASE, and MAPMEM commands that can be used to manage the memory resident utilities. MAPMEM is a full-screen command in color.

Batch Language

- ❑ The batch language in HI-dos has been very enhanced and includes new commands such as ANSWER, BEEP, CHECK, DELAY, KEYIN, LOCATE, and REVECHO. These new batch commands make it easy for the user to make interactive and intuitive batch files.

3. THE COMPETITORS

ITS will be competing with industry giants IBM and Microsoft, and operating system specialist Digital Research. All three competitors have enormous resources in product research and development, yet none of them seems to understand the needs of DOS users. Currently, there is no other product in the market that can match the capabilities and features of HI-dos.

3.1. An Ailing Orphan

IBM and Microsoft are credited with the success of DOS, the single most popular software package ever written. At the same time, they also manage to alienate the largest computer user group, namely, the DOS users. In the last nine years, the personal computer standard has evolved from the PC to the AT to the '386, yet DOS remains virtually unchanged. The deficiencies of DOS are numerous and well-documented. After years of negligence, it is badly in need of an overhaul.

Characteristic of inattentive parents, IBM and Microsoft have relegated the duty of product support and improvements to third-party developers. Through the creative effort of a large number of software and hardware engineers, both DOS and DOS users endure.

In their attempt to keep pace with hardware technology, IBM and Microsoft have spent several years developing OS/2, a multitasking and multi-user operating system for computers which are based on the more advanced microprocessors. It is a logical business move for IBM and Microsoft. However, they make a strategic mistake of positioning OS/2 as a successor to DOS. They are too far out of touch with their customer base to realize that there are many DOS users who do not need the power and capabilities of OS/2. Most '386s in use today are DOS-based single-user systems. Indeed, the advancement in hardware technology has not diminished the popularity of DOS applications. For those users, an improved DOS will be most welcome.

With the advent of the '386s and '486s, it is easy to lose sight of the fact that the 8088/8086s and '286s still account for more than half of the sales of IBM and IBM-compatible computers. Almost all of these machines will be running under DOS. Due to the lack of a better alternative, owners of these systems will have to stay with PC- or MS-DOS, and rely on third-party developers for enhancement products. With IBM and Microsoft focusing on OS/2, and their history of being insensitive to DOS users, the low-end segment of the DOS market is particularly vulnerable, and is left wide open for HI-dos.

3.2. "DR" Calls

The only other competition for HI-dos is DR DOS, which was introduced by Digital Research Inc. (DRI) in 1988, and was marketed as an inexpensive single-user, single-tasking DOS alternative for OEMs.

Headquartered in Monterey, California, Digital Research is a veteran software developer in the microcomputer industry. In addition to DR DOS, it also offers a full line of operating systems including the multi-user, multitasking Concurrent DOS and FlexOS, as well as GEM, the first graphics environment manager for the IBM and IBM-compatible personal computers. Its founder, Gary Kildall, created an operating system for Intel's first microprocessor back in 1974. That program later became known as CP/M, the first standard operating system in the pre-IBM-PC era, and the forerunner of PC- and MS-DOS. Indeed, Microsoft's DOS was derived from a CP/M clone originally developed by a company called Seattle Computer Products. It is no coincidence that the command structure of DOS is very similar to that of CP/M.

Ironically, both the operating system and operating environment markets pioneered by Digital Research are now dominated by Microsoft. Once an innovative company, Digital Research has degenerated into a DOS-clone maker. The opposite fate of the two companies will make a great case study of visions, management, and marketing savvy.

Even with the expertise of Digital Research, DR DOS does not represent a leap in technology. It has been judged to be an adequate "me too" product that will not have significant impact on the industry. In spite of its limitations, DR DOS has managed to take over a large percentage of the new computers for DOS and has produced licensed sales of around 4 million copies since its release, without a major advertising campaign. The fact that DR DOS is ROMable certainly plays a significant role in its market acceptance (see Appendix C).

The market's response to DR DOS is highly encouraging for HI-dos. If the market will respond enthusiastically to a mere alternative, one can be comfortable with the market's response to HI-dos which, in fact, represents a major improvement in DOS technology. According to a recent ITS survey of the OEMs in Taiwan, Digital Research currently sells DR DOS, with manuals, to the OEMs at about $30 per unit, which is about $10 to $15 less than the price of MS-DOS.

4. RISK FACTORS

DOS is the program that controls every aspect of a computer's function. Like it or not, IBM and Microsoft own DOS and they set the standard for the industry. The opportunities are there for HI-dos, but so are the risks:

- ❑ It is a daunting task to keep HI-dos totally hardware and software compatible with the industry standard.
- ❑ Potential HI-dos users, while they may be enthusiastic about the advanced features of HI-dos, will undoubtedly have reservations about the program's compatibility and reliability. Overcoming the users' skepticism of a DOS-compatible program is a major hurdle for ITS.
- ❑ ITS is an unknown. Before the users will switch to HI-dos, they have to be convinced that ITS is a serious contender in the DOS market and it has the credibility and resources to continue product support and future development.
- ❑ DOS is perhaps the most bootlegged software in the industry.
- ❑ ITS must constantly be on the look-out and be ready to play the game of one-upmanship with market leader Microsoft, which plans to release DOS 5.0 before the end of this year. The new DOS is designed to run faster yet uses less memory than the current version, an improvement which has already been accomplished by HI-dos. Some other advanced features will be needed to further differentiate HI-dos from Microsoft's latest offering.

- Digital Research Inc. has a head start in the DOS-clone market with its own program called DR DOS. It recently launched an advertising campaign targeted at the OEMs who are potentially HI-dos's major customers (PC Week, April 9, 1990, p.95). It has also announced an end-user version of the OEM product to be available in June. Called DR DOS 5.0, this version will incorporate many of the key features planned for Microsoft's DOS 5.0.

- The anticipated success of Windows 3.0 is a mixed blessing for HI-dos. On the one hand, it will prolong the useful life of the DOS-based systems, which is important to HI-dos. On the other hand, it could render redundant some of the features incorporated in HI-dos.

HI-dos DEVELOPMENT GUIDELINES

HI-dos is an advanced DOS-compatible operating system. The characteristics that distinguish HI-dos from the competition's are ease of use, speed of execution, parsimonious memory requirement, and functionality.

1. THE ART OF CLONING

A piece of software can only be as good as the programming skills of the software developer. HI-dos is able to achieve the speed and size advantages over the competitions because ITS software engineers are proficient programmers who are capable of writing coherent and efficient source codes. Their mastery of the Assembly language is a definite asset. The fact that HI-dos is an intuitive and user-friendly operating system also reflects the qualities of ITS software engineers, who understand the needs of DOS users.

The development of HI-dos is an on-going project. ITS management must continue to provide the leadership and put special emphasis in sustaining the high standard of its research and development team.

Although it is the technological improvements and functional features which make HI-dos a superior product, HI-dos is nonetheless a DOS-clone. Maintaining a high level of compatibility with the latest offerings from IBM and Microsoft is a crucial factor in bolstering the users' confidence, particularly for those DOS old hands who are familiar with the industry standard. Sure, there is no good reason to use the COPY CON: command anymore when there is a full-screen text editor in HI-dos, but the customers are always right. The "word of mouth" communication among the end users could well determine the future success of HI-dos. Any negative comments from irritated users, regardless of how irrelevant they are, could do a disproportionate amount of damage to other users' perception of HI-dos. It is, therefore, highly desirable to structure the HI-dos commands as a superset of the PC- and MS-DOS commands.

Personal computer users in general have a higher level of resistance to a DOS-clone than, say, to an alternative utility program. In many ways, HI-dos is as much a DOS utility as it is a DOS-compatible operating system. Unlike the traditional utility programs, HI-dos has its own system files and command interpreter. It is, however, possible to set up and run HI-dos on a DOS-based system without having to replace the original system files. As a precautionary tactic, ITS will ensue this possibility in the design of HI-dos. The dual personality of HI-dos is a feature that ITS could exploit in the future, particularly if HI-dos somehow fails to generate sufficient interest in the operating system market. ITS still has the option of marketing HI-dos to the end-users as a "quasi" operating system, or more precisely, a productivity enhancement program consisting of the command interpreter and a set of external command files which can be switched to run under PC- or MS-DOS.

2. KNOW WHEN TO SAY WHEN

The number of functions and features that can be incorporated in a program like HI-dos is practically unlimited. ITS software engineers can use all the time and resources available contemplating and perfecting HI-dos. The reality is, for ITS to stay in business, it needs to have a product in the market soon to generate the much needed cash flow.

A working version of HI-dos has been in existence for quite some time. Already there are obvious improvements in performance and functionality which could clearly distinguish HI-dos from the competition. For reasons discussed in the next chapter, HI-dos will be marketed first through the OEM channel. ITS's initial contact with some OEMs suggests that, while they are interested in the advanced features of HI-dos, their primary concern is the cost of licensing a DOS program. The implication for ITS is that it may already have a product that meets the requirements of the OEMs -- HI-dos will be priced lower than the competition, and it has a sufficient level of sophistication to get the attention of the OEMs.

A successful debut of HI-dos with the OEMs could buy ITS the precious time and resources for further development of HI-dos, perhaps a dressed-up retail version for the end-users who may have a more stringent demand for functions and features than the OEMs. The announcement of HI-dos is set for this year's Fall Comdex. A tentative schedule of operation and product development is found in Table 6. In light of the upcoming release of Microsoft's DOS 5.0, any delay in developing and marketing HI-dos is unwarranted.

To ready HI-dos for market release, there are two areas which require immediate attention. The first concerns HI-dos's compatibility with the industry standard. ITS software engineers need to complete a DOS shell and include a number of commands found in the other DOS programs but are missing in HI-dos. The completion of these tasks is targeted at the end of July.

The second unfinished business involves debugging and testing HI-dos. A startup company like ITS cannot risk the fatal consequence of marketing a product which is known to be bug-ridden. To enhance market acceptance of HI-dos, ITS must also prove that the product is compatible with literally thousands of hardware platforms and DOS software programs. The debugging and testing procedures are both expensive and time consuming, but there is no room for compromise. ITS will spend the time between June and November polishing and making sure that HI-dos will perform reliably, including a two-month NSTL testing for a certification of hardware and software compatibility.

Table 6
Operation and Product Development
Tentative Schedule

May 30, 1990	Move research and development to Seattle
June 15, 1990	Hire 2 software engineers
July 30, 1990	DOS 3.3 compatibility, with many 4.01 features DOS shell ready
August 1, 1990	Start alpha testing
September 1, 1990	Start beta testing Start NSTL testing Hire 1 President Hire product support and sales people
November 15, 1990	Product announcement (Fall Comdex) ROMable version available
December 30, 1990	Establish liaison office in Asia
April 1, 1991	Release retail version

MARKETING STRATEGY

The market for DOS consists of the new computer segment and the installed computer segment. In the new computer segment, DOS is marketed to the end-users either through the OEMs or the retail distributors. In the installed computer segment, the retail distributors and the DOS publishers themselves are the major outlet for DOS.

1. DISTRIBUTION CHANNELS

The OEMs and the retail distributors are two very different distribution channels which require different marketing and sales tactics on the part of ITS.

The OEMs are in the business of selling computer systems. For marketing purposes, they often include a copy of DOS, together with other proprietary utility programs, with the systems they sell. They normally acquire these software packages through licensing agreements with the software publishers. Currently, Microsoft's MS-DOS has a lion's share of the OEM market. The only other known competitor is DR DOS from Digital Research. To the OEMs, the DOS program is a marketing gimmick which adds to their cost. Consequently, HI-dos must be priced competitively. In terms of functionality, HI-dos has a substantial lead over MS-DOS or DR DOS. ITS must place strong emphasis on the fact that HI-dos is an operating system as well as a productive tool in one complete package. With HI-dos, the OEMs will no longer have to bundle other costly utility programs with their computers.

To the retail distributors, HI-dos is just like any other software package they carry -- they want to be sure that there is a demand for the product and they expect to make a reasonable profit. They also need assurance from ITS that there will be active advertising campaign to promote HI-dos. In order to sell HI-dos as a retail product, ITS will have to deliver HI-dos in a complete package with reference manual, quick reference handbook, and diskettes. All these elements add to the cost of the product. Nonetheless, the retail distributors represent an important channel for ITS to reach the end-users in both the new computer segment and the installed computer segment.

2. FOCUSING ON OEMS

For a new product like HI-dos, the initial marketing effort should focus on the OEMs. The OEMs represent a high volume, cost efficient marketing channel that does not require enormous capital resources. Most significantly, getting the endorsement by just one or two reputable OEMs means instant market recognition for HI-dos. It would generate the much needed revenues for ITS, and provide HI-dos an important beachhead for further market penetration.

Focusing on the OEMs also means HI-dos will be marketed initially to the new computer segment. This approach gives HI-dos a better chance for market acceptance. Because the OEMs often have their hard drive systems preformatted and loaded with the operating system, the new owners of these computers will have a first-hand experience with HI-dos. And once they discover the features of HI-dos, they are likely to stay with the program. Recommendations by these satisfied HI-dos users will be the ideal kind of publicity for HI-dos. As a result of the "word of mouth" communication among the end-users, interest for HI-dos may also develop in the installed computer segment.

Before this scenario becomes a reality, there will be substantial resistance to HI-dos in the installed computer segment. Since the existing computer systems must have already been configurated with a DOS program, it will take extra effort to convince the users of these systems to switch to HI-dos, particularly if they have acquired a large number of utility programs and are comfortable with the old setup. It will not be prudent for ITS to pursue this segment of the DOS market before it has achieved some success with the OEMs.

3. OVERSEAS OPERATIONS

The U.S. is a major market for foreign manufacturers in many industries. The personal computer industry is no exception. Thriving on high productivity and low labor cost, computer producers in the Pacific Rim countries such as Japan, Taiwan, and Korea are important players in the highly contested U.S. market. Their products range from computer components to complete computer systems. Many U.S. run OEMs rely on foreign manufacturers for supply of vital components such as memory chips, monitors, storage and input devices, and power supply units. Some OEMs in the U.S. are foreign-owned; they compete directly with U.S. manufacturers with computer systems which are either imported or assembled in the U.S. with imported components.

Despite the foreign manufacturers' prowess in the computer hardware industry, foreign competition is surprisingly lacking in the software market. In the development of operating system and application software, the U.S. companies remain largely unchallenged.

It is of great strategic significance for ITS to establish a close tie with the OEMs who have a foreign affiliation, including both the Pacific Rim and the West European countries. In addition to their substantial sales volume in the U.S., they also provide ITS a vital link to the foreign markets. The DOS users in these markets in general are more cost conscious than their U.S. counterparts, and may be more receptive to a lesser known but competent DOS alternative like HI-dos.

Given the market potential, ITS's operations in the Far East and Western Europe will be given a very high priority, even in the early stage of the company's existence. It is a strength of ITS that the management team and software engineers are knowledgeable about the Asian markets. Two chief engineers of the company, moreover, are European educated. ITS plans to expand its current liaison in Asia and establish a distribution network in Europe.

The liberation of the East European countries could mean new business opportunities for the U.S. computer industry. Through its representatives in Europe, ITS will be ready for the new frontier market, should the personal computer industry there start to take shape. HI-dos will be available in foreign versions, including German, French, and Spanish.

4. PROMOTING HI-dos

One of the priorities in marketing HI-dos is to make the product known to the OEMs, the retail distributors, and the end-users. There are several options:

- ❑ Authoritative reviews in industry publications. A pre-release version of HI-dos has already been reviewed in the French magazine DECISION and was elected the "Clone of the Year" (see Appendix A).
- ❑ Advertising in industry publications. A well-orchestrated advertising campaign targeted at the OEMs is needed to counter the recent effort staged by Digital Research.
- ❑ Major trade shows. They provide the best opportunities to give HI-dos maximum exposure and demonstrate HI-dos to a large number of potential customers.

From a marketing stand point, it is important that HI-dos be assigned a version number that matches or is higher than the latest release of PC- and MS-DOS. A seemingly inconsequential stratagem like this could go a long way to conjure the reputation of ITS as a company that always keeps up with or stays ahead of the competition.

Promoting the company itself is perhaps as important as promoting the product it sells, particularly for an operating system which is, by all measures, the most important piece of software on any computer system. Potential users of HI-dos would certainly demand utmost compatibility and reliability. They would feel more comfortable with HI-dos if they have a favorable perception of ITS.

Since ITS is a late comer in the software business, it is important to establish for the company an upscale image of quality, professionalism, and strong customer support. A public relations company with a proven track record in the software industry will be hired for this purpose.

5. PRODUCT SUPPORT

While there is no question that HI-dos is a technologically superior DOS program, its initial success in the market may well depend on the quality of end-user support offered by ITS. A positive image of the after-sale support will accelerate market entry and will be important in maintaining ITS's market position.

Product support is an important factor for any company involved in the computer industry. Given the poor customer relations image of Microsoft, ITS can gain a strong competitive advantage by establishing a reputation for quality product support. In this sense, customer relations can play an important role in the overall HI-dos marketing strategy.

In addition to being good business practice and gaining an advantage over the competition, effective customer relations and product support will be an excellent source of market information and technical comments. User feedback will help HI-dos stay ahead of the competition. With accurate input from the end-users, ITS will be able to constantly improve its software products.

Several levels of customer support that have been proven to be effective in the computer industry will be implemented, including:

- ❑ Telephone support, including 800 number for sales and technical support in the U.S.A.
- ❑ Facsimile support for businesses.
- ❑ Agent support for overseas customers.
- ❑ Educational seminars at major trade shows.
- ❑ Newsletter for registered owners of HI-dos.
- ❑ BBS service for technical support, product development, announcements, and users feedback.

PRODUCTION COST AND PRICING

There are two major marketing channels for HI-dos: the OEMs and the retail distributors. Each channel has different requirements in regards to packaging. Pricing for the OEM product and the retail product will also be different.

1. THE OEM PRODUCT

Many OEMs of IBM-compatible computers prefer to handle the production of the DOS program themselves. This practice allows them to keep costs down, be able to get their brand name on the DOS package, and be in control of delivery. All they need from the DOS publisher is a set of diskettes with the original DOS binaries and the camera ready artwork for the manual. The OEMs will then take care of copying the DOS program onto diskettes, printing the manual, and packaging the product.

In order to check that the OEMs disclose all sales of the DOS packages, both Microsoft and Digital Research have begun to furnish the OEMs with a holographic label that has to be present on every DOS package to make it a legal product. A holographic label is almost impossible to counterfeit. This way it is easy to keep track of the number of DOS packages sold to different OEMs.

ITS will pursue the OEM market in a similar manner, by supplying the OEMs with the HI-dos master diskettes, holographic labels, and the camera ready artwork for the manual which is about 125 pages and can be printed inexpensively by the OEMs. This method of distributing HI-dos will keep the cost down to around $0.10 for each package licensed to the OEMs. Since handling each OEM account boils down to sending the necessary holographic labels, the OEM market can prove to be very profitable. Inventory control will be an almost unknown factor in this operation. To be competitive in the OEM market, the unit price for HI-dos in quantities of about 10,000 copies should be in the area of $15 to $16, bringing in a gross profit of about $15 or more per copy.

For the OEMs who choose not to produce the package themselves, ITS will offer them a complete, packaged product consisting of the following:

- ❑ 1 Reference manual (OEM version) with approximately 125 pages printed on each side.
- ❑ 1 Registration card, combined with offer for manual upgrade.
- ❑ 2 360K-byte diskettes with labels and sleeves, or 1 720K-byte diskette with label.
- ❑ 1 Holographic label.

The manual will have a soft cover, with the diskette(s) and registration card placed inside. The complete package will be shrink wrapped. Including the material listed above, and the cost for copying the diskettes and packaging the product, the total cost is about $2.0 per unit. In order to cover overhead and inventory expenses, the unit price for this OEM product should range from $19 to $20. As in the case of selling HI-dos to OEMs under licensing agreements, the gross profit for each packaged OEM product will be about $15 or more.

For a fee of about $25, those clients of the OEMs who respond to the manual upgrade offer will receive an expanded version of the reference manual of about 250 pages, together with a quick reference handbook of about 45 pages. The expanded reference manual will have in-depth explanations of the workings of HI-dos.

2. THE RETAIL PRODUCT

Selling HI-dos as a retail product requires ITS to deliver a complete, packaged product with the HI-dos diskettes, the expanded reference manual, and the quick reference handbook. The total cost of the retail product, including overhead and inventory expenses, is about $5 per unit. Each package will consist of the following:

- ❑ 1 Reference manual (expanded version) with approximately 250 pages printed on each side.
- ❑ 1 Quick Reference handbook with approximately 45 pages printed on each side.
- ❑ 1 Registration card.
- ❑ 2 360K-byte diskettes with labels and sleeves.
- ❑ 1 720K-byte diskette with label.
- ❑ 1 Package hard cover.

At the retail level, HI-dos is targeted to a retail price of $99. Retail outlets often reduce the selling price by up to 25 percent of the retail price for low cost products, giving a likely selling price of about $75. To attract the retail outlets to sell HI-dos, they should earn a profit margin of about 45 percent on the retail price, so their buying price should be below $55. This will give them a true profit margin of about 26 percent.

Retail outlets will be purchasing HI-dos from retail distributors. Retail distributors should earn a profit margin of about 40 percent for them to promote HI-dos. Therefore,

ITS should be selling HI-dos at around $30 to $35 to retail distributors in order to make HI-dos profitable to all parties.

For the OEMs who choose to bundle the retail version of HI-dos with their computers, the price will be about $22 to $23 per package.

MANAGEMENT TEAM

Three people currently comprise ITS's management team: Leonard , Thierry , and Michael . Within several months, ITS expects to add a new president and several computer technicians. Each member of the current staff and future additions to the management team are described below.

Leonard O

Mr. O is the current CEO of and primary investor in ITS. He has managed the company since mid-1989, having first invested in the firm in 1988. Mr. O has owned and run his own businesses for the last thirty years, primarily in the construction and real estate development industries. His businesses have been highly successful. He has extensive experience in project management, personnel management, financing, and marketing.

A search is currently underway to bring in a President who has had extensive experience in the computer industry. Discussions with several candidates have occurred, and a new person will be hired in the next six months. This new person will have had experience running a firm in the computer industry and will have significant industry contacts.

Thierry C

Mr. G is a French native and has the equivalent of a M.B.A. in Business Management from Ecole Superieure de Commerce de Reims and the equivalent of a Master's Degree in Computer Science from London University. He speaks fluent French, English, German, and Chinese. He worked for Digitaire-Sfena, a computer telecommunications company in France, as a communications engineer from 1984 to 1987. He then worked as a software manager from 1987 to 1988 for Kortex International in France, which specializes in fax and modem cards for personal computers. His interest in the Chinese language and his experience in computer communications took him to Taiwan in 1988, where he served as a consultant to several major Taiwanese computer equipment manufacturers, including CMP, Tremon, and Best Communications. His consulting work included software engineering and computer marketing.

Mr. G joined ITS in June, 1988. He is the head engineer of HI-dos and has written the major portion of Assembly language for the program. He will continue to work on refining and improving HI-dos so that it exceeds the capabilities of other competing operating systems.

The current engineering team consists of Mr. G and two other software engineers. Three new software engineers will be hired in the next couple months. Two of them will assist Mr. G in research and development of HI-dos, adding new features and refining current ones. The other new employee will be involved in technical support. He will learn the program in detail and respond to OEMs and customers' questions about usage of the program.

Michael A

Danish born, Michael A studied Computer Science at the University of Aalborg. During his college years, he started his own business of selling computers to college students. It rapidly expanded to the point at which he was selling to businesses and selling a considerable number of computers through direct marketing. The rapid growth and success of his business did not allow him to complete his degree. His frequent trips to suppliers in Taiwan allowed him to establish contacts in that country, which eventually put him in touch with ITS. He is fluent in the languages of Danish, English, and German.

Mr. A is responsible for making HI-dos "user-friendly." He is in charge of screen menu creation and the writing of straight forward user manuals. He has also been centrally involved in creating a demonstration diskette and training programs for users. He is basically the person who stands between the technology and the user. He tests all programs to ensure that they run without problems and according to specifications.

FINANCIAL PLAN

Most software companies which sell to broad markets have significant research costs before any sales occur. The majority of costs are fixed once sales commence, and variable costs are low. As a result, the firm must generate significant sales to be successful. These characteristics hold true for ITS.

1. BREAKEVEN ANALYSIS

The initial development costs for HI-dos will reach approximately $1.5 million before sales begin in the fall of 1990. With the opening of an office in Seattle and the addition of quite a few new employees, fixed costs are estimated at approximately $1,850,000 per year for large-scale marketing and support of HI-dos. The only true variable cost is the $2.00 manual/diskette cost for each OEM version of the program. These figures yield a projected annual breakeven point of approximately $2.1 million in sales, or 103,000 units. Projected sales in 1991 are $3.5 million, well above the breakeven point. As sales increase, staff will be added so that total fixed costs will increase. However, this will occur only after sales are gained.

2. CASH FLOW ANALYSIS

A $200,000 loan from Mr. Otten and a $1,000,000 private placement stock offering is required in 1990 to allow a safe positive cash balance throughout the entire year. Sales are projected at $3.5 million in 1991, $7 million in 1992, and $14,000,000 in 1993 (based on a selling price of $20 to OEM's, with a $2.00 variable cost). The 1993 sales figure is calculated based on capturing 14% of the OEM market. Since most of the costs are fixed, these sales increases result in significant positive cash flows. The loan to Mr. O is paid back in 1991. The projected cash balance at the end of 1991 is approximately $1.2 million, in 1992 is $3.8 million, and in 1993 is more than $9.5 million. These figures are after taxes are paid.

3. INCOME STATEMENT

The income statement varies only slightly from the cash flow statement. The primary difference is the five-year amortization of R&D expenditures which are capitalized at $1.5 million. The projected incomes are:

	Before taxes	After taxes	Return (after taxes) on equity [1)]
1991	$1.6m	$1.1m	63%
1992	$3.8m	$2.5m	87%
1993	$8.3m	$5.6m	110%

4. BALANCE SHEET

A striking feature of the balance sheet is the absence of long-term debt, in spite of significant start-up expenses. The lack of debt provides considerable security to the company. Changes in major balance sheet accounts are shown below in millions of dollars:

	1990	1991	1992	1993
Total assets	$2.3m	$3.4m	$6.0m	$12.1m
Total equity	$1.8m	$2.9m	$5.5m	$11.6m

Increases in total assets and equity are dramatic, while short-term debt increases only slightly through accounts payable.

5. PROPOSED COMPANY OFFERING

ITS is offering 1,000,000 shares of common stock at $1.00 per share. 3,500,000 shares are currently outstanding. The new shares issued thus represent 22% ownership of the company. The earnings per share in 1993 are projected to be $1.24. At an estimated P/E ratio of 15, the stock would be evaluated at $18.6. The increase in net worth for any investor will obviously be considerable.

1) calculated with current years profit after taxes divided by beginning of year equity.

FINANCIAL EXHIBITS

Figure 1
Breakeven Analysis for 1991
I.T.S Corp.

COSTS	FIXED AMOUNT	VARIABLE %
Payroll	750,000	
Payroll Overhead	112,500	
Manuals		0.10
Group Insurance	18,000	
Office Rental	18,000	
Office Furniture	10,000	
Utilities	5,400	
Office Supplies	3,800	
Telephone/Fax	9,000	
Postage/Freight	2,400	
Equipment	90,000	
Legal & Accounting	42,000	
Travel	42,000	
Trade Show Expenses	80,000	
Employee Search	5,000	
Consultants	20,000	
Market Research	20,000	
PR Firm/Advertising	150,000	
Asia Office	120,000	
Miscellaneous	60,000	
R&D Amortization	300,000	
TOTALS	1,858,100	0.10

BREAKEVEN POINT	=	2,064,556
Price/Unit	=	20
Breakeven point in units	=	103,228

Figure 2
Breakeven Graph for 1991
I.T.S Corp.

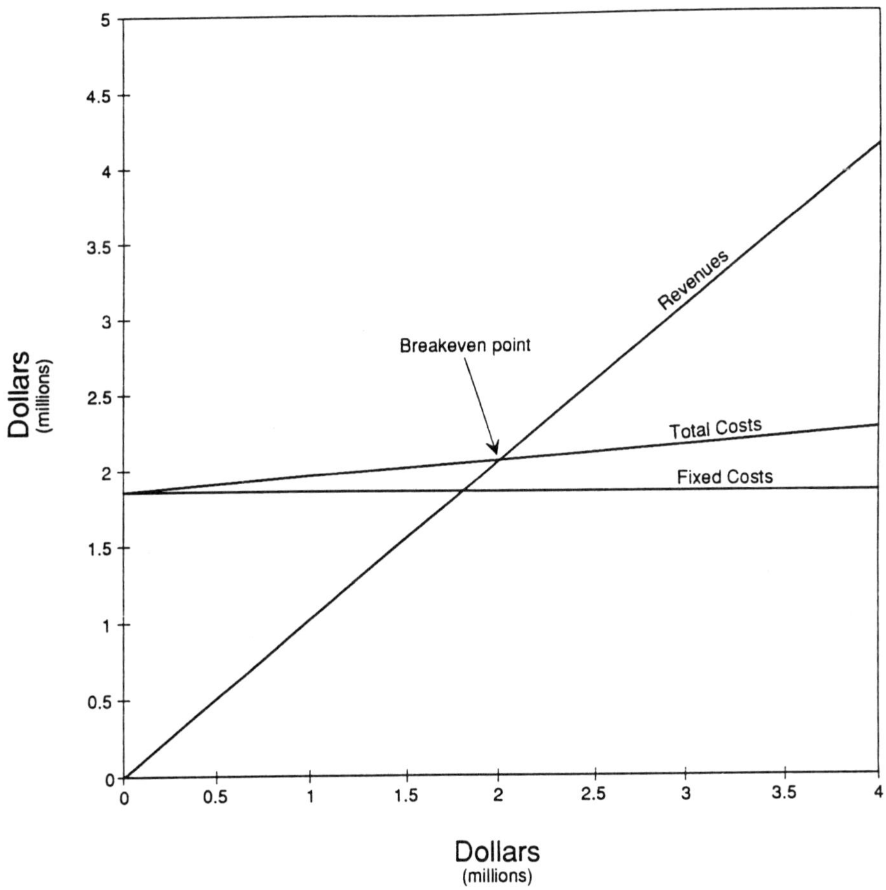

Figure 3
Cash Flow Projection for 1990
I.T.S Corp.

	Apr	May	Jun	Jul	Aug	Sep	Oct	Nov	Dec	Total
Beginning Cash on Hand		169,670	83,915	34,085	474,780	393,625	247,220	609,815	482,760	XXXXXXXXX
Cash Sales										0
Collections								60,000	80,000	140,000
Loan, Investment	200,000			500,000			500,000			1,200,000
Total Cash Inflows	200,000			500,000			500,000	60,000	80,000	1,340,000
Total Cash Available	**200,000**	**169,670**	**83,915**	**534,085**	**474,780**	**393,625**	**747,220**	**669,815**	**562,760**	XXXXXXXXX
Cash Outflows										
Payroll Expense										
T. Giron	1,000	3,500	3,500	3,500	3,500	3,500	3,500	3,500	3,500	**29,000**
M. Aaen	1,000	3,500	3,500	3,500	3,500	3,500	3,500	3,500	3,500	**29,000**
J. Suau (Consultant)	1,000	7,000								**8,000**
R. Huebner	3,200	3,200	3,200	3,200	3,200	3,200	3,200	3,200	3,200	**28,800**
M. Zaoui		3,500	3,500	3,500	3,500	3,500	3,500	3,500	3,500	**28,000**
New Engineer #1			1,750	3,500	3,500	3,500	3,500	3,500	3,500	**22,750**
New Engineer #2			1,750	3,500	3,500	3,500	3,500	3,500	3,500	**22,750**
Additional Employees			2,000	5,000	10,000	35,000	35,000	50,000	50,000	**187,000**
Payroll Overhead	930	3,105	2,880	3,855	4,605	8,355	8,355	10,605	10,605	**53,295**
Manuals							5,000	25,000	30,000	**60,000**
Group Insurance		1,500	1,500	2,000	2,500	3,500	3,500	4,500	4,500	**23,500**
Moving Expenses		6,000								**6,000**
Office Rental		1,500	1,500	1,500	1,500	1,500	1,500	1,500	1,500	**12,000**
Office Furniture		6,000				5,000				**11,000**
Utilities	450	450	450	450	450	450	450	450	450	**4,050**
Office Supplies	200	200	200	200	300	300	300	400	400	**2,500**
Telephone/FAX	500	500	500	500	500	500	500	1,000	1,500	**6,000**

(Continued)

Figure 3
Cash Flow Projection for 1990
I.T.S Corp.
(continued)

	Apr	May	Jun	Jul	Aug	Sep	Oct	Nov	Dec	Total
Office Rental		1,500	1,500	1,500	1,500	1,500	1,500	1,500	1,500	**12,000**
Office Furniture		6,000				5,000				**11,000**
Utilities	450	450	450	450	450	450	450	450	450	**4,050**
Office Supplies/Subscriptio	200	200	200	200	300	300	300	400	400	**2,500**
Telephone/FAX	500	500	500	500	500	500	500	1,000	1,500	**6,000**
Postage/Freight	100	100	100	100	100	100	100	400	400	**1,500**
Equipment										
Software & Books	1,200	500	1,000	500	1,500	3,000	3,000	1,000	1,000	**12,700**
Computer	4,000	4,000		2,000	4,000	10,000		4,000		**28,000**
Network Equipment		3,800								**3,800**
Fileserver		5,400								**5,400**
Other Equipment	2,000	2,000	2,000	2,000	4,000	8,000	8,000	4,000	4,000	**36,000**
Legal & Accounting	3,500	3,500	3,500	3,500	3,500	3,500	3,500	3,500	3,500	**31,500**
Travel	2,000	1,500	1,500	1,500	1,500	1,500	1,500	5,000	10,000	**26,000**
Trade Show Expenses		20,000	10,000					35,000		**65,000**
Employee Search	750		500	500	1,000		1,000			**3,750**
Consultants	2,500				10,000					**12,500**
Market Research	1,000						10,000			**11,000**
PR Firm					10,000	25,000	15,000	15,000	10,000	**75,000**
Source Code Verification				10,000						**10,000**
Compatibility Testing by NSTL						15,000	15,000			**30,000**
Liaison Office in Asia									60,000	**60,000**
Miscellaneous	5,000	5,000	5,000	5,000	5,000	5,000	5,000	5,000	5,000	**45,000**
Total Cash Outflows	**30,330**	**85,755**	**49,830**	**59,305**	**81,155**	**146,405**	**137,405**	**187,055**	**213,555**	**990,795**
Cash Position	**169,670**	**83,915**	**34,085**	**474,780**	**393,625**	**247,220**	**609,815**	**482,760**	**349,205**	XXXXXXXXX

Figure 4
Cash Flow Projection, 1991-1993
I.T.S Corp.

	1991	1992	1993
Beginning Cash on Hand	349,205	1,241,105	3,823,355
Cash Inflows:			
Cash Sales			
Collections	3,500,000	7,000,000	14,000,000
Loan, investment			
Total Cash Inflows	3,500,000	7,000,000	14,000,000
Total Cash Available	3,849,205	8,241,105	17,823,355
Cash Outflows:			
Payroll	750,000	1,125,000	2,000,000
Payroll Overhead	112,500	168,750	300,000
Manuals	350,000	700,000	1,400,000
Group Insurance	18,000	27,000	47,250
Office Rental	18,000	27,000	40,500
Office Furniture	10,000	15,000	26,250
Utilities	5,400	8,100	12,150
Office Supplies	3,800	7,600	15,200
Telephone/Fax	9,000	18,000	36,000
Postage/Freight	2,400	4,800	9,600
Equipment	90,000	135,000	202,500
Legal & Accounting	42,000	60,000	80,000
Travel	42,000	84,000	168,000
Trade Show Expenses	80,000	120,000	180,000
Employee Search	5,000	7,500	13,125
Consultants	20,000	30,000	45,000
Market Research	20,000	30,000	30,000
PR Firm/Advertising	150,000	300,000	450,000
Asia Office	120,000	180,000	270,000
Miscellaneous	60,000	120,000	240,000
Loan Repayment	200,000		
Taxes	500,000	1,250,000	2,750,000
Total Cash Outflows	2,608,100	4,417,750	8,303,075
Cash Position	**1,241,105**	**3,823,355**	**9,520,280**

Figure 5
Income Statement, 1991-1993
I.T.S Corp.

	1991	1992	1993
Sales	3,500,000	7,000,000	14,000,000
Cost of Goods Sold	350,000	700,000	1,400,000
Gross Profit	3,150,000	6,300,000	12,600,000
Expenses:			
Payroll	750,000	1,125,000	2,000,000
Payroll Overhead	112,500	168,750	300,000
Group Insurance	18,000	27,000	47,250
Office Rental	18,000	27,000	40,500
Office Furniture	10,000	15,000	26,250
Utilities	5,400	8,100	12,150
Office Supplies	3,800	7,600	15,200
Telephone/Fax	9,000	18,000	36,000
Postage/Freight	2,400	4,800	9,600
Equipment	90,000	135,000	202,500
Legal & Accounting	42,000	60,000	80,000
Travel	42,000	84,000	168,000
Trade Show Expenses	80,000	120,000	180,000
Employee Search	5,000	7,500	13,125
Consultants	20,000	30,000	45,000
Market Research	20,000	30,000	30,000
PR Firm/Advertising	150,000	300,000	450,000
Asia Office	120,000	180,000	270,000
Miscellaneous	60,000	120,000	240,000
Loan Repayment	200,000		
Depreciation	40,000	65,000	95,000
Total Expenses	1,598,100	2,532,750	4,267,325
Net Profits Before Taxes	1,551,900	3,767,250	8,332,675
Taxes (estimated)	500,000	1,250,000	2,750,000
Net Profit After Taxes	**1,051,900**	**2,517,250**	**5,582,675**

Figure 6
Projected Balance Sheets, 1990-1993
I.T.S Corp.

	END OF 1990	END OF 1991	END OF 1992	END OF 1993
ASSETS				
Current Assets:				
Cash	349,205	1,241,105	3,818,355	9,489,030
Accounts Receivable	120,000	350,000	550,000	1,200,000
Inventory	250,000	500,000	500,000	500,000
Total Current Assets	719,205	2,091,105	4,868,355	11,189,030
Fixed Assets:				
Land				
Building				
Less Depreciation				
Equip & furniture	100,000	200,000	350,000	578,750
Less Depreciation	-20,000	-60,000	-125,000	-220,000
Development Costs	1,500,000	1,500,000	1,500,000	1,500,000
Amortization		-300,000	-600,000	-900,000
Total Fixed Assets	1,580,000	1,340,000	1,125,000	958,750
TOTAL ASSETS	**2,299,205**	**3,431,105**	**5,993,355**	**12,147,780**
LIABILITIES				
Current Debt:				
Accounts Payable	250,000	500,000	500,000	500,000
Notes Payable				
Taxes Payable				
Total Current Debt	250,000	500,000	500,000	500,000
Longterm Debt:				
Notes Payable	200,000			
Mortgage				
Loan				
Total Longterm Debt:	200,000	0	0	0
TOTAL DEBT	450,000	500,000	500,000	500,000
EQUITY		1 = price/share		
Common Stock	4,500,000	4,500,000	4,500,000	4,500,000
Premium on C.S.				
Retained Earnings	-2,650,795	-1,568,895	993,355	7,147,780
Owners Equity (if no stock issued)				
TOTAL EQUITY	1,849,205	2,931,105	5,493,355	11,647,780
TOTAL DEBT + EQUITY	**2,299,205**	**3,431,105**	**5,993,355**	**12,147,780**

APPENDIX A

HI-Dos: THE CLONE OF THE YEAR

A pre-release version of HI-dos has been reviewed in the French computer magazine, DECISION. Regarded by the columnist as a technical revolution in the MS-DOS world, HI-dos was designated the "Clone of the Year." A translation of the original article, which appeared in the July 1989 issue of the magazine, follows:

TECHNICAL REVOLUTION IN THE MS-DOS WORLD

HI-DOS : THE CLONE OF THE YEAR

For the first time, a software house is seriously rivaling the most famous software in the world, MS-DOS. HI-dos, unlike DR-DOS, does not only do slightly better for less money. Almost totally compatible, with a lot of new commands, less memory consuming... you will adopt it very easily.

The first impression of HI-dos is excellent: with the execution of each command, Hi-dos behaves like MS-DOS, with much more functionalities. Everything was thought not only in terms of functionality (dynamic parameters to modify the behavior of a command), but also in terms of ergonomics and aesthetics. The installation of HI-dos is done, using the traditional SYS command, and then the system files are copied. In order to benefit from some extended features of HI-dos, it is necessary to partition the disk using the HI-dos tool, thus allowing partitions up to 2 Gigabytes (2,000 Megabytes!).

The installation program takes care of creating the Autoexec.BAT and Config.SYS files, according to the user's needs. The user won't have to look in manuals for configuration commands and maybe forget some. The user will be asked (in English) : Do you want a virtual disk ? Of which size ? or, more technically, What buffer size ?. Hi-dos will gently replace MS-DOS. By the way, during installation HI-dos automatically does the housekeeping: it creates an OLDDOS directory into which it copies all the files from the DOS directory if a DOS directory already exists prior to installation, then it writes the proper files [the HI-dos files] into the DOS directory.

It is rarely necessary to rely on the manual, well written by the way, in order to activate the commands since most have help describing all valid parameters and their usage.

As far as the aesthetic aspect is concerned, HI-dos utilizes colors a lot : thus, for the DIR command, the files have different colors according to their extensions; the directory display stops at page break and displays the disk usage at the end, whereas COPY displays a real dashboard that indicates the files being read and copied, the chosen options, etc. COPY functions like XCOPY, the files are read by packets and then copied to the chosen destination. The options also manage the copying of files and directories.

The minor incompatibilities

The difference in the screens of the two systems prevents total compatibility, especially if one uses a command that expect certain information to be on the screen the way MS-DOS displays them. With the command EMULATE (EMULATE ON or OFF), Hi-dos becomes nearly compatible : the DIR command is not colored any longer, the COPY command looks like the one from DOS... the regression is reassuring.

Another feature, the command NEWVER changes the version number of HI-dos. Nothing is modified in the functionalities of HI-dos but a software that expects a 3.x version of DOS will read 3.x. The compatibility is not total, even in the emulation mode : Some commands will behave differently, some commands have minor differences; Thus, when DIR is activated in the emulation mode, HI-DOS does not display the available disk space. The command COPY CON <filename> did not work, but some software use this command to create text files from the keyboard. The incompatibilities also affects some memory drivers. More tolerant than DR-DOS that refused all the drivers, HI-dos only had problems with the DESQVIEW memory driver. And to finish with some problems, the HI-dos keyboard had some problems with special characters such as the backslash. We had to use an old KEYBFR.

The Utilities.

Once installed, we noticed that we had gained more than 6 Kb of memory while having access to a number of additional commands and much more sophistication; some of them seem to be internal since there is no corresponding .EXE or .COM file on the disk. Hi-dos uses, just like MS-DOS, a command interpreter, COMMAND.COM, but also has a secondary command interpreter, MAX.COM, which handles commands like DIR, FIND, LABEL...

The DOS users have generally created a personal operating system by using other tools like the NORTON or Paul Mace utilities, besides public domain utilities. It is often a long and tedious task : conflicts between memory resident utilities, operation problems (nothing is guarantied with public domain software), a source for supply... Hi-dos has increased the range of MS-DOS commands with several very famous ones. These emulate classic commands like CED, WHEREIS, CALC, GRABBER, LIST, NCD... (see the frame below [on the following page]) But here, no conflict with one another: The commands are compatible with each other, and for the memory resident utilities, the assigned hot keys are not assigned according to the developers' own fantasy. Thus, <ALT><Ctrl>C will call the calculator, <ALT><Ctrl>A the Ascii table, etc. As an extra luxury: the memory resident utilities are compact and will not consume too much of the precious memory. Finally, to manage memory resident programs, there are the internal commands MAPMEM, MARK, RELEASE. There is no longer any need for the LIST command (TYPE does the job very well), for MAPMEM (this is now an internal command in Hi-dos), for WHEREIS (also an internal command).

The famous NCD command from Norton, which can find any directory in the tree, has simply been incorporated in HI-dos - with some differences - in the CD command. Thus, CD DOC* goes directly to the \LOGICIEL\WORD\DOCUMENT directory. However, and different from NCD, if one chooses a directory that does not exist, Hi-dos will look for it in all the tree: typing mistakes can be costly in time.

Some of the commands are managed by the second command processor, and the resident portion of HI-dos has more features than the one from MS-DOS. The DIR command, managed by MAX.COM, which displays a sophisticated directory catalog, can be replaced, if necessary, with SDIR which outputs a simplified directory catalog. Thus, if one uses Hi-dos from a diskette, one avoids a laborious disk access for simply getting a directory catalog. Likewise, COPY is an external command (COPY.COM), which also has its twin, SCOPY, in the resident portion.

HI-dos places the [partition] barrier at 2,000 Megabytes, enough for the future. But the improvements in the disk management are not limited to that. The FDISK command, totally menu based with context sensitive help,works in a manner that makes partitions visible. It has possibilities to create, destroy, and password protect partitions. Its is possible to install HI-dos quickly onto an MS-DOS disk, but it will be necessary to reformat the disk if one wishes to benefit from the extended HI-dos partitions. Even with so many functionalities, HI-dos is reasonable in both disk or memory usage. Everything fits onto one 360 Kb diskette!

Hi-dos is one of the best surprises we had this year. The high quality of the work performed predicts very few problems with the usage. Now all that is left is for this superb product to be distributed in France.

ANTOINE JENNET

Notes

Notes

Notes

Notes

Order Form

for additional copies of *The Utah Entrepreneur's Guide*
or
other resource materials

Name ____

Organization ______________________________________

Address ____

City ______________________ State _____ Zip _____________

Phone ___________________________________

Enclosed please find: Check ___ Government PO# _____________

VISA/MASTERCARD # _______________________________

Expiration date ____________ Signature _____________________

Please send:

____	copies of *The Utah Entrepreneur's Guide*	$19.95
	plus shipping and handling	$ 3.50
____	copies of Macintosh Financial Templates	$ 5.00
____	copies of 3 1/2" IBM Financial Templates	$ 5.00
____	copies of *How to Write a Questionnaire*	$ 7.00
	Total	_____

Mail to: **University Press**
1719 Dearborn
Missoula, MT 59801

or call: 1-800-243-6840